Constructing Autism

The dramatic increase in diagnoses of autism has paralleled a huge increase in scientific research. At the same time a wide range of information about autism, directed towards popular audiences, is disseminated by the media. Underlying both scientific and popular representations is a premise that autism is a disorder for which we will ultimately find a cure through the ceaseless efforts of scientific enquiry. This quest has inevitably entailed a reductionist search for the origins of the disorder.

In *Constructing Autism*, Majia Holmer Nadesan, herself the mother of an autistic child, argues that although there is without doubt a biogenetic component to the condition we call autism, it is the social factors involved in its identification, interpretation and remediation that determine what it means to be autistic. This book explores the social practices and institutions that reflect and shape the way we think about autism and what effects these have on autistic people and their families. She unravels what appears to be the 'truth' about autism, stepping behind the history of its emergence as a modern disorder to see how it has become a crisis of twenty-first century child development.

This innovative text provides a welcome counter-balance to the predominantly medical and scientific literature on autism, and will be invaluable for anyone studying autistic disorders, child development and child health, modern public health issues and other areas of medical sociology, psychology and health studies.

Majia Holmer Nadesan is Associate Professor of Communication Studies at Arizona State University, Phoenix, Arizona. Her research addresses relationships across institutional forms, cultural practices and individual subjectivity.

Constructing Autism

Unravelling the 'truth' and understanding the social

Majia Holmer Nadesan

Routledge
Taylor & Francis Group

LONDON AND NEW YORK

First published in 2005 by Routledge
2 Park Square, Milton Park, Abingdon, Oxon OX14 4RN

Simultaneously published in the USA and Canada
by Routledge
29 West 35th Street, New York, NY 10001

Routledge is an imprint of the Taylor & Francis Group

© 2005 Majia Holmer Nadesan

Typeset in 10/12 Sabon by J&L Composition, Filey, North Yorkshire

Printed and bound in Great Britain by TJ International Ltd,
Padstow, Cornwall

British Library Cataloguing in Publication Data
A catalogue record for this book is available from the British
Library

Library of Congress Cataloging in Publication Data
A catalogue record has been requested

ISBN 0-415-32180-8 (hbk)
ISBN 0-415-32181-6 (pbk)

Contents

Acknowledgements

The author would like to acknowledge the editorial support of Michael Walker, to whom a great debt of gratitude is held. The author would also like to acknowledge the support of family members and friends whose willingness to discuss the social construction of autism enabled this project. Finally, the author dedicates this book to her family and, most of all, to Kamal.

1   Introduction

This story begins with my son, Kamal, born September 5, 1996. Kamal, a beautiful, alert, and demanding infant, seemed unusually irritable and inconsolable beyond the "normal" period for these typical behaviors of infancy. Repeated visits to the clinic resulted in a diagnosis of an "overly educated" mother who doted excessively on her demanding son, even when Kamal failed to speak at two years. After all, Kamal was alert and clearly understood the words of those around him even if he failed to replicate them. The clinician attributed his behavioral oddities, such as his tendency to bang his head against the wall when frustrated and his clinginess, to his demanding and sensitive "inborn temperament."

Unsatisfied with this account, I began to visit clinical "experts" in an attempt to understand and remediate Kamal's behavioral oddities and lack of expressive language. A speech therapist's suggestion that Kamal might suffer from a "personality disorder" led me to the office of a well-known child psychologist, who declared Kamal to be "autistic" but "probably not mentally retarded." After delivering these incomprehensible and chilling words, the psychologist responded to my objections that Kamal could not be autistic because he was "so clearly affectionate" by asking whether I thought that he "really loved me." I assumed she was implying that Kamal was incapable of love and at that moment my calm assurance in his love (because he was so very affectionate) dissipated. After all, how *could* he love me if he was indeed autistic?

Within a span of three months, my son's "condition" was explained in terms of my mothering—my "over-education" and excessive ministrations—my son's "inborn" temperament, a personality disorder, and finally autism. No words could describe my or my husband's anguish. We felt that Kamal was lost to us. Yet out of this story grew my intense interest in the subject of autism.

Our story is not unusual. There are many autobiographical narratives written by parents of "autistic" children reflecting a similar search for explanations amidst competing diagnoses. Bewildered and desperate, many parents of recently diagnosed "autistic" children immerse themselves in the scientific and medical literatures on autism. Their successes (or failures) with the many therapies and interventions detailed in the "expert" literature are often published as triumphant accounts of parental assaults against the "fortress" of autism that holds captive their inner child. While these stories can be inspiring, they seemed to leave a gap in the existing literature on autism.

The medical and scientific literatures represent autism as a biological facticity that must be explained using the positivist methods and assumptions of the natural sciences. That is, the medical and scientific literatures often assume autism is some *thing or things*, some essential biogenetic condition(s), which will ultimately be unequivocally identified and known as a spatially centered genetic, neurological, or chemical abnormality through the efforts of scientists toiling in their laboratories.

In the literature directed to popular audiences or parents of autistic children (e.g., Maurice's (1993) *Let Me Hear your Voice: A Family's Triumph over Autism*), autism is a biologically based psychiatric condition to be therapied, remedied, assaulted in an effort to "save" afflicted children locked inside an autistic cage. The popularity of this literature is growing and its dissemination encouraged by the proliferation of Internet sites dedicated to autism support groups.

Yet, it became increasingly clear to me that autism, or more specifically, the *idea* of autism is fundamentally *socially constructed*. To make the claim that the idea of autism is socially constructed is not necessarily to reject a biological basis for the conditions or symptoms that come to be labeled as "autistic." Rather, I use the phrase "socially constructed" to point to the social conditions of possibility for the naming of autism as a distinct disorder and to the social conditions of possibility for our methods of interpreting the disorder, representing it, remediating it, and even for performing it.

And yes, autism has a performative component, as known by every parent who struggled to meet the criteria for government and educational services for their child. For the social services agent, I must stress (and even exaggerate) Kamal's maladaptive behaviors. For his teachers, I stress Kamal's high intellect in order to avoid having him labeled as "mentally retarded."[1] For his peers, Kamal performs "normality" in the context of the school playground by stifling his odd interests and masking social awkwardness in order to "fit in" with the other children. For those parents with whom I have shared the "secret" of Kamal, I carefully engineer their interpretation of his diagnosis to ensure their "understanding" for his oddities without engendering their alienation. Although there is a biological aspect to this condition named autism, the social factors involved in its identification, representation, interpretation, remediation, and performance are the most important factors in the determination of what it means to be autistic, for individuals, for families and for society.

This book attempts to redress this limitation in the vast corpus of literature on autism by addressing the social conditions and practices that enabled autism to be identified, labeled, and remediated in the early twentieth century as well as those conditions that prevail today that enable the labeling of childhood autism, particularly high-functioning childhood autism, an "epidemic" with dramatic increases in diagnoses up to 1000 percent.[2] Although much maligned, "autism" as an epidemic has also captured the public imagination as a disorder that is regarded simultaneously as both threatening and fascinating. Therefore, exploration of the social conditions involved in the production, interpretation, and remediation of autism is important not only for people intimately involved with autism, but also for those interested in how social institutions such as medicine, psychology, and psychiatry, and even the popular media, constitute and shape our ideas about normality and difference in the context of economic and political environments. Thus, what is at stake in this exploration extends beyond "autism" as a distinct disorder to include the ideas and practices whereby we constitute everyday life and social institutions, including the processes that will ultimately produce the opportunities for personhood in the early twenty-first century.

Autism, as I will argue, is a disorder of the early twentieth century while the high-functioning variants of autism such as Semantic Pragmatic Disorder (SPD), Pervasive Developmental Disorder (PDD), and Asperger's syndrome (AS) are fundamentally disorders of the late twentieth and early twenty-first centuries.[3] This is to say that as a distinct psychological disorder or psychiatric disease, autism could not have emerged in the nineteenth century, even while I concede that there have been, no doubt, people throughout history who have displayed the symptoms we now group and define as autism.[4] The idea of autism could not have emerged as a distinct disorder because within the diagnostic categories of nineteenth century (and earlier) thought, autism was unthinkable. If autism was unthinkable within the scientific taxonomies, medical nosologies, and medical practices of nineteenth-century thought, "high-functioning" or "shadow" variants of autism were largely unthinkable diagnostic categories until the mid- to late twentieth century.[5] It was not until standards of normality had been formalized and narrowed and standards of pediatric screening extended to a child's earliest years that children with PDD, SPD, or AS (or Attention Deficit Disorder (ADD) and Attention Deficit Hyperactivity Disorder (ADHD)) could be widely identified, labeled, and therapied. And so the history of autism in all of its forms must be contextualized within the evolution and transformation of medical practices, the development of professions such as psychiatry, psychology, social work, and special education, many of which either emerged or were professionalized in the early twentieth century.

The history of "high-functioning" forms of autism must be further understood in the context of new standards for parenting that emerged mid-twentieth century and new economic and social conditions surrounding the purported "information revolution" that began in the 1960s. As I will argue, the public's fascination with autism, particularly its high-functioning forms, stems in large part from the idea that people with autism are technologically gifted and are particularly adept with computer technology.[6]

The scientific search for understanding the essence of autism in the late twentieth century must also be contextualized within a new matrix of practices that seeks to explain social behaviors in terms of genetic markers, which are seen as entities that will ultimately be linked (deterministically) to the whole repertoire of human behaviors. Likewise, the popularization of neuroscience, fueled by the development of new neural imaging technologies, plays an important role in shaping the scientific study and understanding of autism. Late-twentieth-century efforts to link genetics and neuroscience provide a new paradigm for representing and predicting the social significance of human differences that will, no doubt, play an important role in the identity politics of the early twenty-first century.

Finally, alternative explanations for interpreting the rise of autism diagnoses must be explored. In particular, environmental discourses play an important, although somewhat marginal role, in explaining and preventing disease at the end of the twentieth century. These environmental discourses, particularly when coupled with biomedical frameworks, play a role in the political debates surrounding the causes of autism.

In sum, this book addresses the social complexity of autism, embracing the ambivalence and contradictions associated with its interpretations and remediations, not only to understand its social construction but also to gain insight into some of the cultural frameworks of interpretation and social practices that are leading us into the twenty-first century. Moreover, the book pointedly demonstrates that contemporary understandings and practices are inflected by historically rooted philosophical assumptions and theoretical frameworks of interpretation. Historical significations often implicitly shape the problem space and context of understanding for current approaches to studying, representing, and treating autism.

Recognizing the problematics associated with the vocabulary of social construction, particularly when applied to a psychiatric disorder that is undoubtedly real/material in terms of its symptoms and effects, I will attempt to clarify my position and objectives before proceeding further:

- Without denying that autism has a biogenetic component, I aim to explore the *matrices* of social practices and institutions that enabled the identification and interpretation of (the *idea* of) autism and, later and in more depth, (the *ideas* of) high-functioning forms of autism, particularly Asperger's syndrome, as distinct psychiatric disorders.
- I will argue that the matrix of practices and institutions that enabled the identification and interpretation of classical autism was historically specific, as is the matrix that is contributing to increased rates of diagnoses for high-functioning forms of autism. However, the historical specificity of these matrices does not preclude the tendency for current

understandings to be framed in relation to historically rooted interpretive paradigms.

- I will argue that the contemporary matrix of practices and institutions used to identify, label, and therapy autistic people contributes to the production and interpretation of the behaviors, self-awareness, and "other" awareness of people understood as autistic.
- I will explore how ideas about autism reflect and shape societal norms and expectations and opportunities for personhood.

This project, involving an exploration into the social construction of autism, will be organized into the following chapters.

Chapter 2 contextualizes this project in several ways. First, it introduces the reader to current psychological criteria used to identify autistic spectrum disorders and provides a brief history of their emergence in the early twentieth century. Second, it introduces and explores the thesis that biological diseases, particularly autism, and the clinical practices developed to "cure" them are fundamentally cultural in origin and remediation. This thesis does not reject a biological component to autism; rather, the argument forwarded here is that the emergence, identification, and treatment of disease are always infused with cultural practices, values, and frameworks of interpretation. Third, this chapter provides the theoretical framework for exploring how autism can be understood historically as a "niche" disorder whose interpretation, representation in research practices and in the popular imagination, and remediation reflect cultural preoccupations and concerns.

Chapter 3 addresses the historically embedded psychiatric niche conditions that enabled the identification and emergence of autism and Asperger's syndrome in the early twentieth century. Accordingly, the chapter provides a social history of the material institutions, professional identities, and cultural values that enabled Kanner and Asperger to name autism and Asperger's syndrome and frame their meanings in relation to the diagnostic categories of their time. Kanner derived the name for autism from Eugene Bleuler's descriptive account of schizophrenia. Asperger also invoked Bleuler's idea of autism but recontextualized the concept within the framework of a personality disorder. Ultimately through the discussions of this chapter and the next it will be evident that the matrix of institutions and practices that engendered the identification and exploration of autism in the works of Leo Kanner and Hans Asperger in the 1940s was dependent upon the emergence of a new, early-twentieth-century psychiatric model of the medical subject that centered childhood psychopathology, personality, and social relationships/interpersonal dynamics. The role of childhood in this matrix is addressed in Chapter 4.

Chapter 4 addresses the historical niche conditions that enabled early-twentieth-century psychiatrists and physicians to address mental illness in children. In particular, the chapter contextualizes the works of Leo Kanner and Hans Asperger within early-twentieth-century child guidance and mental hygiene movements, which together brought childhood into focus as a legitimate sphere of psychiatric inquiry. Moreover, the chapter traces this new focus to social institutions and professional identities that emerged in the nineteenth century. The chapter argues that the early-twentieth-century interest in childhood was a direct function of the expansion of compulsory education, the late-nineteenth-century interest in childhood "development," and the child-saving movement. The new professionals—child educators, child psychologists, and social workers—all played a vital role in ensuring the convergence of events and institutions that provided the conditions of possibility for Leo Kanner to "discover" autism. These same trajectories enabled Hans Asperger to identify Asperger's syndrome as well, although in the context of European institutional and social relationships.

Chapter 5 explores in depth how autism emerged in professional research and clinical practices as well as in the popular imagination in the United States and Britain in the mid- to late twentieth century. The chapter addresses how two dominant psychological paradigms, psychoanalysis and cognitive psychology, shaped professional and popular understandings of autism in the context of distinct historical circumstances that were specific to the post-World War II period and to the late-twentieth-century "information revolution." Accordingly, the psychoanalytic construction of autism as an ego shipwrecked on the shores of object relations for lack of adequate mothering is historically contextualized when compared to the cognitive articulation of autism in relation to the vagaries of computational intelligences. Cognitive psychology's interest in and research about high-functioning forms of autism are of particular relevance because they point to late-twentieth-century representational practices that center the young child's brain as a locus for research and therapeutic intervention, as well as to "parent-centered" bourgeois practices and interpretive frameworks that articulate childhood as the locus of class mobility, particularly in the context of the "information" age. The chapter will conclude that autism has multiple valences in the context of late-twentieth-century life. Autism signifies pathology and difference in a historical epoch that increasingly emphasizes physical and psychological "health." Yet, autism also signifies technological aptitude as illustrated in this passage from a *Los Angeles Times* article on the prototypical "computer geek": "There is some fascinating speculation going on these days that the well-known stereotype of the computer geek or nerd may actually be a description of mild autism, especially a form of autism known as Asperger's syndrome" (Chapman 1999). As I argue, the simultaneous elevation and denigration of "high-functioning" autistic characterizations speak more to cultural preoccupations than they do to the "essential" autistic personality.

Chapter 6 explores autism in the context of an emergent and increasingly dominant set of research and representational practices labeled (by critics) the "geneticization thesis" (Lippman 1991). Responding to the increased tendency for researchers, clinicians, and the media to interpret psychological problems and individual behaviors in terms of genetic determinism, critics argue that the gene has become reified in science and the popular imagination as the ultimate causal agent for human behavior and forms of sociality (see Hedgecoe 2001; Keller 1995; Rabinow 1999; ten Have 2001). As Novas and Rose (2000) argue, the new "discourse" of geneticization has profound implications, including the production of "new categories of individuals and according genetic risk a new calculability" (486). The intersection of popular articulations of autism—including the presupposition that "high-functioning" people with autism are somehow selected for by the demands of the "information age"—renders exploration of the geneticization thesis in the context of autism particularly relevant for understanding the social construction and transformation of pathology and normalcy in the late twentieth century.

Chapter 7 explores how the bodies of knowledge and practices identified in previous chapters operate upon those people who are labeled "autistic" in the United States. In this respect, the chapter will address how the disciplinary knowledge produced by psychology and medicine are translated into concrete therapeutic practices. Although the effects of these practices are difficult to determine conclusively, I speculate how they might shape the expression of autistic symptoms. This chapter will also explore how individuals with high-functioning autism, particularly AS, inhabit the identities to which they have been ascribed and how they appropriate and/or resist autistic ascriptions in their efforts to promote their sense of personal well-being. Accordingly, the chapter illustrates how the voices of "autistic" people and their relatives speak from and resist the various interpretive frameworks and therapeutic spaces explored in this project. So labeled "autistic voices" will be interpreted as they resound in a variety of media sources including published interviews and personalized web sites.

Chapter 8 concludes the book by considering various effects of the current articulations of autism. This chapter does not attempt to locate the "truth" of autism because, as I argue, there is no fixed, universal biological truth to be located. Autism is produced through the nosological clustering of symptoms and through the clinical practices of remediation. It is "produced" through historically unique institutional and representational practices described in this book. It is also produced through the effects of its articulations and therapeutic remediations on individuals labeled with this disorder. This argument does not deny biological differences: it does not deny that genetics, ontogenetic socialization factors, and environmental chemicals shape the emergence and expression of our experiential embodiment. Rather, the argument made here is that the processes of identifying, interpreting, and remediating embodied differences are cultural and historically specific and socially and materially mediated. Autism is not outside of the symbolic awaiting discovery. Autism is inscribed and produced through the symbolic and an investigation into these processes of inscription/production reveals current desires, anxieties, and opportunities for personhood in the early twenty-first century.

Notes

1 For excellent accounts of how mental retardation has been socially constructed see Trent's (1994) *Inventing the Feeble Mind* and Wright and Digby's (1996) *From Idiocy to Mental Deficiency*.
2 See "Evidence mounts for epidemic of autism" in the 2000 edition of *Autism Research Review*, 14(2): 1. Indeed, "autism" has become such a ubiquitous disorder that the state of California allocated $34 million for autistic spectrum disorders research in 2000 (California 2000).
3 Although first described by Hans Asperger in the 1940s, "Asperger's syndrome" was not defined as such or well known until publicized by Lorna Wing in 1981. Until the popularization of Asperger's syndrome as a diagnostic entity, adolescents and adults with overt social "deficiencies" but "normal" intelligence were often diagnosed with personality disorders, such as "schizoid" personality disorder, from the 1940s onward.
4 For a case study of an individual who has been retroactively labeled "autistic", see Rab Houston and Uta Frith's (2000) *Autism in History: The Case of Hugh Blair of Borgue*.
5 For a discussion of "shadow" syndromes, including shadow forms of autism, see Ratey and Johnson's (1997) *Shadow Syndromes: The Mild Forms of Major Mental Illnesses that Sabotage Us*.
6 For example, in December 2001 *Wired* magazine ran an article titled "The geek syndrome" written by Steve Silberman that speculates that some technologically "gifted" individuals may have Asperger's syndrome and that autism and Asperger's syndrome diagnoses are surging among the children of Silicon Valley. Silberman speculates that "math and tech genes" may be to blame.

2 Constructing autism

A dialectic of biology and culture, nature and mind

Efforts to define the precise *essence* of autism escape the best representational practices of scientists and medical practitioners: consequently, even at the dawn of the twenty-first century, we do not know what autism *is*. That the nature of autism remains ambiguous and elusive seems to spur more efforts to represent it definitively and concretely in biomedical research and in diagnostic nosologies. Yet, these representational efforts seemed doomed to failure if success is measured by the creation of a comprehensive theory for the origins of the disorder. Perhaps because autism is defined and delimited in terms of lack, a lack of "normal" communication skills defined in the broadest possible way, that it is so difficult to pinpoint a definitive etiology and, even, a definitive set of behavioral/expressive "autistic" markers.

Perhaps it is the case that the etiology of autism lies in a multitude of mutually entwined biological and cultural/social factors, including the very standards of normality used in the determination of the disorder. Put another way, perhaps autism is not a *thing* but is a nominal category useful for grouping heterogeneous people all sharing communication practices deviating significantly from the expectations of normalcy. These communication practices are becoming, increasingly, standardized, codified, and widely distributed. Such an approach to autism need not reject the idea that so-labeled "autistic" people's biochemistry impacts their communicative practices. Rather, this approach opens up the opportunity space for exploring how socially constructed standards of normalcy embedded in cultural values and practices not only shape our interpretations of autism but also contribute to the production and transformation of people labeled with the disorder. Thus, rather than attempting to unlock the biogenetic "key" of autism, this chapter takes the first step in exploring the cultural processes involved in its production. First, the chapter introduces the reader to current psychological criteria used to identify autistic spectrum disorders and provides a brief history of their emergence in the early twentieth century. Second, it introduces and explores the thesis that biological diseases, particularly autism, and the clinical practices developed to "cure" them are fundamentally cultural in origin and remediation. This forwards the argument that cultural practices, values, and frameworks of interpretation always infuse the emergence, identification, and treatment of disease. Third, this chapter provides the theoretical framework for exploring in subsequent chapters how autism, particularly high-functioning forms of autism, can be understood historically as a "niche" disorder whose interpretation and remediation reflect cultural preoccupations and concerns.

Diagnostic autism: classical readings and contemporary nosologies

In this section, I introduce readers to "autism" as a diagnostic category by providing a brief history of its popularization in the 1940s and by introducing the various diagnostic categories and criteria used to carve up the "spectrum" of autistic disorders. The diagnoses of an autistic spectrum disorder are broadly applied to children who have widely divergent life histories, although different labels are applied to differentiate children based on age of onset and severity of impairments.

Classical readings in autism

Writing in Baltimore, Maryland, in 1943, Leo Kanner delimited autism as a distinct psychiatric disorder.[1] One year later, writing in Vienna, Hans Asperger also identified and described a syndrome, which has come to bear his name: Asperger's syndrome. It is instructive to return to these original writings before moving to contemporary definitions of autistic spectrum disorders.

In 1943 Leo Kanner published an essay about eleven children in his clinical practice. The essay was titled "Autistic disturbances of affective content" and described a previously unreported syndrome, which he described in terms of an

> *inability to relate* themselves in the ordinary way to people and situations from the beginning of life. Their parents referred to them as having always been "self-sufficient" . . . This is not, as in schizophrenic children or adults, a departure from an initially present relationship; it is not a "withdrawal" from formerly existing participation. There is from the start an *extreme autistic aloneness* that, whenever possible, disregards, ignores, shuts out anything that comes to the child from the outside.
>
> (Kanner 1943: 41)

Kanner was particularly struck by the fact that all of the mothers of the eleven children studied reported that as infants these children failed "*to assume at any time an anticipatory posture* preparatory to being picked up" (41). They also experienced communication delays and were inclined to take a literal approach to language comprehension and usage, as illustrated by their practice of "*delayed echolalia*", whereupon the child would affirm a parent's question with a literal repetition of the question (43). Personal pronouns, such as I and you, were exceedingly difficult for these children to apply appropriately. Despite these handicaps, Kanner noted these children exhibited an "*excellent rote memory*" and were able to read, although some exhibited problems with comprehension (42). Perhaps above all, Kanner stressed the children's fear of intrusions from the outside world (e.g., loud noises) and their "*anxiously obsessive desire for the maintenance of sameness*"(44).

In his struggle to provide an adequate label for this syndrome, Kanner drew upon Eugene Bleuler's (1908) clinical description of dementia prae-cox, a more general category of psychiatric distress eventually narrowed to those patients who exhibited the symptoms we now associate with schizo-phrenia. Bleuler used the term autistic to describe his psychotic patients' tendency to withdraw from the external world into fantasy (see Alexander and Selesnick 1966; Berrios 1996). Kanner recognized that his use of the term "autistic" differed from Bleuler's, but felt unable to find a more concise definition (Kanner, in Donnellan 1985: 2).

Within one year of the publication of his 1943 essay, Kanner's "early infantile autism" entered the psychiatric nomenclature and soon captured widespread psychiatric attention (Neumarker 2003). In the mid-1950s, Kanner and Eisenberg (1956) modified the diagnostic criteria for autism to stress (1) a profound lack of affective contact and (2) elaborate, repetitive, ritualistic behavior in the absence of psychotic symptoms (Wing 1993). However, to Kanner's dismay, for the next several decades "early infantile autism" remained sub-categorized under "schizophrenia, childhood type," according to the American Psychiatric Association's (APA) *Diagnostic and Statistical Manual of Mental Disorders* (DSM) versions I (1952) and II (1968).

It was not until 1980 with the third edition of the DSM (DSM-III), that autism was formally distinguished from schizophrenia by the APA with the advent of the general category of "Pervasive Developmental Disorders" (PDD). PDD encompassed autism and related disorders characterized by deficits of social interaction, social communication, and social/symbolic play. "Infantile autism" was a subgroup of PDD defined by lack of respon-siveness to others, language difficulties, resistance to change or attachment to objects, the absence of schizophrenic features, and onset before 30 months (Wing 1993). DSM-III had categories for late onset (after 30 months) and for atypical PDD (Wing 1993).

In 1987, the APA again revised the diagnostic criteria for autism with the publication of the DSM-III-R. This version loosened the autism criteria to recognize variations in the degree of deficits across the three key areas: (1) reciprocal social interaction, (2) communication (verbal and non-verbal), and (3) repetitive, stereotyped or ritualistic behavior. The DSM-III-R thus allowed children with more subtle symptoms to be diagnosed with autism and related disorders such as "high functioning Autistic Disorder" or "Pervasive Developmental Disorder Not Otherwise Specified" (PDD-NOS). Age of onset was de-emphasized, and diagnosis was to occur independently of level of intelligence or the presence of associated conditions (Wing 1993).

Asperger's syndrome did not arrive into the DSM's taxonomies until the 1994 revision. Accordingly, the DSM-IV included Asperger's syndrome—formally "Asperger's Disorder"—as a separate heading under the general classification of Pervasive Developmental Disorders. The DSM-IV also substituted "autistic disorder" for "infantile autism" (Bishop 1989). I turn now to the history of the inclusion of Asperger's syndrome within the psychiatric nosologies some fifty years after its articulation by Hans Asperger.

Writing his doctoral thesis in Vienna in 1944, Hans Asperger pondered a group of four boys whom he described as having an "autistic psychopathy" form of personality disorder (see Wing 1981). Although unaware of Kanner's work because of the war, Asperger's description closely mirrored Kanner's, except that Asperger's group of four boys was less communicatively impaired and exhibited intensely developed special interests not noted in Kanner's pioneering work. In later years, Asperger described the difference between children with Kanner's autism and those with the disorder of his name in the following terms:

> Kanner's early infantile autism is a near psychotic or even psychotic state, though not identical with schizophrenia. Asperger's typical cases are very intelligent children with extraordinary originality of thought and spontaneity of activity though their actions are not always the right response to the prevailing situation. Their thinking, too, seems unusual in that it is endowed with special abilities in the areas of logic and abstraction and these often follow their own cause with no regard for outside influences.
>
> (Asperger 1979: 48)

According to Asperger's account, these children share many of the maladies described by Kanner (including stereotypes of movement, obsessional attachments, lack of adaptability, and monotonous speech) but their social prognosis is much better. Moreover, their particular cognitive profile may lead to professional success despite engendering social handicaps, as illustrated by Asperger's statement that: "Indeed, it seems that for success in science or art a dash of autism is essential" (Asperger 1979: 49). However, Asperger noted that parallel to Kanner's children with autism, those with Asperger's syndrome have great difficulty learning and using the pronoun "I" leading him to comment that: "It shows that the children do not find themselves at all at home with others and are even strangers to themselves in spite, or because of their extraordinary abilities" (50).

Asperger (1979) felt the term "autistic" could apply to "disturbances in behaviour of quite different origin which can and should be differentiated" despite the fact that "autistic behaviour has its own particular flavour which is unmistakable for the experienced" (50). In trying to reconcile the relative uniformity of autistic expression with the heterogeneity of autistic causes, Asperger wrote: "It is possible for man to behave in an autistic way though nature has given him the tools to be part of the human community" (51). Asperger thus argued that the disorder of his name was a "personality" disorder, whose "type" was distinct from other psychological diagnoses, that could be caused by a variety of factors, both physical (including an inherited or "constitutional basis") and emotional (46).

Speaking in 1977, Asperger argued that his contribution to the development of psychological/psychiatric pediatric thought in the 1940s was his identification of a specific pediatric "personality disorder" whose impact is relatively independent of intellectual functioning (Asperger 1979). And yet, Asperger's contribution remained in relative obscurity for decades before it was included in the widely used psychiatric classifications systems, DSM-IV and the World Health Organization's (WHO) *International Classification of Diseases* (ICD-10).

In 1981 Asperger's work was introduced to a wider audience through Lorna Wing's essay "Asperger's syndrome: a clinical account" published in the journal, *Psychological Medicine*. Wing drew upon Asperger's observations to describe children and adults who exhibit normal intellects yet experience relatively severe impairments in their abilities to understand and relate to others. She coined the phrase "Asperger's syndrome" to refer to their impairments, which she summarized in terms of lack of empathy, one-sided or naive interaction, difficulty with friendship formation processes, pedantic, repetitive speech, poor non-verbal communication, intense preoccupation with certain subjects, and poor gross motor coordination (Burgoine and Wing 1983). Wing modified Asperger's descriptions somewhat as she viewed the children in her practice as more afflicted communicatively in their earliest years (e.g., more delayed speech and social withdrawal than observed by Asperger) and less capable of imaginative play.

Wing saw strong similarities between Asperger's "autistic psychopathy" and Kanner's autism. Accordingly, she felt that Asperger's syndrome ought *not* to be viewed as "personality disorder," even while acknowledging that many people who fall under Asperger's syndrome would previously have been diagnosed as "schizoid," a personality disorder. Instead, in 1988 Wing suggested viewing both Asperger's syndrome and autism in relation to a continuum of developmental disorders. She named this continuum the "autistic spectrum" and described it in terms of "a continuum of impairments of the development of social interaction, communication and consequent rigid, repetitive behavior" (Wing 1991: 111). Wing argued the autistic continuum ranges from the most profoundly retarded to the "most able, highly intelligent person with social impairment in its subtlest form as his own disability" (111).

Wing (1991) rejected classifying Asperger's syndrome as a personality disorder because she felt that its identification within the autism continuum had more practical value for management and prognosis. Her views prevailed; however, the "schizoid" personality disorder remains in contemporary psychiatric nosologies and its exact relationship with, and diagnostic distinction from, Asperger's syndrome remain somewhat ambiguous. Technically, Asperger's syndrome's differential diagnosis from the schizoid personality type is based in the former's tendency toward stereotyped behaviors and interests and more impaired social interaction.[2] However, the boundaries between and across eccentricity, the schizoid personality, and the developmental disorder, Asperger's disorder remain fraught with contention (see McCallum 2001; Rapin 2002; Sowell 1997, 2001).

Asperger's syndrome is now technically classified under the DSM-IV's category of PDD but is typically considered as part of the autistic *spectrum* disorders, which broadly include (classical) Autism, High Functioning Autism (HFA), Asperger's syndrome (AS), Semantic Pragmatic Disorder (SPD), Childhood Disintegrative Disorder (CDD), and sometimes Attention Deficit Disorder (ADD) and Attention Deficit Hyperactivity Disorder (ADHD). Classifying the relationships between and across these disorders remains fraught with contention (e.g. see Mayes et al. 2001). The determination of diagnoses and the problem of overlapping diagnostic criteria bedevil researchers and clinicians. Worse, the etiology of these diverse but purportedly related disorders remains unclear, leaving researchers unable to determine whether all of these disorders share a common etiology (to explain overlapping symptoms) or whether the phrase "autistic spectrum disorders" is merely a nominal category, a short-hand indicator, that refers to nothing *real* in the sense of a biologically unified and cohesive disorder. Thus, given this confusion, a diagnosis such as autism or Asperger's disorder is contingent on the interpretive work of the clinician's endeavors to match an individual's symptoms to the diagnostic criteria provided by the APA's DSM-IV and the WHO's ICD-10. It is to these that I turn to provide a more detailed discussion of contemporary diagnostic criteria and procedures.

Diagnosing autism

As explained above, a simple answer to what autism *is*, that is, what constitutes its essence, is unattainable. As explained by medical experts, "autism is heterogeneous with respect to clinical symptoms and etiology, and varied presentations of the disorder may be the final common pathway of environmental factors (e.g., infections, birth trauma) and genetic factors (e.g., fragile X syndrome)" (Hollander et al. 1998: 22). Heterogeneity in autistic symptoms and, possibly, the etiology (or cause) create confusion about diagnostic differentiation of the autistic spectrum disorders (e.g., Childhood Disintegrative Disorder, autism, Rett's disorder), as well as differentiation of these disorders from other related disorders such as Childhood-Onset Schizophrenia (with psychosis), Obsessive-Compulsive Disorder, Schizoid Personality Disorder, and Schizotypal Personality Disorder, among others. The DSM-IV and the ICD-10 provide general guidelines for diagnoses (despite subtle variations in categories and descriptions) but construct the autistic disorders as dichotomous categories, which problematizes actual diagnoses when symptoms vary in their degree of expression across individuals and across individual life spans.

The DSM-IV stipulates a diagnosis of autism (299.00 Autistic Disorder) requires the patient exhibit symptoms (a total of six or more items) from a triad of behavioral/communication impairments including: (1) impairments in social interaction, including impairments in non-verbal behaviors ("eye contact," "facial expressions," "body postures," "gestures to regulate social interaction"), impairments in ability to develop appropriate peer relationships, and impairments in emotional reciprocity (e.g., pleasure in other people's happiness), (2) impairments in communication including delays in expressive language, impairments in conversational competence, use of stereotypic or repetitive language, and lack of spontaneous make-believe play, and (3) "restricted repetitive and *stereotyped patterns of behavior, interests, and activities.*" Onset of delays and/or impairments must occur before the age of three for a diagnosis of autistic disorder (70–71). With few substantive differences, the diagnostic criteria stipulated in the ICD-10 by the World Health Organization basically mirror these criteria.[3] Neither system specifies that mental retardation be an essential diagnostic feature of autism.

Because of the heterogeneity of autistic expressions, both the ICD-10 and the DSM-IV include a diagnostic category for atypical expression: "Atypical Autism" in the ICD-10 requires the patient meet fewer of the diagnostic criteria stipulated for autism as does Pervasive Developmental Disorder: Not Otherwise Specified (299.80 PDD-NOS) in the DSM-IV. In DSM-IV, late age of onset requires a diagnosis of PDD-NOS in the absence of other diagnostic possibilities (e.g. schizophrenia). A variety of disorders related to "atypical" autism are subsumed within this category including Nonverbal Learning Disability, Developmental Learning Disability of the Right Hemisphere, and Semantic Pragmatic Processing Disorder (see Klin and Volkmar 1997).

"Asperger's Disorder" has its own diagnostic sub-category in both the ICD-10 and the DSM-IV.[4] However, as noted above, clinicians and researchers find it very difficult to sort out the differences across autism disorder, PDD-NOS (atypical autism), and Asperger's syndrome. Indeed, the DSM-IV lists basically the same diagnostic criteria for Asperger's disorder as it does for autism disorder, excepting delays and impairments in communication. Asperger's disorder also stipulates the requirement of near-normal intelligence and self-help skills. However, both Hans Asperger and Lorna Wing reported AS patients who were either speech delayed as small children or evidenced mild mental retardation (Tsai 2004). Other researchers have found that patients diagnosed with Asperger's disorder invariably evidence communication impairments because of their social deficits and restricted interests (Mayes et al. 2001). Szatmari et al. (1995) went so far as to argue that a diagnosis of Asperger's disorder is impossible using the DSM-IV because the clinical presentation of features would require a diagnosis of autistic disorder. And Miller and Ozonoff (1997) suggest that present diagnostic criteria for Asperger's disorder do not necessarily capture the syndrome described by Asperger. Finally, the presence of co-morbid psychiatric disorders such as Tourette's disorder, psychosis, and schizophrenia in some individuals diagnosed with Asperger's disorder undermines the exclusivity of psychoses and PDDs (Tsai 2004).

As one can infer from this rather confused discussion of related diagnostic categories and overlapping diagnostic criteria, autism has yet to be fully understood in terms of its symptoms or etiology. The best efforts towards revising the ICD and the DSM have not fully eliminated diagnostic confusion and overlapping categories as illustrated by the unfortunate overlap of Disintegrative Psychosis in ICD-9 and Autistic Disorder in DSM-III-R (see Volkmar et al. 1997b: 48). Thus, at best, autism is understood as a multiplex disorder encompassing at least three continua of impairments. Individual differences in the degree of impairment along these continua results in multiple diagnostic categories designed to group individuals with similar patterns of variance. Often, clinicians forgo investigation into the origins of their patients' disorders unless warranted by the need to make a differential diagnosis such as in the case of Fragile X syndrome.

Etiological analysis, in contrast, is left to researchers who often work on isolated strands of research focusing on: (1) research attempts to identify the genetic markers that cause, identify, or predict autistic behaviors in individuals, (2) research attempts to use advanced neural scanning techniques to identify neurological topological or electrical abnormalities in the brains of autistic patients, and (3) research attempts to identify unique metabolic and/or immunological profiles of autistic people. These research orientations are discussed further in later chapters, but for now it suffices to say these research efforts typically search for definitive and generalizable origins for autistic disorders. Further the research tends to be largely disconnected from the clinical practice of diagnosing patients.

In order to make this rather abstract discussion of diagnostics and etiology more concrete, let me provide several real examples of autistic diagnoses. In a newsletter for parents of developmentally delayed children, one parent reports on her son's autistic diagnosis:

> Jeremy, one of our twins, was born with severe heart defects. His doctor told us that there was nothing that they could do for him, and he would soon die. However, when he was just one week old we found a doctor in Los Angeles who performed Jeremy's first surgery, and it

saved his life. Six months later, Jeremy endured a second surgery leaving him weak, unable to lift his head, and behaving differently. Little did we know then, our world was changing and it would never be the same. Two years later, our son was diagnosed with autism.[5]

Although lacking a clinical history, the reader is led to infer that Jeremy suffered some unalterable brain damage during his second surgery, causing the onset of his autistic symptoms. Asperger (1979) himself observed that brain damage could produce autistic-like symptoms and, unlike Kanner, he did not feel that such "acquired" forms of autism should not be classified as such. In the case of Jeremy, however, the root source of his symptoms remains undiagnosed.

Compare Jeremy's story with the story of Joel, reported in the same newsletter:

Born in 1974, Joel seemed to be a normal baby well into his second year of life. At 21 months, he seemed to change overnight. Joel stopped talking, didn't look directly at anyone, seemed selectively deaf, and no longer played with his toys. It took my husband and me two full years, and going to a dozen specialists, before he was diagnosed with autism.[6]

Based on the brief description provided here, Joel may meet the diagnostic criteria for the particularly disabling form of autism termed Childhood Disintegrative Disorder (CDD) described in terms of a delayed onset of symptoms, which are themselves marked by significant regression (Volmar et al. 1997b). CDD may be particularly tragic for parents who watch their apparently "normal" child undergo massive and irreparable regression. For example, a child diagnosed with CDD may have lost the ability to speak in full sentences within a very short period of time and while that child may ultimately regain some communication skills these tend to be limited in terms of expressive and pragmatic abilities.

The relation between CDD and classical or Kanner's autism is particularly ambiguous because while Kanner's patients typically exhibited "autistic" symptoms from birth, more contemporary accounts of autism often describe the manifestation of "late onset" autistic symptoms as occurring between two and three years of age. In an effort to distinguish CDD from late onset autism, Volkmar et al. (1997b) observe that clinical characteristics of late onset autism tend to be described as higher functioning with more intact cognitive abilities when compared to those described in the case of CDD, whose overall prognosis may be worse. For example, the CDD cases were more likely to be mute. However, the authors observe that efforts to differentiate CDD from autism cause confusion and are ultimately subject to "some degree of judgment on the part of clinicians" (Volkmar et al. 1997b: 50). In all cases, late onset autism and CDD are particularly devastating for parents and the search for answers has increasingly targeted exogamous factors—for example, immunizations or acquired autoimmune disorders—as catalyzing or causing autistic deterioration.

My son's history is quite unlike the ones reported for Jeremy and Joel. His history more closely matches the history of children who are labeled with PDD, SPD, or AS. By the time that Kamal was one year old, I was aware of his subtle differences from other children his age. Although he seemed to understand the language of those around him, he made absolutely no effort to produce speech. Also his use of non-verbal gestures to signal desires seemed stunted compared to his peers. At the same time, he seemed intelligent and was able to point to named items in picture books. Although affectionate and sociable with family members, he was easily frustrated and prone to tantrums at an early age. By age two, he was aggressive with other children and banged his head against walls when frustrated. However, he seemed typical, even precocious, in other respects: he loved being read to and pointed to letters and numbers; he recognized and sorted shapes and colors. He also seemed quite able to convey his wants despite lacking expressive language. A very demanding and difficult child, he also was quite affectionate and bright, as confirmed by a formal non-verbal assessment of his intelligence conducted by a speech therapist. My observations of his communication skills were particularly nuanced as I received my PhD in communication studies. Perhaps my tendency to provide detailed accounts of his "oddities" to the pediatric staff at the clinic led to their diagnosis of me as an "overly educated mother."

Kamal did, and continues to, fit the diagnostic criteria of autism disorder, AS, PDD-NOS, and SPD but his impairments are relatively "mild." That is, nowadays Kamal has relatively normal expressive and receptive language but he has some difficulty with peer relationships (particularly in unstructured venues with unfamiliar children), his language use can at times be stereotypic and monotonous, his interests tend to be circumscribed, and he formerly suffered from a mild form of obsessive-compulsive disorder. Kamal has been classified or described by a bevy of clinicians and educators as having PDD-NOS, AS, and SPD. The classification of SPD (Semantic Pragmatic Disorder), while not an officially accepted diagnostic category, is particularly useful for grouping children such as my son who exhibit subtly impaired social-pragmatic skills but are otherwise "normal" or "above normal" in intellectual development. The relationship between AS and SPD has not been adequately clarified.

Whether PDD-NOS, AS, and SPD are etiologically distinct disorders, each with a clear pathological profile, or simply reflect nominal categories useful only for grouping symptoms remains unclear. However, children and adults who meet the classificatory criteria for these disorders particularly trouble and intrigue clinicians, researchers, and the public. They are typically, and definitionally, normal or even above normal in intellect. Yet they seem to lack or be deficient in those skills culturally regarded as most natural and intuitive, those skills for decoding and encoding nuanced communications addressing the relational, rather than the report function of communication. Since the relational component of communications addresses social expectations and implicit social routines that facilitate everyday unstructured interaction, individuals lacking the ability to encode and decode the relational component of non-verbal and verbal communication find themselves socially handicapped. And yet, one hundred years ago Kamal and many children like him would not meet any diagnostic criteria for a psychiatric or neurological disorder. Unlike Jeremy and Joel, who, because of the severity of their symptoms, would have ultimately been diagnosed with some form of dementia or "idiocy," society would have regarded Kamal as mildly eccentric.

As I later argue in more depth, the emergence of autism as a diagnostic category in the 1940s must be understood in relation to a matrix of professional and parental practices marking the cultural and economic transition to the twentieth century just as the popularization of high-functioning forms of autism must be understood in terms of the matrix of practices that mark late-twentieth-century and early-twenty-first-century life. The conditions of possibility for diagnosing Jeremy or Joel as autistic and Kamal as high-functioning autistic are ultimately less rooted in the biology of their conditions than they are rooted in the cultural practices and economy of their times. For example, in the 1800s, the standards for classifying individuals as disordered were much less nuanced, the standards of normality much broader, and the mechanisms for social and individual surveillance that we take for granted today simply did not exist. Indeed, it was not until the 1930s that developmental guidelines and cognitive profiles were created and used in tracking children's "developmental" progression.[7] Prior to the late 1800s, children, in particular, would not have been subject to any form of "developmental" or psychological examination unless their conditions were particularly severe and their parents particularly economically privileged. Certainly, there were few formalized, standardized instruments for measuring their cognitive skills or assessing whether they suffered from a personality disorder before the 1930s. This raises questions about the relationship between the biological and the cultural, about the relationship between disease and social representation.

Disease and representation

In the search for its essence, the *being* of autism, researchers debated whether autism is a psychological disorder of ego attachment (e.g., Bettelheim 1967), a biological disorder of the brain or metabolism (e.g., later Kanner), a personality disorder (e.g., Asperger), or some combination. Although present-day researchers represent autism as a continuum or as several continua of communicative and cognitive impairments, and pay lip service to the idea these impairments may stem from different etiologies, autism continues to be implicitly and explicitly theorized as a definitive entity whose origins can be found in faulty genetics, neurological impairments (e.g., of the amygdala), or impaired biochemistry. The implicit but dominant model seems to be that there is a visual-spatial-topological autistic center that will ultimately be discovered. This view of autism implicitly invokes a model of medicine in which disease is ontological, *a thing in itself*, which can be distinguished from the afflicted patient whose ontological status is unrelated to the disabling disorder.[8] Now while this model of autism as disease has certain strengths, it also has attendant weaknesses and definitely implies a lack of reflexivity about how autism is constructed through our representational practices in research, in therapy, and in popular accounts. I believe this visual-spatial-topological ontological model prevails because it draws upon our common sense understanding of disease and medicine.

In our everyday thinking and communication, most of us visualize disease as either caused by a scientifically discernible agent such as a virus or bacterium (e.g., AIDS or meningitis) or as emanating from a detectable, localized bodily dysfunction (e.g., heart disease or diabetes). The disease-causing agent or diseased bodily system is seen as objective, available to visual representation, and ultimately, treatable; even if the "cure" eludes current medical understanding. In effect, disease is represented in our everyday understanding as available to "empirical" identification, interpretation, and intervention. This everyday understanding of disease is partially rooted in nineteenth-century "positivistic" thought holding that humankind can identify and understand the laws of nature unequivocally through detached, empirical inquiry. Positivist conceptions of medicine presume a mind–body dichotomy in which diseases are primarily if not exclusively located in the biological body and presume that each disease is caused by a specific and, ultimately, identifiable element.[9] Although medicine, as a professional field, has long rejected many of the positivist assumptions about the nature and origin of disease, our popular understandings and much medical practice continue to invoke these assumptions in the ways we diagnose and treat various diseases.

In contrast to this positivist approach to health and illness, many scholars have demonstrated that disease is partly, or largely, socially constructed. There are, of course, different ways of approaching the social construction of disease. One can explore the social conditions producing disease, such as the role of diet in producing diabetes. Or, one can explore how ideas about disease constrain medical researchers' observations, interpretations, and interventions. This latter approach can oscillate between two positions: first, an extreme constructivism (form of idealism) whereby the disease itself is an unknowable facticity rendered intelligible only through its various representations, which are themselves culturally produced and contingent; or second, a moderated materialism that sees disease in terms of the interaction between the biological and cultural practices of interpretation and remediation.

For example, David Armstrong's (2002) *A New History of Identity* takes a moderated social constructionist approach in tracing changing perceptions of the origin and treatment of disease. Armstrong is less concerned with the biological reality of disease than in the representational practices used to identify, diagnose, and cure it. Accordingly, he argues that prior to the nineteenth century, disease was understood in terms of a "shifting collection of symptoms" lacking "spatial localization" while the origins of disease were understood to be found in the weather, the soil, and various aspects of the physical environment (Armstrong 2002: 58). However, medicine in the late eighteenth and early nineteenth centuries began to localize disease in the form of a "pathological lesion, a specific abnormality of structure (or later, function) situated somewhere in the corporal space" (58).

Whereas pre-nineteenth-century efforts to contain infection focused on the creation of a *cordon sanitaire* designed to regulate people's access to the diseased geographical terrain, the move to visualize disease in terms of a corporal lesion led to what Armstrong (2002) describes as a new regime of hygiene, which demarcated the diseased body from its environment. Medical clinicians of the nineteenth century sought to develop techniques enabling them to identify the nature of the disease/lesion from the telltale signs it inscribed on the body. The actual voice of the medical subject was considered largely irrelevant until, according to Armstrong, the early twentieth century. Indeed, it was not until 1938 that protocols for soliciting the patient's personal history were added to the medical editions of *Physical Diagnosis* (Cabot, Adams 1938) as a means for gaining insight into the origins of a patient's disease. As Armstrong argues, the emergence of the speaking patient as a source of medical information must be understood in relation to the emerging power of the fields of early-twentieth-century psychiatry and psychology to identify, differentiate, and explain individuals' behavior in terms of psychic dysfunction. For psychiatric and psychological experts, disease had to be understood in relation to psychosomatic disturbance and somatopsychic dysfunction and so by 1938 medical experts were advised to attend to the patients' words, in addition to the lesion's signs, for insights into the nature and origins of disease. Armstrong's account of changing conceptions about the nature and origin of disease, as well as its clinical diagnosis and treatment, highlights how social beliefs, values, and institutions influence medical practice.

The accounts of Armstrong (2002) and others demonstrate how illness and health are not simply biological attributes. However, the question typically arising in discussions on the relationship between culture and illness (in all of its forms including mental illness) is whether the cultural component is simply built upon a foundational and determining biological component or, conversely, whether the biological component exists at all.[10] Is culture merely the clothing within which the diseased body appears? Or, does culture—through its practices of hygiene and diet *and* through its medical vocabularies and institutions—produce disease in its entirety? For those versed in academic debates, one can recognize the eternal battle between realists in the materialist camp and nominalists in the idealist camp having their say about the nature and origins of health and disease. At issue are the seemingly inescapable dualisms in western thought between mind and body, culture and biology.

These dualistic frameworks—mind–body and culture–biology—have particularly plagued the study and treatment of illnesses we dub "mental." Although the contemporary fields of psychiatry and psychology trace common roots to Augustine and beyond, their current modes of operation are predicated upon, and reinforce, the mind–body dualism. From at least the 1700s onward, the predecessors of contemporary psychiatrists, alienists and physiologists, tried to explain mental illness in relation to biological disorders and their efforts to categorize symptoms into mental diseases stressed somatic signs, as opposed to the patients' subjective experiences, well into the nineteenth century. Although twentieth-century psychiatry acknowledges the role of the speaking medical subject in the diagnosis of disorders, it continues to target the patient's physiology—particularly in relation to the brain—as opposed to the patient's psychology, for intervention and treatment. In contrast, contemporary psychology, although indebted to many philosophical traditions including positivism, tends to center the "mind" of the speaking subject for investigation and intervention. In contrast to psychiatry's emphasis on somatic processes, contemporary psychology emphasizes mental processes, interpersonal relationships, and behavior, all of which are believed malleable and subject to non-medical therapeutic interventions (Herman 1995). In effect, psychiatry is sovereign over body–brain and psychology over mind. Though rejected philosophically by advocates in both fields, this object–subject dichotomy continues to dominate clinical practice.

The twentieth-century study of autism has been particularly plagued by these dualisms. Derived in relation to schizophrenia, autism was first thought to be organic in nature. However, psychoanalytic thought was becoming increasingly popular in North America and Europe at the time that Kanner first identified and labeled autism. Thus, the ascendancy of psychoanalytic thought, soon after the formalized identification of autism as a distinct disorder, led to speculation that psychic distress brought on by "frigid mothering" caused autistic symptoms. This psychoanalytic orientation to interpreting the etiology of autistic symptoms led to a variety of psychologically directed therapeutic interventions. Today, however, the pendulum has again swung in the direction of organic causes, although contemporary causal agents may be considered exogamous (e.g., mercury poisoning) as well as endogamous (e.g., genetics). Given this organic orientation, autistic patients today are likely to be treated with a variety of drugs ranging from anti-psychotic to anti-yeast agents. This tendency to center the body–brain (perhaps in an effort to erase finally the lingering agony of the "refrigerator mother") often reifies autism in the visual imagination of nineteenth-century medicine whereupon it is a disorder characterized by distinct physical symptoms spatially localized in origin. Such reification and spatial localization may be initially emotionally reassuring to desperate parents and eager researchers but it ultimately leads to frustration as efforts to trace definite and consistent biological markers (such as genetic deviations or neurological pathology) prove impossible and efforts to remediate symptoms through biological agents prove unreliable at best.

Although research and therapies targeting autism have value, in my opinion they are extremely unlikely to be successful in identifying a definitive set of biogenetic factors mechanistically causing or capable of curing all, or even most, forms of autism. What is more, the current tendency for researchers and clinicians, but ironically not insurance companies, to emphasize the biological component of autism can lead to a devaluation of psychologically based therapeutic interventions such as behavioral modification therapy (rooted in behaviorist psychology) or "play therapy" rooted in psychoanalysis. The social construction of "ideas" about the origin and remediation of the "autistic" patient is imbued with material consequences for parents, researchers, therapists, and physicians.

In *Beyond Health*, Fox (1999), among other sociologists of health and medicine, argues that rather than becoming locked within the dualism of nature–biology and culture–mind, a more productive route would be to reject a search for the "truth" of how the body (or brain) "really is." In other words, reject a search for the body's facticity, and instead focus on the *becoming* of the body–mind as constituted by and in relation to cultural processes. Fox's approach need not be construed as necessitating a rejection of the role of biology. Rather, it entails viewing the biological and the cultural as mutually constitutive, inseparable in their constitution of personhood. This approach would not emphasize the mechanistic and reductionistic search for definitive origins, but would instead focus on the *becoming* of autism as it is interpreted, experienced, performed, and resisted. Although there are many avenues of investigation suggested by this orientation, I have narrowed my focus to exploring the cultural articulations within which autism was, and continues to be, identified, performed, and therapied. In an effort to demonstrate how this approach need not reject a biological component to the disorder, I turn to some preliminary efforts by Ian Hacking to resolve the material–ideal conundrums associated with the positivist–constructionist paradigms.

In *The Social Construction of What?* Hacking (1999) sets out to demonstrate the interaction of biology and culture, materiality and ideas, through a variety of examples including schizophrenia, child abuse, and childhood autism. Hacking contrasts the idea of "interactive kinds" with "indifferent kinds" to explain the mediation of socially constructed ideas and material existence: "'Interactive' is a new concept that applies not to people but to classifications, to kinds, to the kinds that can influence what is classified. And because kinds can interact with what is classified, the classification itself may be modified or replaced" (Hacking 1999: 103). Unlike "indifferent kinds," which refer to the classifications of entities not affected by their classifications as such, "interactive kinds" are fundamentally affected by, and produced in relation to, the categories and labels used to describe them. For example, Hacking notes that the indifferent kind "plutonium," although manufactured by humans, does not interact with the "idea" of plutonium. "Indifferent kinds" do not possess "self-awareness" or "self-conscious" knowledge (108).

Interactive kinds, in contrast, are affected by the process of classification to such a degree that classification may require eventual modification or replacement. The construct of child television viewers, Hacking observes, illustrates the kind of classificatory "looping" effect specific to interactive kinds: the classification and research of children as child viewers irrevocably changes the behavior of child television viewers. Interactive kinds are classificatory systems that emerge within complex matrices of institutions and practices. Once articulated, these classificatory systems engender practices and institutions having the effect of producing what was classified. However, the process of producing human beings is subject to effects unintended because, among other factors, of the reflexive nature of consciousness. Awareness of one's classification as a particular kind of being, a particular kind of subject, can engender resistance and/or behavioral variation.

Hacking (1999) goes on to distinguish the kind of classificatory looping illustrated by child viewers from another form of looping he describes as mind–body "biolooping," which he illustrates in relation to the brain chemical, serotonin (109). Serotonin levels, as Hacking observes, are correlated with depression. However, behavioral treatments directed toward reducing depressive states can be as effective as chemical therapy in raising serotonin levels. Biolooping thus refers to the process whereby mental states, individual comportment, and cultural practices can affect biological outcomes (e.g., serotonin levels). Hacking argues that biolooping and classificatory looping could both be at work, simultaneously, in some forms of psychopathologies, particularly schizophrenia and childhood autism. Hacking starts with a discussion of schizophrenia in order to demonstrate the interaction of biology and culture before moving to address childhood autism.

As Hacking observes, there exists considerable debate within the literature whether schizophrenia constitutes a unified and coherent disorder. Scholars such as Mary Boyle (1990) argue that the people who share the label of schizophrenia, as Hacking (1999: 113) puts it, "are not of a kind" and lack a common etiology. However, individuals classified as schizophrenic will be shaped and produced in relation to the construct's (i.e., schizophrenia) classificatory schema and the matrix of practices and institutions schizophrenia is embedded in and contributes to the reproduction of (i.e., looping effect). Moreover, the psychotropic drugs used to alleviate the "symptoms" of schizophrenia will themselves alter the disease and the so-classified individual's experience of it (i.e., through biolooping). Psychotropic drugs increase the ability of those classified as schizophrenic to reflect actively upon their diagnoses, leading to potential transformations in their disorder through their interpretive engagement with it. In effect, the schizophrenic patient hermeneutically engages with their disorder and thereby engenders its metamorphosis. Therefore, as Hacking (1999) argues, it is not surprising that the symptoms used to identify and diagnose schizo-phrenia have changed significantly across time. In effect, schizophrenia is an "interactive" kind that evidences both looping and biolooping effects.

Hacking (1999) observes that autism, like schizophrenia, is an interactive kind that may be subject to looping effects as a consequence of the inter-pretive work done by parents, caregivers, therapists, and autistic patients. To demonstrate his point, Hacking notes that many of the symptoms iden-tified by Kanner and Asperger are no longer regarded as the primary symp-toms demarcating "autistic" children; illustrated by the decreased relevance of "flat affect," which was observed and remarked upon by both original researchers and yet is no longer regarded as a determinate diagnostic crite-rion. Autism, for Hacking, is a particularly compelling example of the inter-section of biology and culture because although it is arguably an interactive kind, it also evidences the characteristics of an indifferent kind in that its symptoms are in some way rooted in genetics or molecular chemistry. These biogenetic factors, however, do not "motivate" fixed, uniform symptoms, such as "flat affect." Moreover, the underlying biogenetic factors are not themselves fixed or uniform. The effects of parental expectations, therapy programs, and the individual's experiences loop back to affect/constitute the expression of biogenetic factors. Further, the use of drugs such as Prozac do not merely reduce symptoms but may actually alter the brain chemistry and neural topography of autistic patients, illustrating what Hacking describes as biolooping. Although my discussion of the interactive dimen-sion of autism extends beyond Hacking's formulation, it demonstrates the complex interaction between disease and representation, biology and culture, neurology and communication.

Although Hacking's works point to many compelling avenues of research for those interested in approaching autism from a communication perspec-tive, I am most interested in the emergence of autism in the early twentieth century and the emergence of more high-functioning forms of the disorder in the late twentieth century as "niche" disorders. In *Mad Travelers*, Hacking (1998) investigates "niche" disorders through the example of "transient" mental illness:

> By a "transient mental illness" I mean an illness that appears at a time, in a place, and later fades away. It may spread from place to place and reappear from time to time. It may be selective for social class or gen-der, preferring poor women or rich women. I do not mean that it comes and goes in this or that patient, but that this type of madness exists only

at certain times and places. The most famous candidate for a transient mental illness is hysteria.

(Hacking 1998: 1)

Hacking (1998) ponders whether a variety of neuroses such as pre-menstrual syndrome (PMS), ADHD, and multiple personality disorder are real or whether they are culturally produced in relation to specific socio-cultural events and practices. Hacking notes that the so-called "shadow syndromes" such as subclinical autism and depression are particularly suspect disorders in this regard (see Ratey and Johnson 1997).

I feel that autism exemplifies the niche effect that Hacking sees as oper-ating in transient mental illness, even while it undoubtedly has a biological component. In the section that follows, I briefly introduce my thesis of autism as a disorder that emerged and was created in relation to cultural practices and discourses specific to particular points in time, the transition from the nineteenth to the twentieth centuries and, more recently, the transition from the twentieth to the twenty-first centuries.

Constructing autism in the twentieth century

Reflecting back on his career, Hans Asperger (1979) observed that his research reflected and extended the scholarly investigation of children that emerged in the 1930s:

> Let us remember the early thirties. At that time psychological problems in children had become fashionable. Karl and Charlotte Buehler and their pupil Hildegarde Hetzer did some pioneering and fundamental work and Piaget had made himself known. Tests were coming into use for getting to understand anomalies of the intelligence. But none of this helped with the children I am about to describe. The disturbance was elsewhere and made one think of personality traits which the then cur-rent psychiatric circles did not describe or clarify. The disturbance was not so much intellectual, but lay more in the child's relationship with other human beings; in his lack of *contact*. But at that time this lack of contact was not recognized and it had no name. So how was a doctor trained to observe and categorise, to describe the pecularities of these children?

(Asperger 1979: 46)

Asperger's recollections are significant in that they point to the niche con-ditions that enabled the emergent identification of autism as a distinct dis-order. First, Asperger observed that the study of children had become "fashionable" in the 1930s, implicitly suggesting that research on children had previously lacked broad support or general interest. Second, Asperger observed that his analysis focused on "personality" in contrast to the prevailing approach that focused exclusively on the intellect (e.g., retardation) and in contrast to approaches that focused on psychoses. The emergence of "personality" as a distinct and legitimate sphere of investigation in the early twentieth century, as a phenomenon unto itself, is of historical import for the emergence of autism.[11] Prior to Freud's popularization of the neurosis, psychiatry had relatively little interest in behavioral peculiarities unless they were linked to psychoses or extreme social deviance. Finally, Asperger described the personality disorder, autism, in terms of interpersonal relations or, as he puts it, in terms of "*contact*." Asperger's move to identify autism as a disorder of interpersonal relations is particularly significant when viewed in relation to Armstrong's (2002) observation that the construction of individual identity and pathology around interpersonal dynamics was a distinct innovation of early-twentieth-century medicine. In sum, Asperger's characterization of autism implies that it is a niche disorder emerging out of a constellation of institutions and practices specific to the early twentieth century that include (1) the emergence of the child as a research focus, (2) the emergence of personality as a research focus and clinical locus, and (3) the emergence of interpersonal dynamics as a research focus and clinical locus as a source point for individual pathologies.

In Chapters 3 and 4, I take up the niche conditions enabling the particularized identification of autism, as described by Kanner and Asperger, in the early twentieth century. As observed by Armstrong in *A New History of Identity*, the early twentieth century engendered a new approach to medical subjectivity centering on mental hygiene, the child, and interpersonal dynamics. This expression of medical subjectivity, and the institutions and practices involved in its constitution, enabled the identification of autism as both a medical diagnostic category and as a social construct for interpreting "normal" and "pathological" social relationships. Accordingly, what follows describes the historically specific niche conditions—the matrix of social institutions and practices—providing the conditions of possibility for the emergence of autism as a diagnostic and social category.

Notes

1 Kanner's (1943) text is often cited as his first published reference to the disorder he describes as autism. However, Alexander and Selesnick (1966) argue that Kanner makes a brief reference to autism as a disorder of the mother–child relationship in his 1935 text, *Child Psychiatry*. Since Kanner eventually rejects a psychodynamic explanation for the origins of the disorder, it is possible that he and other researchers disregard the 1935 reference.

2 Personality disorders are viewed as "enduring patterns of perceiving, relating to, and thinking about the environment and oneself, and are exhibited in a wide range of important social and personal contexts" according to the DSM-III (cited in Coolidge and Segal 1998: 591). The relationship between (1) personality disorders and (2) pervasive developmental disorders remains unclear to me, although numerous efforts are made in the clinical literature to distinguish schizoid personality types *from* high-functioning forms of autism, usually by

linking autistic disorders to more pervasive social awkwardness and communication difficulties. However, Lorna Wing noted in her 1981 essay that, "There is no question that Asperger's syndrome can be regarded as a form of schizoid personality disorder. The question is whether this grouping is of any value" (121). The relationship between high-functioning autism and obsessive-compulsive disorder (an anxiety disorder) is also a bit ambiguous.

3 For a detailed discussion of the similarities and differences between the ICD-10 and the DSM-IV see Volkmar et al.'s (1997a) essay, "Diagnosis and classification of autism and related conditions: consensus and issues."

4 Autistic Disorder has the classificatory code of 299.00 within the DSM-IV and PDD, AS, and Rett's Disorder are classified as 299.80.

5 "Parent perspective in raising special kids" (September–October 2002) *Connect Connecting*, 7(5), 12.

6 "Parent perspective in raising special kids" (September–October 2002) *Connect Connecting*, 7(5), 13.

7 See Rose (1989) *Governing the Soul* and Armstrong (2002) *A New History of Identity* for discussion of the emergence of childhood norms of development.

8 For a discussion of the distinction between this ontological model of "disease" and a more holistic model of "illness" that rejects the distinction between the invading "disease" and the individual, see Hudson (1983).

9 See Freund and McGuire's (1991: 6–7) discussion of the western medical model.

10 See Fox's (1999) *Beyond Health: Postmodernism and Embodiment* for a particularly insightful account of this discussion between the biological and the cultural.

11 Although psychiatric publications such as Appel's and Strecker's (1936) *Practical Examination of Personality and Behavior Disorders: Adults and Children* had formalized criteria for the clinical diagnosis of personality disorders, Asperger either was unaware of this work in the 1930s or believed these criteria were inadequate for explaining the unique constellation of behaviors/attributes specific to the disorder he described.

3 Psychiatric niche conditions

Autism is a twentieth-century disorder because it is clearly absent from the diagnostic nosologies of nineteenth-century psychiatry. And yet, it seems very likely that the disorder predates its twentieth-century formulations by Kanner (1943) and Asperger (1979). Why did autism emerge so late in the psychiatric imagination? And further, what unique conditions of possibility enabled its identification in the early twentieth century?

This chapter addresses the historically embedded psychiatric niche conditions that enabled the identification and emergence of autism. Accordingly, the chapter provides a social history of the material institutions, professional identities, and cultural values that enabled Kanner and Asperger to name autism and Asperger's syndrome and frame their meanings in relation to the diagnostic categories of their time. Kanner, as already explained, derived the name for autism from Bleuler's (1908) descriptive account of adolescent onset psychosis—schizophrenia. Asperger, on the other hand, relied on the idea of the personality disorder when generating his formulation of the disorder that bears his name.

The institutional histories implicated in the creation of autism and Asperger's syndrome as diagnostic labels are complex and interwoven and conjoin to form a tapestry of events and persons that resists representation through a simple chronology of events. Therefore, in this chapter and in the next the reader will encounter multiple institutional histories—histories of psychiatry, childhood, and education—that contributed to the production of the specific conditions of possibility for the emergence of autism in the early twentieth century.

In order to establish the relevance of these institutional histories and to help the reader navigate their complex relations, the chapter begins with a very brief overview of historical attitudes about mental illness. After establishing the historicity of twentieth-century attitudes about mental illness, the chapter moves back in time to chronicle the development of the psychiatric terms ultimately involved in the articulations of autism and Asperger's syndrome. Chapter 4 will take up the history of childhood and integrate these psychiatric histories with those institutional practices and professional identities that enabled childhood-based psychiatry to emerge.

Setting the stage: the history of madness

In the late twentieth century, psychiatry and medicine provide expert authorities' complex diagnostic nosologies for differentiating among forms of adult and childhood-specific mental illness and developmental delays. The DSM-IV and the ICD-10 are, for example, systematic and nuanced nosologies that provide exclusively defined diagnostic codes, each of which invokes a complex description of symptoms and differentiating criteria. And yet, the sophistication of these nosologies, the clinical and apparently objective nature of their diagnostic criteria, tends to obscure the complex institutional histories that enabled their production. But when contextualized historically, it readily becomes apparent that these seemingly *transhistorical* nosologies are, in fact, temporally *contingent* documents that have roots in centuries of psychiatric and medical efforts to classify and understand forms of mental illness in both adults and children.

Subsumed within the history of western civilization is a history of efforts to carve up the terrain of mental and behavioral differences across people. From the Greeks onward, western physicians have been fascinated with the boundaries between normality and pathology in human behavior and belief. Efforts to identify, categorize, and systematize differences were particular significant within the European enlightenment movement, which sought during the seventeenth and eighteenth centuries to forge clear distinctions between reason and unreason. However, the nature and causes of differences in thought and behavior resisted simple schemes of identification and explanation and the distinctions drawn in pre-nineteenth-century psychiatry seem, in retrospect, to have been quite molar in character.

In the nineteenth century, early psychiatrists and neurologists struggled to make finer and standardized distinctions across classes of pathology. For example, mental "illness" was qualitatively distinguished from mental "retardation" in the mid-nineteenth century. Forms of psychoses were somewhat clarified and distinguished from classes of neuroses by the end of the nineteenth century. And "psychological" origins of mental disorders were tentatively distinguished from purely organic ones by the beginning of the twentieth century.

But perhaps one of the most significant innovations in nineteenth-century psychiatric efforts to divide human populations was the systematic inclusion of children within newly formalized categories of pathology. Although relatively late in coming, the nineteenth century's willingness to recognize mental illness in children paved the way for the subsequent creation of new diagnostic categories and the institution of new classes of professionals. Childhood "idiocy" was distinguished from madness in childhood. Madness in adults was distinguished from madness in children. And ultimately, madness in children was distinguished from other forms of "unreason," especially personality neuroses.

By the end of the nineteenth century, new classes of professionals—educators, psychiatrists, psychologists, social workers—were created to identify and manage proliferating forms of childhood pathology. And yet, as was the case with adult psychopathology, the project of carving up the territory of childhood psychological differences was an ongoing process that was subject to constant reformulations and revisions. The impetus for replacing old categories of understanding and professional identities with new ones was motivated as much by historical and cultural happenstance as it was by progressive understandings.

The goal of this chapter and the next is to clarify many of the conditions of possibility for the creation of autism as a diagnostic category. It will become clear that the creation of autism as a diagnostic category specific to childhood had to await the completion of nineteenth-century historical recognitions and categorical distinctions. This chapter provides a chronology of psychiatric events, persons, and syndromes which played important roles in the historical recognitions and categorical distinctions that enabled the conditions of possibility for naming and interpreting autism in young children at the onset of the twentieth century.

Normality and pathology: dividing nineteenth-century populations

Nineteenth-century innovations in psychiatric thought were indebted to new social and economic conditions that led to increased social surveillance and control over populations. The nineteenth century engendered new strategies for monitoring, dividing, and acting upon populations in order to foster and ensure social stability in a time of rapid urbanization and industrialization in both Europe and in North America (see Rose 1989). Increasingly, nineteenth-century state and religious authorities set up poorhouses and workhouses, hospitals and madhouses, to sequester and administer indigent and/or troublesome populations that were seen as threatening social and economic security (see Richardson 1989; Trent 1994). Accompanying the formation of these institutions were administrative efforts to divide the criminal from the mad and the poor from the feebleminded, and to sequester these groups in order to adapt them to particular social and economic needs.

In effect, as the nineteenth century progressed, formalized state and professional forms of social surveillance and control were increasingly extended over social life as populations were divided, sequestered, and institutionalized according to the various parameters of normality and pathology. Thus, private life became subject to governmental and professional scrutiny, particularly in the extension of surveillance over populations regarded as "deviant" and in the extension of surveillance over a person's earliest childhood years. Efforts to sequester deviant populations, coupled with the surveillance that ensued, created the conditions of possibility for the field of psychiatry to engage in more systematic study of deviant populations, allowing for the production of new forms of knowledge about mental illness. Heightened nineteenth-century efforts to identify and understanding increasingly nuanced categories of difference and pathology also gave birth to new forms of psychopathology. In particular, forms of difference that had escaped the earlier, more molar categories of pathology were scrutinized, identified, and systematized. For example, individuals who exhibited disturbances of affect, in addition to disturbances of logic and reason, were identified and classified. Out of these new conditions emerged a disorder labeled "dementia praecox," which became an important reference point for both Kanner's and Asperger's descriptions of autism.

In what follows, I briefly trace these developments, beginning with the social construction of ideas about madness and sanity, normality and pathology.

The great internment and the institutional asylum: from molar distinctions to descriptive psychopathology

Historians working in the area of mental retardation and developmental disabilities note that prior to the modern era, the standards for assessing psychological or social "abnormalities" were quite gross compared to present-day standards: indeed, many people who are today judged as having a developmental disorder would not have been judged so before the nineteenth century and few distinctions were made between the mad and the "feeble-minded." Moreover, in the pre-Cartesian world no *ontological* distinction was made between physical and mental disease and, once made, such distinctions were slow in codification (Berrios 1995).[1]

Early pre-nineteenth-century "alienists" and neurologists did study mental disorders but they primarily focused on the most profound or unusual cases of mental illness and relied heavily on psychiatric taxonomies inherited from the Greeks that, by the enlightenment period, had been expanded to include the following categories: melancholy, paranoia, idiocy, amnesia, epilepsy, dementia, and mania (Stone 1997).

One of the first systematic efforts to distinguish mental and physical diseases was made by William Cullen in 1777. Although he retained the somatic model that located disease in bodily processes, Cullen was also inspired by the empiricist philosophies of Locke and Hume. The influence of empiricist thinking led Cullen to distinguish physical illnesses from mental ones by citing the role of disturbed thinking (in the nervous system) in producing the symptoms of madness (Porter 2002). Specifically, Cullen believed that the source of mental illness derived from an "unusual and commonly hurried association of ideas" leading to "false judgment" and "disproportionate" emotion (cited in Porter 2002: 128). Cullen used the term "neurosis" to categorize these forms of mental illness. It is important to keep in mind that Cullen's understanding of the term differs significantly from our own (or even Freud's) because his criteria for neurosis encompassed conditions such as stroke, autonomic dysfunctions, as well as intellectual impairment (Alexander and Selesnick 1966). Moreover, although many enlightenment alienists such as Cullen viewed the brain/nervous system as the locus of mental illness, it—the brain—was regarded simply as "just another viscus (like lungs or heart)" until after 1800 (Berrios 1995: 4). It was not until well into the nineteenth century that "consciousness" became a criterion used to distinguish among forms of mental illness, particularly between temporary, illness-induced delirium and pervasive insanity and that the study of psychosis was distinguished from the study of neurosis (Berrios 1995; Berrios and Mumford 1995), that insanity was distinguished from epilepsy, and that mental retardation was distinguished from insanity (Porter 2002).

Although Cullen helped advance eighteenth-century psychiatric knowledge, the actual practice for diagnosing mental illness probably relied more on "common sense" knowledge than it relied on expert authority. Houston's and Frith's (2000) detailed account of the trial of Blair of Borgue in *Autism in History* documents that in the eighteenth century the formal governmental (i.e., court) process for judging mental incapacity typically relied on the testimony of family members and neighbors. These witnesses were interrogated about the habits and behavioral oddities of the person whose mental status was under determination. Lacking few, if any, formal or professional standards, the court's decision was based on overt and remarkable deviance in behavior. As summarized by Berrios (1996), the diagnoses of idiocy, insanity, and dementia were still made in the most molar of terms revolving around overt behavioral criteria that largely excluded the subjective (experiential) symptoms of the afflicted individual. Mental disorders or incapacities were regarded as "obvious" in nature (Berrios 1996: 16).

However, psychiatric knowledge and practice advanced significantly in the nineteenth century. For example, by around 1820, systematic efforts were undertaken to create a standardized and systematic description of forms of psychopathology, although this project would take more than one hundred years to complete (Berrios 1996). Enabling advances such as these were a number of historical circumstances, including the enlightenment ethos of scientific thinking and the transformation of institutions designed to house the "insane." The development of the madhouse—later the asylum—in the seventeenth century paved the way for the subsequent professionalization and systematization of psychiatric knowledge. In addition to sequestering those regarded as socially deviant and enabling psychiatric observation, the madhouse played a role in the creation of new forms of social control that extended state and scientific authority, particularly into realms regarded in earlier times as private.

Prior to the fourteenth century, people designated as mad or simple typically lived in the confines of their family or were allowed to roam the countryside unfettered. However, Foucault's (1965) *Madness and Civilization* observes that as the medieval threats of leprosy and plague receded in the mid-fifteenth century, madness came to be seen as the primary threat to social welfare. In response to this threat, those seen as afflicted were sometimes confined to ships that sailed without destination, designed merely to rid the land of undesirables. The task of isolating and confining the mad and feebleminded had begun.

Later, by the seventeenth century, madhouses emerged in great number to confine the mad, the "fool," and the "somber melancholics," among others (Foucault 1965: 36). The 1656 decree founding the Hospital General in Paris illustrates the founding of such institutions and the beginning of what has come to be called "the great confinement." The madhouse directors exercised enormous authority over the administration of inmates' lives, who often lived chained and in great misery. These madhouses added a new institutional element to ongoing governmental efforts to sequester and confine the criminal, the poor, and the unemployed. As the field of psychiatry grew, the madhouse was transformed into the institutional asylum wherein the mad could not only be sequestered but they could also be systematically observed.

In France, the reforms of Philippe Pinel (1745–1826) helped in this transformation of the madhouse into the more humane institutional asylum as the goal of psychiatry slowly expanded to encompass therapy in addition to classification (see Porter 2002). In addition to freeing the "insane" from their chains, Pinel's efforts in 1801 refined the then extant system of classifying mental illness (Alexander and Selesnick 1966; Berrios 1996). His new system of classification included only four categories: mania (with and without delirium), melancholia, dementia, and idiocy. Specific disorders were located within these broad categories (Berrios 1996). Like Cullen, Pinel understood "idiocy" as a form of mental disorder—a neurosis—akin to insanity (but distinguished from it) and believed that a person could be born with it or it could be acquired (Berrios 1996). Along with his contemporaries, Pinel believed that idiocy was largely unalterable and this view was not to change until the mid-nineteenth century. However, Pinel did contend that some forms of mania (e.g., *manie sans delire*) were amendable to treatment through psychological means (Porter 2002). Although his modes of therapy were modeled on Locke's associationist philosophy, Pinel addressed the role of affective associations, in addition to intellectual ones, in causing psychiatric distress (Porter 2002).[2] Jean-Etienne-Dominique Esquirol, a follower of Pinel's approach and an advocate of the role of the "passions" in mental illness, attempted to put Pinel's reforms into practice by incorporating a "therapeutic community" into the asylum that secluded patients from their previous life while substituting it with the community of patients and physicians (Shorter 1997: 13).

Foucault's works (1965, 1979, 1991) suggest that the growth of institutions such as those operated by Pinel and Esquirol constituted a transformation in the form of social control. Social control, Foucault (1991) argued, was transformed beginning in the sixteenth and seventeenth centuries from a form of absolute, but geographically and temporally, limited power embodied in the person of the monarch to a diffuse but more pervasive form of power—governmental power—that is signified by the growth of government (bureaucracy) and the development of the institution, but whose effects are more ubiquitous and pervasive than the limited power of such authorities. "Governmental" power focuses both on the administration of populations and their behavioral normalization. This extension of the finality of state control to include influence over everyday affairs constitutes an important shift that he termed the shift from "sovereignty" (over a territory) to "government," which is concerned with the disposition of things such as people, customs, habits, etc. (Foucault 1991).

Unlike sovereignty, which operates primarily through law, the practices of government include the development of administrative apparatuses that accumulate "knowledge of things, of the objectives that can and should be attained, and the disposition of things required to reach them" (Foucault 1991: 96). This knowledge accompanies and engenders tactics, "programmes" for reorganizing institutions, spaces, and behaviors. The psychiatric taxonomies—nosologies—created by Cullen and Pinel coupled with the transformed madhouse—the asylum—together illustrate how new forms of knowledge were concomitant with the reorganization of social space so as to divide, sequester, and administer populations.

The extension of governmentality over the disposition of private life was particularly pronounced throughout the nineteenth century as populations were divided along ever more refined dimensions—dimensions of age and dependency, criminality, and sanity, insanity and mental retardation. And, it was the ubiquitous nineteenth-century asylum that enabled thorough and systematic observation of "deviant" populations and their division along various dimensions of abnormality (Porter 2002). As early-nineteenth-century psychiatry distinguished among the mad, the simpleminded (idiocy), and the epileptic, government and church authorities responded by creating special institutions to house these newly distinguished populations. While some of these institutions were brutal and inhumane, others, under the directorship of psychiatrists, sought to rehabilitate their less afflicted populations, particularly in the early part of the nineteenth century in both Europe and North America. However, towards the middle to end of the nineteenth century, a new pessimism about the prospect of rehabilitating the insane grew.

Many factors played a role in affecting this new pessimism. In part, the ascendancy of the "medical" model in medicine and psychiatry in the mid- to late nineteenth century undermined support for psychologically based therapeutic interventions. Coupled with Darwinist ideas about "natural selection" the medical model's contentions that mental illness was biologically based and potentially heritable functioned to transform madness into a social contagion. Buttressing this interpretive framework was the real failure on the part of asylums to "cure" many of their patients (Porter 2002).

The psychiatric work of Benedict Morel (1809–1873), who approached both madness and mental retardation as regressive, degenerative, and heritable, reflects this pessimism (Barrett 1998). Working from this view, Morel wrote: "Degenerations are deviations from the normal human type, which are transmissible by heredity and which deteriorate progressively towards extinction" (cited in Alexander and Selesnick 1966: 162). By articulating mental illness within a somatic/medical framework and by linking "madness" and "idiocy" with heritable degeneracy in behavior and mind, Morel helped ensure that "madness" would become a critical social policy issue.

Social welfare, and the welfare of the species, demanded intensification of efforts to identify and sequester the mad and feebleminded. Thus, fearing the reproductive capacities of such "degenerates," the asylum took on more social import due to its ability to sequester the "organically" mad, even while its therapeutic aspects were regarded as suspect. Public asylums grew in Europe and the United States and quality of care declined (Porter 2002). As observed by Porter (2002: 122): "The institutionalization drive was a sign of the times. It combined the imperatives of the rational state with the expedients of a market economy." Efforts by social and professional elites to treat unfortunates were not limited to institutionalizing those deemed as insane.

Late-nineteenth-century psychiatric accounts of mental retardation as regressive, degenerative, and heritable also fueled efforts to institutionalize those regarded as mentally deficient, even when they were relatively self-sufficient, in order to prevent their procreation. Public alarm at the "degenerative" aspects of "madness" and "idiocy" was spurred also by the new categories of deficiency that were being created toward the end of the nineteenth century. For example, in 1877, idiocy was formally differentiated from "imbecility," which was intended to denote a condition akin to idiocy but characterized by a lesser degree of impairment (Rafalovich 2001). Forms of "idiocy" were also carved out in relation to the idea of the "moral idiot" or "moral imbecile" wherein the person in question was believed to lack the ability to distinguish between "right and wrong" even when "rising above the state of *mental* idiocy" (Trent 1994: 20).[3]

Accompanying the new categories of "idiocy" were also new categories of mental illness that also debuted toward the end of the twentieth century. Particularly important for this chapter are two developments in the nineteenth-century psychiatric nosology and their implications for the creation of community-based psychiatry. The first development involved progressive efforts to distinguish mental illnesses that involved hallucinations and delusions from those forms of illness that did not. The nineteenth-century solution to this categorical issue centered on the articulation and differentiation of the psychosis from the neurosis and the creation of new classifications of disorders of personality and character. Psychiatric refinements in understanding the psychosis ultimately led to the articulations of dementia praecox, schizophrenia, and Kanner's autism. The second development of import involves efforts to refine understandings of neuroses and other "personality disorders." Greater psychiatric attention to less overt forms of mental illness—such as those characterized by neuroses—facilitated the establishment of community psychiatry in community-based clinics and hospital wards. Each of these developments will be addressed.

New relationships: from demence precoce to schizophrenia and from the institution to the mental hygiene clinic

As observed above, the "great confinement" provided new opportunities for physicians and alienists to observe the insane, which by the nineteenth century had created considerable data on the expressions of insanity. The sheer amount of data and the confusing proliferation of diagnostic terms led ultimately to efforts to standardize and systematize psychiatric classifications. Pinel's efforts in 1801 were just the beginning of the great nineteenth-century project to systematize and standardize forms of psychopathology. Although it is beyond the scope of this project to provide a detailed history of these efforts, it is worthwhile to trace the development of key psychiatric concepts that would subsequently frame twentieth-century psychiatric knowledge about autism and to explore the changing institutional relationships for identifying and treating mental illness.

Accordingly, one key nineteenth-century innovation in psychopathology involved distinguishing those forms of mental illness that involved delirium and hallucinations from those that did not. As mentioned previously, throughout the nineteenth century a range of "character" disorders including *manie sans delire* (Pinel), monomania (Esquirol), and moral insanity (Prichard) were coined to encompass wide ranges of abnormalities in behavior or affect not characterized by delirium and hallucination (Berrios 1993). As interest in these disorders grew, psychiatry devised ever more strategies for distinguishing disorders characterized by "psychosis" from more subtle abnormalities of affect, social relations, and subjective experience. During the late nineteenth and early twentieth centuries, Freudian psychoanalysis increasingly claimed authority over the latter territory while more organically inclined psychiatry sought to refine understanding of psychosis-linked forms of illness characterized by hallucinations and delusions.

However, these distinctions between biological and psychoanalytic psychiatry tended to blur in a number of ways. When Eugene Bleuler coined "schizophrenia" in 1908 he blended elements from both psychiatric frameworks, thereby extending the explanatory framework of the (psychoanalytic) neurosis to the psychogenesis of the psychosis. Moreover, early-twentieth-century efforts to identify the precursors of mental illness and criminality often blended psychoanalytic formulations of the psyche with biological psychiatry in describing the constitutional types of individuals prone to psychosis and/or neurosis. Out of this interest in constitutional types emerged the study of neurosis-linked character types, schizoid and schizophrenic personality types, and ultimately, the emergence of distinct personality theories.

Accordingly, what follows traces the conceptual histories and chronologies of events implicated in the following events:

- *Refining psychosis:* the turn-of-the-century transformation of the psychosis and its role in shaping Kanner's autism and Asperger's autistic psychopathy.
- *The Freudian neurosis: developmental character disorders and personality disorders:* the articulation of the neurosis, the role of the psyche, and the Freudian identification of childhood-based affective disorders.
- *Personality disorders: twentieth-century innovations:* the creation of the psychopathic personality disorder in the environment of character disorders and personality neuroses.
- *Community psychiatry: the mental hygiene movement:* the emergence of the mental hygiene movement as a synthesis of preventive medicine, psychoanalysis, and biological psychiatry.

Refining psychosis

Nineteenth-century efforts to standardize understanding of the psychosis within biological psychiatry, particularly pervasive forms of psychosis unrelated to other forms of illness, are typically traced to Benedict Morel. Morel's investigation of degeneracy ("madness") led him to conclude that pervasive insanity characterized by delusions and/or hallucinations often first manifests in young adulthood (what we now term "adolescence") and therefore he coined the phrase *demence precoce* to refer to adolescent onset of mania or delusional states, which he characterized in terms of severe cognitive impairment and psychosocial incompetence (Berrios 1996).

In 1893, the great classifier, the German psychiatrist Emil Kraepelin (1856–1926), extended Morel's concept of *demence precoce* by combining the specific disorders of catatonia, with dementia paranoids, simplex, and hebephrenia (madness of youth, not childhood): this new disease he labeled dementia praecox (Berrios 1996). Kraepelin's innovation was significant because it helped clarify psychiatric nosology by replacing the old concepts of pervasive madness with the two newly designated categories of dementia praecox and manic-depressive insanity. At a diagnostic level, Kraepelin distinguished these categories in terms of their prognosis because he regarded manic-depressive insanity as periodic and curable and dementia praecox as progressive (i.e., degenerate) and incurable (Barrett 1998). Following the Lockean, empiricist tradition, Kraepelin believed that many of the symptoms specific to dementia praecox were disorders of thought association, although he rooted the cause of these disorders in organic dysfunctions

(Berrios 1996). For Kraepelin, dementia praecox was a disease entity specific to the brain (Ovsiew 2000). This neurophysiological orientation led Kraepelin to be deeply pessimistic about the long-term prognosis of dementia praecox. Kraepelin's nosological legacy remains with us today, particularly the nosological distinction between dementia praecox (schizophrenia) and manic-depressive insanity, although the concept of dementia praecox was reframed in the work of Bleuler.[4]

In 1908 and again in 1911, Eugen Bleuler (1857–1939) appropriated Kraepelin's concept of dementia praecox and helped pave the way for the disorder's reconceptualization within a psychological (as opposed to strictly organic) framework. Bleuler's rearticulation of dementia praecox as schizophrenia blended elements from Kraepelin's biological psychiatry with aspects of Sigmund Freud's and Carl Jung's psychoanalytic approaches to mental illness (Hoenig 1995; Stotz-Ingenlath 2000). Bleuler's formulation of schizophrenia provided the context from which both Leo Kanner and Hans Asperger derived their conceptualizations of autism and autistic psychopathy.

Following Kraepelin, Bleuler viewed the psychotic states associated with dementia praecox primarily in terms of a disorder of thought and affective associations (Berrios 1996). Accordingly, Bleuler described the disorder's manifestations in terms of a "rupture of fission of mental functions" (cited in Scharfetter 1996: 23). To capture the significance of this rupture, Bleuler renamed dementia praecox as "schizophrenia," reflecting "the dislocation of the diverse psychic functions" (cited in Gueguen 1996: 2).[5] Bleuler recognized that schizophrenia could be caused by multiple causal agents, both organic and psychological in origin. Therefore, rather than attempt to describe the disease in terms of its etiologies, Bleuler focused on the content of its psychological symptoms, symptoms of the loosening of the associations of mind. Bleuler identified and described four primary psychological symptoms—the four As—that he believed best characterized schizophrenia: association loosening, ambivalence, affect inappropriateness, and autism. Bleuler relegated hallucinations, delusions, catatonia, negativism, and stupor to the category of secondary symptoms that he believed were derivative from the four As.

Unlike Kraepelin who stressed empirical observation over theory building, Bleuler developed a systematic conceptual framework for explaining the psychological processes involved in producing the primary symptoms (Hoenig 1995). Although it is beyond the scope of this chapter to address the totality of Bleuler's framework, his formulation of autism has direct relevance for this project.

Accordingly, for Bleuler, autistic withdrawal signified the patient's delirious break with reality, although this condition was believed to be an outcome of the primary disassociation (of mental functions) that had occurred (Gueguen 1996).[6] Bleuler claimed that schizophrenic autistic thinking is "random" and occurs "independent of reality," although more moderate forms of autistic thinking include daydreams and fantasy (cited in Gundel and Rudolf 1993: 295). Bleuler believed that the (schizophrenic) autistic break with reality, coupled with the other disassociations of affect and thought, ultimately leads to dissolution of personality. Personality was, in Bleuler's time, understood in relation to self-awareness and subjective experience (Berrios 1996) so schizophrenia constituted a fundamental threat to the self. However, unlike Kraepelin, Bleuler was optimistic that the course of schizophrenia could be influenced if the autistic break with reality was countered with therapeutic interventions that increased the schizophrenic's ability to relate to his or her social environment (McCarley et al. 2004). Thus, for Bleuler, autism was engendered by and exacerbated cognitive and affective disassociations but autistic tendencies could be countered through psychoanalysis.

The nature of autistic thinking and its relationship to schizophrenia and other forms of mental illness were subsequently debated in the 1920s and 1930s in psychiatric circles (Gundel and Rudolf 1993). Ernst Kretschmer, for example, distinguished between autism in which patients suppress external stimuli in order to pursue a dream existence and autism characterized by lack of emotion and affective responses to the environment (Gundel and Rudolf 1993). In 1932, Hans Gruhle described the autistic personality in terms of the "sense of not fitting into the world, standing outside of it" (cited in Gundel and Rudolf 1993: 297). As the meanings of autism proliferated it became increasingly possible to discuss the presence of autistic thinking in individuals who did not evidence the delusions and hallucinations of psychosis. In particular, autistic thinking was associated with newly coined character and personality types whose deviance in behavior and affect was seen as warranting new social and psychiatric surveillance, although these individuals did not exhibit psychosis. This was the age of the "schizophrenic personality" (Faris 1934) and the schizoid psychopath. Indeed, as early as 1926, a paper was published on the schizoid personality in childhood (Wolff 1996), in which autistic thinking was fundamentally characteristic. The issue of the relationship between schizoid and schizophrenic personality forms and psychosis was never fully resolved, nor was the psychogenesis of autistic thinking as both psychoanalytic and biological psychiatry provided contrasting accounts of its etiology and expressions.

It is not surprising given this context that Leo Kanner and Hans Asperger elected to describe their patients in terms of the concept of autism. Autism was a phrase with wide currency and applicability, particularly in the German psychiatry of which both Kanner and Asperger were familiar. Although schizophrenic autism clearly signified a break with ordinary attitudes and thinking, the term "autism" also embraced nuanced interpretations thus enabling wide applicability. Chapter 4 explores further the genesis of autism in the works of Kanner and Asperger so for now discussion will turn to that other category of mental illness, the neurosis whose psychological frame of reference was forged in turn-of-the-century Freudian psychoanalysis.

The Freudian neurosis: developmental character disorders and personality disorders

Although many late-nineteenth-century psychiatrists followed the work of Kraepelin, who believed that almost all forms of mental disorders, particularly psychoses, were *disease entities* caused by biological factors, other psychiatrists acknowledged the role of social and/or psychological factors in causing the symptoms of mental disorders, particularly when those symptoms were linked with "neurotic" states not characterized by delusions or hallucinations. The work of Sigmund Freud was, of course, important in extending this latter view of the causality of anxiety and "personality" or "character" specific neuroses. And, as explained above, Freud's optimism about the role of psychoanalysis in combating neuroses was adopted by Bleuler in his understanding and treatment of schizophrenia. Bleuler also appropriated and reframed Freud's concept of auto-eroticism when developing his ideas about autistic thinking.

Working with Joseph Breuer in private practice in Austria, Sigmund Freud (1856–1939) encountered and studied many patients who were diagnosed with what were then regarded as nervous disorders, particularly hysteria. Following Breuer's insight that people with such symptoms could recover, Freud was particularly interested in using "cathartic hypnosis" in the treatment of more mildly affected patients, which eventually led him to speculate about the psychological role of repression in causing patients' psychiatric distress (Alexander and Selesnick 1966). In 1895, Freud broke with Breuer, whom he actually credited with the discovery of psychoanalysis, and began developing his theory of the unconscious, repression, and psychoanalytic therapy. Freud's theory was innovative in many ways but most relevant for the purposes of this project was its approach to studying neurotic "disorders" (such as hysteria) as an outcome of psychic processes and sexual conflicts specific to childhood.

In particular, Freud's ideas about the relationship between auto-eroticism and neurosis have relevance for this project and for subsequent thinkers' understandings of the nature and source of autism, including those forwarded by Bleuler and the object relations school of psychoanalysis (see Chapter 5). In Lecture Four of his *Five Lectures on Psychoanalysis* (1910/1957), Freud outlined his theory of infant sexuality and identified the role of auto-eroticism in satisfying instinctual drives prior to the formation of the ego. Accordingly, Freud argued that prior to the formulation of the ego, the infant takes sexual pleasure in bodily erotogenic zones. Because the infant lacks a unified sense of self, these sexual experiences are not coherently experienced or organized. However, as the child matures she/he becomes subject to the dictates of culture and henceforth the genital zone becomes the sexual focal point. The process of transforming the expression of libidinal forces is fraught with perils, and developmental regression back towards auto-eroticism and away from the sphere of reality can occur in response to outer circumstances or inner lack of adaptability. Various forms of "perversion" and neuroses stem from such regression. Eventually, Freud's work led him to classify the various forms of neuroses into the categories of anxiety neurosis, depressive neurosis, hysterical neurosis, and obsessive-compulsive neurosis (Stone 1997).[7]

Freud's work was highly innovative in several ways. First, it "psycholo-gized" relatively overt forms of mental illness such as hysteria that many nineteenth-century psychiatrists and alienists had believed to be organic in origin and irreversible in character. Second, Freud's interest in his patients' subjective experiences led subsequent psychoanalysts to link the study of per-sonality to the study of developmentally mediated personality neurosis. Moreover, with the works of Jung and Bleuler, Freud's emphasis on person-ality and inner experience was extended and applied to the psychological dimensions of psychosis (i.e., dementia praecox/schizophrenia), particularly as they applied to the characteristics of autism and ambivalence. For exam-ple, Bleuler's autistic thinking suggests the developmental regression and rejection of reality Freud described as "auto-eroticism." Third, Freud offered psychoanalysis as a therapy that could reverse the path of neurosis by identi-fying its psychological origins in childhood trauma. Because patients were often unable to remember the childhood experience responsible for their symptoms, Freud hypothesized their repression and subsequently developed the idea of the unconscious. Finally, Freud's psychoanalytic or "talking cure" incorporated subjective experience into the symptom repertoire of descriptive psychopathology thus paving the way for the medical model of the twentieth century to accept the relevance of inner experience in diagnosing and treating patient mental and physical illness (Berrios 1996). In effect, as described by Berrios (1995), the metaphor of the "inner eye" in self-observation became an important diagnostic framework (Berrios 1995: 3). Although application of the inner eye framework was more common in practice with adult popu-lations, it had the implication of bringing into focus the inner psychic life of childhood, a state whose complexities and crises demanded careful parental care guided by professional expertise (Cunningham 1995).

Freud's work significantly influenced the psychiatric study of children. First, Freud inaugurated the psychoanalytic study of children in Europe. Although Freud's actual work with children was limited to Little Hans, this case illustrates how psychoanalytic principles came to be applied to the treatment of childhood-based "character" neuroses in affluent European populations (particularly in the case of hysteria).[8] Moreover, Freud's daugh-ter, Anna Freud, was particularly responsible for developing the relevance of psychoanalysis for the treatment of anxiety disorders—neuroses—in children. Her work and that of Melanie Klein created new ways of viewing the child's psyche—in terms of instinctual urges and conflicts—and helped formalize and legitimize psychiatric inquiry and treatment of childhood mental illness. Chapter 5 takes up the role of psychoanalysis in shaping twentieth-century perceptions of autism.

By shifting psychiatric attention to the child's psyche—as the origin of many forms of psychopathology—and by stripping childhood of its romantic era of innocence, Freud facilitated subsequent decades of psychiatric inquiry into a whole range of forms of childhood "deviance." Some of this subsequent psychiatric inquiry loosely appropriated Freudian and/or Darwinian concepts of instinctual drives but did so within the framework of biological psychiatry. In the United States, much of this late-nineteenth-century work addressed the supposed moral degeneracy of lower-class children, children whose purportedly flawed biological constitution rendered them incapable of surmounting instinctual drives. However, by the early twentieth century, the moral indiscretions and character neuroses of middle-class children became subject to the psychiatric gaze. This shift marked a transformation from a psychopathology of (heritable) delinquency to a broader study of child psychiatry—childhood psychoses, neuroses and personality disorders —that included and linked school psychology, community psychiatry, and family counseling services (Richardson 1989). Chapter 4 addresses this latter movement, "child guidance," which was part of the mental hygiene movement (Horn 1989; Jones 1999; Richardson 1989). Before turning to introduce the mental hygiene movement, I briefly chronicle an important innovation in the conceptual understanding of personality disorders.

Personality disorders: twentieth-century innovations

As explained above, in the early twentieth century, the idea of a personality disorder occurred in two primary contexts: (1) within the context of psychoanalytic formulations of the personality/character neurosis and (2) within the context of the Bleuler's schizophrenia, within which efforts were made to describe the affective and social disturbances of individuals who were pre-schizophrenic or were schizophrenic-like, or schizoid. Despite the dominance of these approaches, an important alternative framework to the study of personality was developed in Germany in the 1930s by the phenomenological psychologist, Kurt Schneider, working with Karl Jaspers in Heidelberg. Asperger's ideas about personality may have been indebted to Kurt Schneider's formulation of personality "types."[9]

Schneider's (1923) text, *Psychopathic Personalities*, articulated an ontology of distinct personality types whose deviation from the norms of behavior results in extreme social difficulties. That is, according to Schneider, persons with "psychopathic" personalities exhibit such behavioral and attitudinal irregularities that they cause considerable distress for social others and for themselves. Schneider believed that these personality types were not caused by psychiatric diseases of the kind suggested by Kraepelin's dementia praecox. Moreover, Schneider strongly believed that these personality types were not "developmental syndromes" understood in the psychoanalytic sense. In other words, Schneider went against the prevailing tendencies to regard personality irregularities in terms of psychotic tendencies or character neuroses (cited in Berrios 1993: 22). Instead, Schneider forged a new approach to understanding psychopathology: an approach that blended aspects of phenomenology, Gestalt psychology, psychoanalysis and biological psychiatry.[10]

Schneider defined personality as the stable "composite of feelings, values, tendencies and volitions" whose integration in the "psyche" defined a normal personality (cited in Berrios 1996: 431). For Schneider, abnormal personalities were disharmoniously integrated in relation to the normal personality. Although Schneider's interest in the psyche and its integration illustrates the Freudian legacy, Schneider rejected the idea of the Freudian unconscious as the source for these disharmonies (Schneider 1953). Rather, for Schneider these disharmonies were integral to the personality type, a type of being.

Schneider's work helped inaugurate alternative directions in the study and treatment of "borderline" individuals who did not meet clear-cut diagnostic criteria for psychosis and whose personality characteristics escaped the parameters of neurotic-disorders. Schneider was not alone in addressing such individuals. As early-twentieth-century psychiatry escaped the confines of the asylum in the forms of community clinics and psychiatric hospital wards, more attention was afforded to individuals who evidenced symptoms of "disharmoniously" integrated personalities but whose "illnesses" did not warrant institutionalization. In the guise of prevention, psychiatrists and psychologists increasingly sought to identify, classify, and treat such individuals, thereby engendering the proliferation of psychiatric disorders and the dissemination of new understandings of mental illness throughout popular culture. The institutional matrix of professionals, expert knowledge, and institutional apparatuses that embraced these trends is termed the "mental hygiene movement."

Community psychiatry: the mental hygiene movement

The mental hygiene movement was a turn-of-the-twentieth-century movement by American psychiatrists to improve the mental health of American adults and children that operated primarily by identifying, defining, and treating "pre-psychotic" symptoms and neuroses-linked developmental syndromes. The movement was inspired in part by a book that humanized the plight of psychiatric patients titled, *A Mind that Found Itself* (1908), written by a former psychiatric patient, Clifford Beers (Shorter 1997). Although popularized by a former patient, the movement was formalized and institutionalized by medical and psychiatric professionals who combined psychoanalytic principles and biological psychiatry in an emphasis on treatment and prevention. These twin emphases led to the creation of psychiatric wards in general hospitals and the establishment of community-based clinics (Horn 1989). These physical moves signified the symbolic move away from full-scale commitment to Kraepelin's organic approach to mental illness as the psychiatrists who staffed the new wards and clinics hoped to treat patients who were not yet fully "insane" and, further, sought to *prevent* mental illness and, importantly, social deviance in the community (Horn 1989). And so it was that the physical move away from the asylum engendered a new social programme, the *mental hygiene movement*, that sought to promote mental health and combat mental illness through, in part, community-based psychiatry.

One psychiatrist who was instrumental in this movement, indeed who named it, was Adolf Meyer (1866–1950), a European émigré who founded the Henry Phipps Psychiatric Clinic at Johns Hopkins Hospital in 1913. Meyer incorporated Freudian approaches to psychoanalysis into his developmental, psychobiological approach to psychiatry. Because psychoanalysis stressed the role of childhood in adult mental health, Meyer and his associates at the new psychiatric wards may have been more interested in and receptive to the possibility and forms of mental illness in children. As will be explained in the next chapter, Meyer's most notable protégé was Leo Kanner. In addition to being influenced directly by Meyer, Leo Kanner was probably exposed to European psychology and psychiatry during his years in Berlin, 1906–1924 (Neumarker 2003).

An important contribution of the mental hygiene movement to the history of psychiatric innovations was its formal recognition that adult forms of mental illness existed, albeit in incipient form, in pre-adolescents. The establishment of school-based psychology to identify personality or character disorders in children and the creation of child guidance clinics for treating these disorders disseminated the principles and practices of psychiatry throughout popular culture. This dissemination engendered ever more psychiatric inquiry into childhood-based forms of "deviance" and eventually led to the creation of new forms of psychiatric illness specific only to children.

The medicalization of childhood deviance that was achieved by the mental hygiene movement significantly revolutionized popular notions about the nature of children and childhood. As will be discussed presently and further in Chapter 4, the idea that children are susceptible to mental illness awaited nineteenth-century innovations in education, medicine, and practices of social surveillance. What follows provides a brief history of the prehistory of child psychiatry before exploration turns in Chapter 4 to the social conditions of possibility for the innovations cited above.

Children and madness

As evidenced by the history of psychiatry chronicled above, children are strangely missing from the history of madness in psychiatry until the nineteenth century (Stone 1973). There are many reasons for this absence of children from pre-nineteenth-century psychiatric texts and institutions. First, there existed a widely held belief that children were not susceptible to mental illness. The origins of this belief may have been rooted in the general lack of public attention afforded to children as distinct beings, qualitatively different from adults, until sometime late in the eighteenth or early in the nineteenth centuries. Moreover, since pre-nineteenth-century asylums did not typically admit children, psychiatrists would have had little opportunity to systematically observe childhood "pathologies." In fact, it was not until the expansion of public and private schooling in the nineteenth century that children came under any systematic observation and control. Consequently, "deviant" behavior in young children would probably have occasioned relatively little interest unless it interfered significantly with family affairs. In such cases, the children would probably have been sequestered by the family or left to their own devices. Moreover, hallucinations and other seemingly bizarre behavior in children (e.g., anorexia) in the pre-enlightenment period would not necessarily have been regarded as invariable signs of madness, particularly if they were accompanied by religious ecstatics (Stone 1973). Second, given the incredibly high rates of infant abandonment in pre-nineteenth-century Europe (Cunningham 1995), it seems quite likely that overtly abnormal young children may have been "exposed" and, therefore, not have attained adulthood. In the early nineteenth century this was to change as European alienists increasingly focused on children's psyche's and by century's end the invention of psychoanalysis had so expanded the idea of childhood mental disorders that it became possible to conclude that intellectually "normal" children might also suffer from mental pathology. In what follows I briefly trace key developments in the "prehistory of child psychiatry" (see Stone 1973; Treffers and Silverman 2001; Walk 1964).

As stated above, psychiatric history reveals little about mental illness or retardation in children before the nineteenth century. For example, the records of early psychiatrists such as Benjamin Rush (1745–1813) indicate a decided unwillingness to recognize the potential for children to develop adult forms of madness and/or insanity, although Rush did observe phobic anxiety in children (Treffers and Silverman 2001). Undeniable deviance in childhood behavior was ascribed to spiritual possession, idiocy, or illness-induced delirium.[11] However, childhood increasingly took on a new import in the nineteenth century due to a variety of factors including the growth of the institutional asylum, the professionalization of psychiatry, and the expansion of that form of power Foucault described as governmentality. Together these forces contributed to the creation of a new division, the division between madness and idiocy in childhood.

One factor that ultimately enabled new "expert" understandings of children was their gradual admittance to the nineteenth-century institutional asylum. Although children were generally barred from the institution, some were admitted due to the direness of their illness or, perhaps, due to their class standing. Psychiatric reluctance to recognize mania in children was gradually transformed as the alienists who administered mental hospitals had increased opportunity to observe child populations, as illustrated in the records of the English psychiatrist, John Haslam (1764–1844), who in 1809 included the case histories of three "insane" children as part of his textbook, *Observations on Madness and Melancholy* (Stone 1973). Haslam's experiences as a psychiatrist in Bethlem Hospital reinforced his belief that most forms of madness in childhood were symptomatic of some underlying organic dysfunction, as illustrated by his record of a 30-month-old girl who had been well until she received a smallpox inoculation, after which she developed convulsions and became delirious. By nine months after the inoculation she had lost speech and could recognize few sounds. A similar story was recorded for a seven-year-old boy who, although mildly retarded from birth, experienced severe deterioration of intellect after contracting measles (Stone 1973). When Haslam did encounter a child whose mania could not be linked to a clear somatic legion, he released the boy as untreatable due to the "functional" or purely psychological etiology of the condition. Although Haslam and others may have regarded such cases as untreatable, they did indicate the possibility for "mania" in childhood (as opposed to youth). Still, during the early nineteenth century, manic symptoms in children were seen as symptomatic of adult disorders rather than ones specific to children.

Professional medical and psychiatric scrutiny of children was fueled by additional factors. Inspired by enlightenment ideals, nineteenth-century medical "experts" made children the subjects of experiments designed to prove the supremacy of reason over nature. In 1806, Jean-Marc-Gaspard Itard's work with a mute and "savage" foundling child exemplified this project. Itard attempted to rehabilitate the eleven-year-old "Wild Boy of Aveyron," who had presumably been abandoned in the wild as an infant (Stone 1973). Although Itard regarded his experiment a failure, popularization of his efforts contributed to a new interest in children, rendering them increasingly subject to the psychiatric gaze.

Accordingly, for the reasons mentioned above, the mid-nineteenth century witnessed a new interest in childhood disorders among European alienists, neurologists, and physicians. That interest resulted in the inclusion of children in mid-nineteenth-century psychiatric texts such as those produced by Wilhelm Griesinger (1817–1868) in Germany and Jean Esquirol (1772–1840) in France. Griesinger's (1861) textbook on psychiatric disorders included a short section on childhood psychosis under the etiological heading of "Age" (Walk 1964). As was the case with Haslam, Griesinger did not regard childhood psychosis as qualitatively distinct from adult forms. Esquirol's comprehensive 1540-page text on psychiatry dedicated only a few pages to children with "functional" psychoses. Considerably more attention was dedicated to describing various forms of "idiocy" among children including cases of cretinism, albinism, and leprosy (Stone 1973).

For reasons that will be discussed further in the next chapter, the classification of childhood idiocy rather than childhood "mania" captured nineteenth-century psychiatric attention. Idiocy was taken up, divided and fragmented, and recontextualized throughout nineteenth-century psychiatric discourses as changing cultural and economic circumstances afforded the label iterations of new meanings across time and space.

Professional willingness to recognize childhood "idiocy" as distinct from forms of insanity was formalized in Esquirol's *Maladies Mentales* (1838).[12] This early-nineteenth-century distinction encouraged the work of those such as Itard's student, Edouard Seguin (1812–1880), who in the spirit of the enlightenment, sought to "rehabilitate" retarded children in the mid-nineteenth century. However, changing social and economic circumstances toward the end of the nineteenth century led to a pessimistic attitude about rehabilitation. The medical model of inherited degeneracy replaced the enlightenment humanism. New social valuations of mental retardation engendered new symbolic divisions among "forms" of "idiocy" and new institutional relationships. By the end of the nineteenth century, the ideas of imbecility and moral idiocy became linked to a new category of child, the "feebleminded" child who would serve as the foundation for important new institutional and professional arrangements, which will be explored presently in Chapter 4.

Eclipsed by the social and professional interest in "idiocy," madness in children was pushed to the margins of psychiatric discourse until almost the beginning of the twentieth century. That is, although some references to childhood madness exist in nineteenth-century texts, the idea that children are susceptible to diseases qualitatively distinct from adult ones awaited the end of the nineteenth century.

The first psychiatric text to dedicate an entire chapter to childhood psychosis was Henry Maudsley's (1879) "The insanity of early life," in *Physiology and Pathology of the Mind* (Walk 1964). The chapter details various forms of "moral" "insanity" including "affective insanity," applying to cases of disturbances in the "mode of feeling generally and not of moral feelings only" (cited in Walk 1964: 761). Alexander Walk's (1964) "The pre-history of child psychiatry" observes that Maudsley's account of mental illness adopted the Freudian view of childhood aggression and instincts but did so within a decidedly pessimistic frame of mind that reflected the late-nineteenth-century preoccupation with degeneracy.

Maudsley's work was quickly followed by the more optimistic work of Hermann Emminghaus (1845–1904), who believed that children's and adults' disorders were qualitatively distinct. Unlike many of his contemporaries who adopted Kraepelin's organic approach, Emminghaus believed that childhood psychoses could be caused by either environmental or biological factors (Stone 1997). Emminghaus' work was also notable for its endorsement of collaboration between pediatrics and psychiatry (Walk 1964).

In addition to recognizing full psychosis in children, late-nineteenth-century psychiatry also began to recognize and treat childhood-specific anxiety disorders, among other less pronounced forms of mental illness—e.g., personality disorders and/or neurosis—in children (see Treffers and Silverman 2001). For example, in 1887 Karl Kahlbaum (1829–1899) described what he believed to be three types of "partial pathology" that could affect children, including paranoia, dysthymia, and diastrephia, which affected judgment, mood, and the will respectively (Stone 1997: 83). Pharmacotherapy, including opium and cannabis, was often prescribed by these late-nineteenth-century psychiatrists (Treffers and Silverman 2001).

Despite these late-nineteenth-century innovations the widespread practice of child psychiatry was not fully established until early in the twentieth century. In concluding his comprehensive review, "Child psychiatry before the twentieth century," Stone (1973) remarked:

> It would seem that before 1900 the eccentricities of children were simply tolerated, with indulgence or irritation, as the case might be, unless their behavior made them impossible to ignore. Thus the only children deviant enough to win notice, from the psychopathological point of view, were (1) the feebleminded (Itard, Seguin), (2) the destructive (Haslam, Esquirol), (3) the epileptic (Griesinger) or (4) the bizarre (Weyer, Baddeley, Voisin). Even bizarre children were able, for a long while, to escape the stigma of mental illness, if their "bizarre" behavior (by current standards) fit neatly enough into some schema that was acceptable to the period in which they lived.
>
> (Stone 1973: 298–299)

And so the legitimization of child psychiatry awaited the creation of new symbolic and institutional arrangements that were specific to the twentieth century. And yet, as I shall explain in the next chapter, these arrangements stemmed less from a new interest in child psychosis than they stemmed from the effects of nineteenth-century efforts to control indigent and feebleminded child populations. Chapter 4 chronicles the expansion of social surveillance and institutional control over such children throughout the nineteenth century. Although this movement was inspired primarily by social concerns and anxieties over children deemed mentally deficient, the effects would have implications for those who exhibited signs of mental illness as well.

Notes

1 See Berrios (1995) for a discussion of how mania was distinguished from the temporary, illness-induced delirium associated with phrenitis. However, delirium was a term employed for many uses. In its initial uses, it referred simultaneously to an acute organic disorder (phrenitis) and also to a symptom, "delusion" (Berrios

1995: 12). The two meanings were eventually distinguished according to dura-
tion, reversibility, presence of fever and confusion. The idea of psychosis did not
emerge until distinctions had been made between forms of delirium. Berrios
(1995: 13) claims that psychoses was eventually "modeled upon the symptom
structure of delirium."

2 Berrios (1996: 72) describes the two models for the etiology of mental disorders
that vied for supremacy during the nineteenth century. The "associationistic"
model was the legacy of British empiricism and appropriated Locke's description
of simple and complex ideas. Simple ideas were believed to be based on sensations and complex ideas were based on reflection, which was defined as the combination of simple ideas. Laws of association were employed in thinking
processes to link ideas together. The associationistic model influenced both
Kraepelin and Bleuler.

The second model was rooted in Greek thinking but came to be called "Faculty
Psychology" through its articulations by Kant and by the Scottish philosophers
of common sense. Its development by these latter thinkers was motivated as a
reaction against the presumed "passivity" of the associationist model. The
Scottish philosophers' work would influence the phrenological view regarding the
existence of an independent "intellectual faculty" that comprised perceptive,
reflective and germane functions all situated at the front of the brain (Berrios
1996: 72).

3 Trent is citing Howe's work published in 1874. It is unclear whether Howe's formulation of moral idiocy was derived from Prichard's (1835) articulation of
"moral insanity," a heterogeneous clinical concept used by Prichard to describe
individuals who evidenced a "perversion" in feelings and moral dispositions in
the absence of other overt forms of madness:

> madness consisting in a morbid perversion of the natural feelings, affections,
> inclinations, temper habits, moral dispositions, and natural impulses, with-
> out any remarkable disorder or defect of the interest or knowing and
> reasoning faculties, and particularly without any insane illusions or
> hallucinations.
>
> (cited in Sass and Herpertz 1995: 635)

Stone (1997: 107–108) claims that Prichard's idea of moral insanity included
manic depression as well as melancholy, various personality disorders, and
conditions characterized by a lack of compassion or excessive violence.

4 Although Kraepelin's work is foundational to present-day psychiatric nosology, it
has come under serious scrutiny in two regards. First, some psychiatrists feel that
the distinction between manic-depressive states and schizophrenic ones is useful
at a diagnostic level but problematic at an ontological level (see Jablensky 1999b;
Ovsiew 2000). Some suggest that a continuum relationship should replace the
molar distinction that currently prevails (Ovsiew 2000). Second, some psychiatrists exhibit doubt about whether schizophrenia is a disease since no replicable
disease markers have been found (see Jablensky 1999a for review). Similarly, it is
unclear whether schizophrenia is a disease, a syndrome that expresses a "final
common pathway" for a variety of pathological processes, or a collection of
symptoms and syndromes of multiple underlying causes (Jablensky 1999a: 245).
Additionally, it is worth noting that Kraepelin himself eventually distinguished
the description of schizophrenic symptoms from the "disease" of dementia praecox
(Jablensky 1999a).

5 Although Bleuler's formulation of schizophrenia involved disassociation, it did
not equate with the "split personality" conception that dominates popular perceptions of the disorder today (Turner 1995). Additionally, Bleuler did not believe

that schizophrenia was specific to adolescence and did not extend his research to address the disorder's precursors in childhood.

6 Importantly, one finds within Bleuler's work two understandings of the meaning of autism (Gundel and Rudolf 1993). Daydreams, superstition, and fiction are expressions of autistic thinking found in "normal being" (cited in Gundel and Rudolf 1993: 295). More extreme forms of autistic thinking, at the other end of the autistic continuum, demarcate "schizophrenic autism" (295). Schizophrenic autism occurs "totally independent of reality, using and creating concepts composed of random characteristics and capable of changing at random from one moment to another" (cited in Gundel and Rudolf 1993: 295).

7 Although the most recent DSM (APA 1994) has replaced the diagnosis of "neurosis" with the various anxiety disorders and some personality disorders (e.g., avoidant, obsessive-compulsive, and histrionic), the term is still employed by psychoanalysts (Stone 1997: 303). Accordingly, present-day understandings of, and distinctions among, personality disorders, affective disorders, and neuroses are twentieth-century innovations that are inconsistent with important aspects of late-nineteenth- and early-twentieth-century psychotherapy in which personality and neurosis were deeply connected. In describing the history of the conceptualization of the personality disorder, Berrios (1993, 1996) suggests that Kurt Schneider's representation of the personality type as an innate form of being characterized by psychic disharmony—not a developmental neurosis—contributed significantly to present-day formulations. However, present-day formulations are again in transition as syndromes that have been regarded as personality disorders—e.g., schizoid personality type—are being reclassified as developmental disorders.

8 Application of Freudian principles to child development and parenting occurred earlier in Europe than it did in North America but by the publication in 1938 of Mary Aldrich's *Babies are Human Beings*, behaviorism's influence had been replaced by those of psychoanalysis and psychodynamic approaches in North America (Jones 1999).

9 In Uta Frith's (1991) translation of Asperger's (1952) textbook, Asperger acknowledges the resemblance between his description of autistic psychopathy and Carl Jung's introverted personality. I have elected to focus on Schneider's work instead because the parallels are so unmistakable and the phenomenological influence apparent.

10 Tracing the diverse philosophical influence on Schneider's ideas is no easy task for the non-German speaker. However, a conceptual history of influences is implied in tutelage. Schneider completed his doctoral dissertation in philosophy under the tutelage of Max Scheler, who was embedded within the tradition of German phenomenology and applied this tradition to the problems of emotional life (Strasser 1957). Like Scheler and Jaspers, Schneider emphasized the value of phenomenological analysis in revealing the empirical features of psychopathology, particularly with respect to emotion and social relations. Although Schneider's works are sometimes represented as "empirical" and "atheoretical," these representations are not accurate. Schneider's implicit model of the psyche and its integration invokes complex phenomenological and psychoanalytical legacies. When tracing phenomenological trends in European psychology, Strasser (1957) identifies Henri Bergson (1859–1941), Wilhelm Dilthey (1833–1911), and Sigmund Freud (1856–1939) as seminal thinkers that influenced subsequent generations of phenomenological psychologists. Of course, Freud was himself a student of Franz Brentano (1838–1917), whose ideas also significantly influenced humanistic and phenomenological psychological developments. These diverse but also integrally related philosophical traditions find expression in subsequent generations of

German-influenced European psychologists including Bleuler, Schneider, Jaspers, and (I argue), Hans Asperger.

11 The exception to this generalization involves childhood cases of "hysteria," although this "disorder" was primarily regarded as specific to young girls and in such cases was attributed to the action of the uterus on intellectual capacities (Trillat 1995). Thus, the prescribed treatment for hysteria typically involved marriage and pregnancy (Stone 1973). Although hysteria would eventually be transformed into the contemporary category of the "neurosis," this development did not occur until relatively late in the nineteenth century.

12 This differentiation between the child afflicted with mania and the child afflicted with idiocy was enabled by Georget's argument in 1820 that "idiocy" was not a form of "insanity" (cited in Berrios 1996: 161).

4 The history of childhood
Ontologies, institutional divisions, child saving and child guidance

By the end of the nineteenth century, new ways of understanding various forms of childhood deviance and pathology had engendered new institutional forms and new cadres of professionals. The historical matrix of events, knowledge, and professional identities that emerged out of the end of the nineteenth century set the stage for the creation and expansion of twentieth-century child psychiatry, and ultimately provided the conditions of possibility for autism to emerge as a diagnostic category.

As explained in Chapter 3, the creation of autism as a diagnostic category specific to childhood had to await the completion of nineteenth-century historical recognitions and categorical distinctions. Autism could not have emerged in the nineteenth century as a diagnostic category because the pediatric experts—Leo Kanner and Hans Asperger—who produced it were a twentieth-century phenomenon. Moreover, the institutionalization of child psychiatry was indebted to other social institutions that were specific to the early twentieth and late nineteenth centuries, including the formalization of compulsory education and the creation of the child guidance movement.

The increased forms of social surveillance over childhood posed by compulsory education and nineteenth-century "child saving" led to public concern over increasingly nuanced understanding of childhood pathology. As the newly established child psychologists, pediatricians, and child psychiatrists reported ever more forms of childhood deviance, the public responded with new forms of surveillance over, and intervention with, "deviant" children who purportedly posed a new threat to social stability. In effect, efforts to engineer social stability through child saving, and later child guidance, coupled with increasingly nuanced understandings of normality and pathology in mental health, led to the creation of community clinics and special schools for children newly recognized as in need of psychiatric evaluation and support. It was within these schools and clinics that a new cadre of experts—child psychiatrists and psychologists—encountered a class of children who escaped the increasingly narrow parameters of normality but whose apparent pathologies could not be satisfactorily explained by the extant psychiatric categories.

Leo Kanner and Hans Asperger each required a new label for classifying and understanding the children they encountered. Although each found Bleuler's description of "autism" useful for describing their patients' lack of social involvement, neither felt entirely comfortable with Bleuler's model of adolescent psychosis. And so each created a new label, a new way of understanding, a population of children who in previous centuries would have been regarded within different frameworks of interpretation, if they were regarded at all.

Accordingly, the history of autism is intricately bound up with the sociological history of childhood as well as the history of psychopathology. And so, efforts to understand the emergence of autism as a personality disorder of childhood, symptomized by defects in affect and interpersonal relations, must be contextualized within a complex matrix of social practices, interpretive frameworks, and institutions that are specific to the early twentieth century but have complex roots in previous historical periods. Whereas Chapter 3 traced the matrix of psychiatric practices, interpretive frameworks, and professional identities implicated in the eventual "discovery" of autism, this chapter explores the niche conditions that pertain to the history of childhood. These conditions of possibility involve (1) the identification of childhood as a discrete phase of life in the nineteenth century, (2) the emergence of pediatric medicine, child psychology and psychiatry, and (3) the creation of new ways of thinking about childhood "deviance" in the late nineteenth and early twentieth centuries. These complex and divergent institutional histories converge in the early twentieth century in the pediatric psychiatry and medicine within which Leo Kanner and Hans Asperger practiced.

Accordingly, tracing the professional and institutional foundations of early-twentieth-century pediatric psychiatry requires investigation into several distinct but related historical strands. First, one must explore the emergence of childhood as a recognized social stage, both qualitatively and quantitatively distinct from adulthood. This entails investigating the historical process whereby western European ideas about childhood were constructed in and through social practices and in relation to educational philosophy and reform. Second, one must explore new categories of childhood deviance and the various professional movements and social reforms that brought childhood into focus in the early nineteenth century.

As the economic import of children changed in the early nineteenth century, as their mortality rates decreased, and as their symbolic significance in social life as *children* increased, childhood was brought into focus as a legitimate object of medical, psychiatric, and legal inquiry as well as a focus for governmental action. In Europe, the United States, and Canada, deviant children—simple-minded children, neurotic children, and ultimately troublesome children—became an important rallying call for late-nineteenth- and early-twentieth-century research, institutionalization, and social reform. The late-nineteenth-century establishment of pediatric medicine, the development of "mental hygiene" and the child guidance movement, the professionalization of social work and child psychology and psychiatry, and the institutionalization of the clinic for middle-class children all created the conditions of possibility for the early-twentieth-century identification of autism as a distinct childhood disorder of interpersonal relations. These institutional histories organize this chapter. The concluding section will draw these histories together to produce a synthetic discussion of the niche conditions that enabled the identification of autism in the early twentieth century.

The emergence of the child: constituting childhood, formalizing education

The history of childhood demonstrates that childhood is not a natural and universal phenomenon. Rather, determination of the identification and significance of children *as "children"* is contingent upon historically specific social and economic conditions. In what follows, I narrate the history of childhood as it has been analyzed and interpreted in the academic literature. Although this review is far from exhaustive, it illustrates the historical specificity of social understandings about childhood and it documents how these understandings are always constituted in relation to unique historical economic and social conditions. This analysis will ultimately support my contention that the idea of childhood psychopathology—particularly autism—was contingent upon the emergence of social institutions, economic relations, and cultural value orientations that were specific to the nineteenth century. Out of these conditions, autism was born as a diagnostic category in the early twentieth century. I begin this discussion with a brief look at some seminal studies of the history of childhood and with several historically significant philosophies of childhood.

Ontologies of childhood

Aries' *Centuries of Childhood* (1962/1992) is perhaps the most often cited source on the history of childhood. Drawing upon French historical records, Aries argued that the idea of childhood did not even exist in medieval society: even the smallest children were regarded as preformed adults. After leaving behind an extended infancy at the age of six or seven, children entered adulthood, engaging fully in adult forms of work and social interaction. DeMause (1974) proposed that the aim of infant care during this pre-enlightenment period focused on the physical molding of children into adults. Largely in agreement with Aries, DeMause's psychoanalytically based investigation of medieval childhood stressed that while infants were regarded physically as preformed adults, they were often perceived as spiritually deficient and were therefore believed to be (potentially) subject to the devil's machinations. Although Aries' and DeMause's accounts have been criticized for understating the degree of affection that medieval parents held for their children as beings unique unto themselves, their accounts do reflect the historical fact that childhood as we understand it today is historically specific to our period and that children had relatively little social stature or public significance prior to the nineteenth century.[1]

One of the first writers to suggest formally that children might be qualitatively different than adults was John Locke (1632–1704). Locke (1690) argued that children are not intrinsically evil; rather, they are born *tabula rasa* and are subject to the socialization effects of training and experience. Locke's ideas about the sensory, or empirical, basis of knowledge acquisition no doubt played a significant role in developing his *tabula rasa* approach to the infant's psyche. Accordingly, Locke's philosophy stressed the role of education, and particularly the inculcation of self-control, in the transformation of children into thinking adults, as codified in his text, *Some Thoughts Concerning Education* (1693). Although innovative in many ways, Locke's view of the child was influenced by the ideologies of his time, in particular, by mechanistic views of power and force:

> Locke rewrote the child as a different kind of becoming. It was a shift that took the child out of its Aristotelian unfolding of natural potential and its medieval Christian sinfulness and located it in regard to possession of interior powers in which the child was given an active, resistive, and mobilizing capacity to apply its own force against other human particles.
>
> (Baker 2001: 121)

Although mechanistically formulated, Locke viewed the child as an agent unto itself. Locke described the boundaries of the child's force in relation to the circumscribing limits of the then emerging nuclear family (Baker 2001).

Although secular in orientation, Locke's ontology of the child and attitudes toward childrearing were consistent with new religious attitudes about children. Between the seventeenth and eighteenth centuries, the belief that children were innocent and spiritually pure replaced the idea of children as bearers of original sin. As summarized by Aries, children were increasingly regarded as "fragile creatures of God" (1992: 40) whose spiritual growth required careful tending.

The idea that children need careful cultivation was forwarded still further by the contradictory ideals of Jean Jacques Rousseau (1712–1778) (see Baker 2001: 243–260; Pollock 1992). Rousseau is generally regarded as having romanticized childhood by suggesting that children are not, in fact, *tabula rasa*, but instead possess a unique and "naturally" based way of thinking, which is stifled through the inculcation of adult education (e.g., see Crain 1992). Rousseau's *Emile* (1762) articulated a stage-based developmental model of childhood, which borrowed from the empiricists an emphasis on (sensory) experience in the acquisition of knowledge. Rousseau believed that up until about the age of twelve, children are primarily pre-social in orientation and that knowledge is best acquired through their empirical involvement in the natural world, as prompted by nature's plan for its apprehension. However, although Rousseau touted a child's "natural inclinations," he also stressed the role of the tutor who has the responsibility of guiding the child morally so as to protect him/her from corrupting influences (Baker 2001; Pollock 1992). Accordingly, Rousseau advised the tutor: "Let your pupil always believe that he is the master, but in fact be the master yourself. No other subjection is so complete as that which keeps up the pretense of freedom; in such a way one can even imprison the will" (cited in Singer 1992: 39). The contradiction in Rousseau's value orientation between his valorization of natural inclinations and his perceived necessity for tutorial guidance remained, philosophically, unresolved and led to further efforts during his time and after to theorize the role of childhood education. Accordingly, Rousseau's work inaugurates a moment in which children become inscribed within the purview of public discourse about social policy (Baker 2001). This inscription within public discourse may have been motivated in part by parental angst about polluting childhood innocence: "Once a child is seen as innocent, any faults which emerge have either been implanted by the caretakers, or the caretakers have failed to protect the child from social contamination" whereas before the mid-eighteenth century, a "parent could always take refuge in the notion of original sin" (Pollock 1992: xix). Consequently, the role of parenting and childhood education became important social issues, at least for the wealthiest segments of society.

Although children became the object of philosophical inquiry by the late 1700s, in everyday life most children had little time for engaging in the practices of unstructured play endorsed by Rousseau: practices that we today understand as constituting childhood. Poor children worked daily, for long hours, in the factories of the cities and on the farms of the country. Indeed, as observed by Pollock (1992), before the nineteenth century, poor children were seen as either potential criminals or hard-working artisans and the public devoted little attention to the idea of child labor as problematic. Indeed, the diffusion of Rousseau's romanticized ideals of childhood during the nineteenth century coincided ironically with unprecedented industrial childhood exploitation (Brown 2002).

While most poor children labored, children of the growing middle class engaged in household chores, learned the trade of their parents or were apprenticed out, and were increasingly schooled, as were their more affluent counterparts. The expansion of schooling coupled with the increased social import afforded to children in philosophical and religious thought contributed to more surveillance of childhood. Moreover, as standards of social "politeness" became more exacting parents, and mothers in particular, spent more time attempting to teach children proper manners and comportment, as illustrated by this account of the role of mothering written by an American woman in 1813:

> There is scarcely any subject concerning which I feel more anxiety, than the proper education of my children. . . . The person who undertakes to form the infant mind, to cut off the distorted shoots, and direct and fashion those which may, in due time, become fruitful and lovely branches, ought to possess a deep and accurate knowledge of human nature. It is no easy task to ascertain, not only the principles and habits of thinking, but also the causes which produce them. It is no easy task, not only to watch over actions, but also to become acquainted with the motives which prompted them. It is no easy task, not only to produce correct associations, but to remove improper ones, which may, through the medium of those nameless occurrences to which children are continually exposed, have found a place in the mind. But such is the task of every mother who superintends the education of her children.
>
> (cited in Reef 2002: 16)

These statements illustrate how the project of nineteenth-century child-rearing involved careful monitoring of the sources of action and deliberate interventions designed to elicit desired outcomes.

DeMause (1974) describes this orientation toward childhood as marking the emergence of a new phase of childrearing in the early nineteenth century he labels the "Socialization Mode." In this mode, the process of rearing a child became "less a process of conquering its will than of training it, guiding it into proper paths, teaching it to conform, socializing it" (DeMause 1974: 52). In effect, new strategies of control and discipline accompanied emergent nineteenth-century conceptions of childhood. And these nineteenth-century conceptions can be traced back to eighteenth-century enlightenment and religious ideals, which themselves engendered new strategies of control and discipline. Thus, power, as it acted upon children's bodies (and "souls"), was transformed from being merely repressive, to being productive as well. Accordingly, the proper goal of childrearing in the socialization mode was to produce a mannered, rational adult through careful surveillance and deliberate intervention.

Studying children

Nineteenth-century efforts to properly socialize children led ultimately to a new interest in children *as children*. Charles Darwin fostered this interest by legitimizing "scientific" inquiry into the child's nature and evolutionary stature. Educational psychology subsequently emerged as a formal field of scientific inquiry, spearheaded by the work of Stanley Hall (1904, 1907). The turn-of-the-century interest in childhood "development" led to the work of Arnold Gesell (1941, 1952) whose laboratory research at Yale introduced new divisions among children based on their degree of apparent normality in relation to newly created and standardized developmental norms. Invention of the standardized "intelligence" test added to these efforts to measure purportedly innate childhood differences. I turn to address briefly each of these disparate threads in the constitution of social surveillance over children's lives.

As the nineteenth century waned, Charles Darwin afforded childhood new importance by adapting his evolutionary approach to child psychology in "A Biographical Sketch of an Infant" (1877). Darwin's work brought childhood into focus as a legitimate area of scientific research, as illustrated by one observer's comments made in 1881: "The tiny occupant of the cradle has had to bear the piercing glance of the scientific eye" (cited in Cunningham 1995: 169). Many early accounts of children's maturational processes, particularly as they were articulated in relation to the idea of child "development," recapitulated Darwin's ideas about evolution (Morss 1990). In particular, Darwinian ideas about evolution influenced the work of Stanley Hall, who has been credited with founding educational psychology and the child study movement in North America (Jones and Elcock 2001).

Hall founded one of the first research laboratories in American universities and established the journal *Pedagogical Seminary* in 1891 to publish research on educational psychology and child development (Alexander and Selesnick 1966). At Clark University, Massachusetts, Hall used data about children's thoughts, dreams, and play activities generated from questionnaires to develop an evolutionary model of child development that recapitulated his view of (phylogenetic) human developmental stages into ontogenetic development (Macleod 1998). Although largely deterministic, Hall's evolutionary-based model stipulated that proper education was necessary for children to acquire the needed skills at each developmental stage. Hall's educational psychology brought childhood into focus as a phase of life qualitatively distinct from adulthood, while stressing that childhood "development" would determine adult characteristics. By emphasizing the role of proper education, Hall's theories contributed to subsequent efforts to link childhood experiences and behavior to adult deviance and thereby helped open the door in the North American context for childhood to become a social welfare issue and the focus for Progressive reforms.

Most importantly for this discussion, Hall helped to pave the way for the systematic and "scientific" study of child "development" to become the raison d'être of the emerging social sciences at the turn of the century, particularly in the fields of psychology and psychiatry.[2] Much of this early phase of child study research focused on profiling the "natural development" of children or applied theories on natural laws to child development (Singer 1992: 68). Both forms of research required subjecting children to the measurement devices of scientific inquiry: children thus became the object for the collection of "empirical" data about "natural" developmental processes.

Arnold Gesell's work in 1911 at the Yale Psycho-Clinic was influenced by this empirical approach to studying the "stages" of child development. At his Yale clinic, Gesell studied and treated children who were having problems at school. However, work was not restricted to these "deviant" youngsters, as Gesell also addressed the "normal" developmental patterns of infants and toddlers. Based on his research with these populations, Gesell created standardized developmental scales that, as summarized by Nikolas Rose,

> Introduced a new division into the lives of small children, a division between normal and abnormal in the form of the differentiation of advanced and retarded. . . . Norms of posture and locomotion; of vocabulary, comprehension, and conversation; of personal habits, initiative, independence, and play could now be deployed in evaluation and diagnosis.
>
> (Rose 1989: 147)

These scales were widely disseminated within the medical community and became institutionalized as "objective" measures of "normal" development.

Creation of the standardized intelligence test by Alfred Binet, with Victor Henri and Theodore Simon, in 1905 contributed to these efforts to divide children according to "scientifically" derived measurement standards. Efforts to explain children's cognitive and developmental profiles ranged from approaches stressing heredity and eugenics to those stressing environmental influences, with the latter approach ultimately gaining more support by the 1920s and 1930s, during the second phase of child studies. This second phase of North American child study, often associated with the first Child Welfare Research Station founded at the University of Iowa in 1917, gained momentum in the inter-war period as education was once again seen as the instrument of social progress (Singer 1992).

In sum, the expansion of state authority to include governance over (publicly funded) childhood education and the expansion of professional interest in childhood were expressions of new forms of social control that began in the seventeenth century but found full expression in the late nineteenth and early twentieth centuries. These new forms of control involved new methods of observing and governing populations that gradually transformed monarchical systems of governance into professional and bureaucratic ones (see Foucault 1979, 1991). As childhood became more widely recognized as a distinct phase of private life, it became subject to these new forms of inquiry and control.

Educating children, dividing children, sequestering children

It seems no historical accident that the full-blown expression of DeMause's nineteenth-century socialization mode of childhood coincided with the extension of formalized public and private education for many children in Europe, the United States, and Canada throughout the nineteenth century. Although this extension of education was uneven in place and time, it gradually led more children of all social classes to enter the expanding educational systems. Of course, this is not to suggest that most poor children did not continue laboring in factories or in agriculture. However, by 1900 thirty-two states in the United States had compulsory education (Preston and Haines 1991). Historical observers suggest that the purpose of early formalized education, particularly publicly funded forms, lay less in the objective of "liberating minds" than it lay in efforts to reinforce social gender and class distinctions (Pollock 1992: xviii). This was particularly true for indigent children as illustrated by this account published in 1897: "It is now conceded on all sides that, if we would make social progress and strengthen the foundations of good government, into the minds of this unfortunate class must be instilled principles of morality, thrift, industry, and self-reliance" (cited in Preston and Haines 1991: 32). As the state shifted attention to indigent children, so did it also, in cooperation with the growing professions of psychiatry and medicine, increasingly attend to those children who were regarded as abnormal, uneducatable, or otherwise deviant.

Thus, expansion of formalized education led to more surveillance over children of all classes, and to more formalized and disciplined approaches to cultivating their manners and minds. This, in turn, demanded the creation, codification, and distribution of standards of normality. Contributing to the process of profiling "normal" development was the field of educational psychology, spearheaded by the work of Hall and others of the early phase of the child study movement. In sum, evolving government authorities, the establishing professions of educational psychology, medicine, and psychiatry, and the early social reformers all saw the child as the locus of adult health and social stability. Children who resisted such efforts or did prove amendable to them for whatever reason were increasingly singled out as "feebleminded" or "delinquent" by the end of the nineteenth century (see Jones 1999; Richardson 1989; Trent 1994). The following discussion chronicles some of these developments.

One early example of the extension of state authority over children's lives can be found in the work of Donzelot (1977). A student of Foucault, Donzelot explored the incarceration of indigent children in France as a project of social engineering in the early nineteenth century. As explained in *The Policing of Families*, the transformation of pre-enlightenment (monarchical) sovereignty into (state/economic) governmental authority and control was motivated in large part by an unraveling of the authority and normative constraints of the traditional patriarchal family. Within France, this unraveling of the family was itself an outcome of the social dislocation affected by the industrial revolution. Vast numbers of mobile, poor, and uneducated people who worked infrequently, according to the whims of industry or the whims of personal inclination, threatened state stability. Although forceful domination was employed to control this population, other means were also needed. "Pacification" and "social integration" promised greater long-term results, particularly if targeted towards society's youth (Donzelot 1977: 55). Therefore, in the service of state security, France passed a series of bills in the mid-1800s aiming to protect children from economic exploitation or abandonment by their itinerant parents. Accompanying these bills were a series of programs designed to generate institutions that would be responsible for the moral transformation of these unfortunate children into good citizens of the state. Children were represented as the crux of social reform, as illustrated by this passage from an authority of the time: "So long as society will not begin this reform at the base, that is, through an untiring vigilance over childhood education, our manufacturing cities will be constant centers of immorality, disorder, and sedition" (cited in Donzelot 1977: 72). Unlike the charity of days past, these programs were "philanthropic" in that they served a purpose in the long-term rehabilitation of the family and, simultaneously, facilitated state, economic, and social security. Donzelot's summary captures the intent and practices of "relief" during this period:

> This relief must also serve some purpose; it must also contribute to the rehabilitation of the family. That was why, in every request for aid, one had to locate and bring to light the moral fault that more or less directly determined it: that portion of neglectfulness, laziness, and dissolution that every instance of misery contained. In this new policy, *morality was systematically linked to the economic factor*, involving a continuous surveillance of the family, a full penetration into the details of family life.
>
> (Donzelot 1977: 72)

In effect, in the name of state security, government authority was extended slowly over more and more realms of life, demanding that the everyday intimacies of living be rendered more visible and more subject to intervention, particularly in the case of childhood.

Accordingly, throughout the nineteenth century, government and professional efforts to monitor, divide, and sequester children expanded. The idea of childhood as a separate stage of life thus demanded both its normalization through the inculcation of manners and education and, concomitantly, an extension of governmental authority, particularly over children who were regarded as problematic or abnormal since they were increasingly seen as constituting a direct threat to social stability.

Children of all kinds and manner of background constituted a threat to nineteenth-century sensibilities. As discussed above, indigent children posed a threat to social and economic stability and therefore in the early nineteenth century, one finds in Europe and North America, a greater willingness on the part of administrative authorities to allow children into the various almshouses and workhouses. One also finds the institution of schools and orphanages for indigent children (Trent 1994). But indigent children alone did not exhaust the threat posed by apparently aberrant nineteenth-century children. As discussed in Chapter 3, early-nineteenth-century psychiatrists began to accept the possibility of madness in children and efforts were made to formalize distinctions between children who were mad and those who were "idiots" (see Stone 1973; Walk 1964).

Childhood "idiocy" became a particularly important category for dividing normal from abnormal childhood populations. The "idiot" child, later the "mentally defective" or "feebleminded" child, was regarded as innocuous enough in the early 1800s but by the end of the nineteenth century, this stereotype had been transformed into a threatening apparition. The threats posed by these children were twofold. First, they constituted a potential economic threat since their purported waywardness made them unsuited for the routinized and disciplined practices of factory labor in a time of rapid industrialization and social dislocation. As illustrated by Donzelot's account, the perceived economic and social threat posed by these children was regarded as profound. Second, by the late nineteenth century, poor urban children were designated as "feebleminded" irrespective of their actual intellectual standing and were regarded as constituting a threat to the survival of the human race because their supposed degeneracy threatened species evolution. Here one sees the influence of Benedict Morel's biological psychiatry (see Chapter 3), Darwinist thinking, and the nascent ideology of the eugenics movement influencing social policy and reform. As I will briefly outline, from the mid- to late nineteenth century, one finds significant transformations in the ways that "feebleminded" and/or "dependent" children were constructed by professional systems of knowledge and subject to governmental authority.

As explained in Chapter 3, early-nineteenth-century views of childhood "idiocy" were inspired by enlightenment thinkers such as Edouard Seguin, who sought to rehabilitate retarded children. Seguin established special schools in France designed to "normalize" retarded children and inspired their institution in the United States. Although the educational quality of these schools varied, some focused more on "normalizing" "defective" children through a specialized educational curriculum, while others simply trained their charges to engage in menial labor, the schools' overall educational focus waned as a new pessimism informed psychiatric ideas about retardation and mental illness toward the latter half of the nineteenth century. Trent's (1994) *Inventing the Feeble Mind* chronicles the development and transformation of these schools in North America and illustrates how they contributed to the creation of new classes of experts—educators, administrators, and psychiatrists (to a lesser extent)—who studied and governed these children.

The function of these experts and their institutions shifted in the latter half of the nineteenth century as childhood "idiocy" was increasingly associated with lack of morality, criminality and degeneracy. For example, Trent found that after the American Civil War, American conceptions of "feeblemindedness" diverged from the educational model promulgated by the

French as the former increasingly regarded the "feebleminded" as burdensome, morally degenerate, and pathological. So began the transformation of the child "idiot" or "imbecile" into the "feebleminded," "delinquent" child. As commentators point out, although this transformation was not even in place and time, its system of operation almost always involved application of (purportedly) scientific medical models to explain the "degenerate" and "heritable" "pathologies" of the poor and afflicted (see Dekker 2001; Jones 1999; Richardson 1989; Trent 1994).

By the 1880s, American psychiatric and medical observers extended the "medical" model used in explaining degeneracy in madness to the "pathological, typological, and degenerative properties" of purportedly "feebleminded" children, particularly those from recently immigrated families (Trent 1994: 16). As observed by Sibley (1995), this nineteenth-century medical model largely prevailed throughout the twentieth century in North America and fostered a "disease based metaphor" that enhanced "anxiety" and the "threat of contagion" (Sibley 1995: 25). The social anxiety and threat that the feebleminded (and mad) posed stemmed from beliefs about their morally unfettered reproduction, the lack of economic self-sufficiency, and their purported susceptibility to criminal exploitation due to lack of moral judgment (Trent 1994). These linkages—across intellect, dependence, deviance, and class—converged in the eugenics movement, a movement articulated and forwarded by the works of Francis Galton (1822–1911).[3] Although most pronounced in the United States, the tendency to construct the children of the poorer classes as unfit, feebleminded, and potentially delinquent grew in Europe as well, as documented by Jeroen Dekker in his analysis of nineteenth-century European "re-education" homes for children "at risk." In sum, one finds across nineteenth-century Europe and North America a new matrix of "scientific" and "medical" practices and institutions that were aimed at identifying, sequestering, and administering problematic children, particularly poor and purportedly "feebleminded" children. This matrix involved the efforts of nineteenth-century "child savers," emergent pediatric physicians, juvenile courts and the rehabilitative clinics they fostered as well as the efforts of members from the newly instituted professions of educational psychology and psychiatry.

Child guidance, child psychiatry, and new categories of childhood pathology

Motivated both by the perceived threat that lower-class immigrant children posed and by pity for their plight, late-nineteenth-century "child savers" began pushing for child welfare, including greater educational and recreational opportunities for the poor children of North America's inner cities and orphanages and special schools for "re-educating" children in Europe. Although some reformers were motivated by eugenics logics, others maintained the enlightenment belief in social rehabilitation. These latter reform efforts were afforded legitimacy by psychiatrists such as Hermann Emminghaus who suggested that delinquency was an outcome of poor home conditions, rather than inherited moral degeneracy (Stone 1997). And across continents, the child savers' efforts conjoined with those of medical professionals who sought to decrease child mortality through better practices of physical and food hygiene. In North America, pediatric physicians, a medical specialization that established itself in the 1880s, adopted the newly developed germ theory of disease to spearhead its efforts toward social reform through the establishment of publicly funded "safe" milk supplies. The reformist efforts of late-nineteenth-century child savers and pediatric physicians, conjoined with the educational psychology of individuals such as Stanley Hall, created the social conditions of possibility that produced in the early twentieth century what has been described as the child guidance movement (see Horn 1989; Jones 1999; Richardson 1989).

The child guidance movement was motivated by fears about the purported delinquency of "feebleminded" children but largely rejected the biological and heritable explanation for delinquency in favor of an environmental explanation that stressed the child's impoverished background. The movement would establish child psychiatry as a professional field and lead to the institution of mental hygiene clinics (see Chapter 3) throughout the United States that first addressed juvenile delinquency but soon extended their focus to all forms of "troublesome" behavior in children, behavior that was believed to lead to adult deviance and/or mental instability (Horn 1989; Jones 1999; Richardson 1989). The twin emphases on mental health and prevention demonstrate the close connections between the child guidance movement and the mental health hygiene movement in general.

Child guidance

Most observers locate the first institutional apparatuses of the child guidance movement in the early juvenile courts and clinics that were established for that new class of childhood, the "delinquent." The purportedly "feebleminded" lower-class delinquent child that inspired such fear and pity warranted a special class of court protections by the early 1900s (Richardson 1989). Perceiving a need for clinical rehabilitation of these delinquent children, William Healy opened the Juvenile Psychopathic Institute in the United States in 1909 (Horn 1989; Richardson 1989). Implicitly applying the heritable model of degeneracy, Healy presumed that these lower-class delinquents would be feebleminded and began experimenting with the newly devised Binet-Simon intelligence scales to confirm his presuppositions. However, the scales revealed that most of the delinquents possessed "normal" IQs as measured against the scales' standards. Healy then adopted an environmentalist explanation to account for the children's "delinquency" and subsequently incorporated the medical model of preventive hygiene as a rehabilitative framework (Jones 1999; Richardson 1989). In 1915 Healy published his conclusions in *The Individual Delinquent*, in which he argued that delinquency was caused by psychological factors such as "emotional maladjustment" or "mental abnormalities" (cited in Horn 1989: 15).

And so, as illustrated by Healy's work, the medical model of preventive hygiene based on the germ theory of disease was reframed to encompass a loose conceptualization of delinquency as caused by the "contagion" of adverse and/or degenerate social (i.e., "environmental") circumstances, including but not limited to the moral failings of adverse parental influence. The child guidance movement that emerged from this synthesis of perspectives thus saw delinquency as a socially or environmentally caused "disease" that could be prevented or treated through application of "expert" knowledge. In this sense, the child guidance movement was founded in the same philosophy as the mental hygiene movement established by Beers and Meyer (see Chapter 3).

Accordingly, following Healy's lead, and funded by the Commonwealth Fund in the early 1920s, many community-based psychiatric clinics were established to handle references from the juvenile courts with the intent of therapeutically rehabilitating delinquent children. The manner of therapeutic remediation primarily involved behavior modification, reflecting the dominance of the behaviorist paradigm in the early 1920s (Horn 1989). Charitable and public support for these programs was no doubt influenced by the popularization of the mental hygiene movement and its preventive approach to mental health as an instrument against social deviance. Although remedial in form, the child guidance clinics reflected this preventive intent in that they aimed to prevent child delinquents from becoming adult deviants.

As the psychiatric clinics grew in number, so did their referrals, particularly as more psychological screening devices were introduced into the public schools. With the expansion of psychological screening in the public schools, the very definition of delinquency was expanded to include "predelinquent" behaviors that were regarded as troublesome and/or as having the potential of causing social deviance or mental illness in adulthood (Jones 1999). Accordingly, by the mid-1920s, the child guidance clinics shifted their focus from lower-class delinquent to the so-called problem children of the middle class whose development required careful monitoring and therapeutic intervention. Increasingly, interpersonal skills and relationships in the home and at school were scrutinized for the factors "motivating" the child's delinquent behaviors (Kanner 1972).

The child guidance clinic's shift in focus accompanied a wider shift that occurred in the fields of psychiatry and psychology as psychoanalytic principles and orientations slowly filtered across North America. As will be explained in the next section, incipient recognition that emotional and interpersonal (i.e., psychodynamic) factors influence development and trigger neuroses led psychiatry and psychology to address the psychic troubles that might afflict the otherwise "normal" development of middle-class children. Of course, some psychiatrists retained their commitments to child delinquents. And psychiatrists in clinics such as the one at Johns Hopkins Hospital treated children with more profound forms of mental illness as the newly established profession of child psychiatry focused on uncovering neuroses and psychoses in child populations. However, even while such commitments were extended, the child guidance clinics themselves became less associated with these populations and more focused on the mental health, developmental progress, and educational psychology of relatively "normal" middle-class children.[4]

Ironically, this new emphasis on "normal" childhood development did not preclude investigation into "deviant" behavioral or cognitive development. In fact, quite the opposite was true. The emphasis on "normality" functioned to delineate "abnormality" as never before. Indeed, the "development" of "normal" middle-class children gradually came to be regarded as fraught with peril and as in need of careful study and intervention. In effect, parents and professionals alike scrutinized the psychic and behavioral progress of children. By the 1930s, psychological neuroses and personality disorders became the new threat to social order.

Childhood neurosis and personality disorders: child guidance for the middle class

As explained earlier in this chapter, the idea of childhood as a separate stage of life thus demanded both its normalization through the inculcation of manners and education and, concomitantly, an extension of governmental authority, particularly over children who were regarded as problematic or abnormal since they were increasingly seen as constituting a direct threat to social stability. While institutions, child savers, and pediatricians directed their efforts at salvaging "feebleminded" and "delinquent" children in the late nineteenth century, by the mid-1920s the growing academic and professional fields of "child" psychiatry, psychology, and pediatrics directed their attention toward the mental life, particularly the social development, of the middle class (Jones 1999; Richardson 1989; Singer 1992). As with their nineteenth-century predecessors, these twentieth-century professionals also saw in the child the locus of adult health and social stability. However, while the nineteenth century extended state and professional authority over the lives of poor, "feebleminded," and psychotic children, twentieth-century efforts eventually extended state and professional authority over the lives of middle- and upper-class children who had heretofore escaped systematic professional scrutiny. Thus, early-twentieth-century efforts to study and remediate the previously untherapied mental and personality "afflictions" of middle-class children simultaneously extended social surveillance over more aspects of private life and extended the nineteenth-century project of dividing populations. And yet, although turn-of-the-century programs of mental hygiene and child guidance increasingly divided populations according to ever-nuanced measures of mental health, they also problematized the boundaries between normality and pathology in mental functioning. In what follows, I briefly summarize the events and personas implicated in the twentieth-century child guidance movement in North America and the general turn in both American and European psychiatry towards subjective and child-based experiences.

As established in Chapter 3, Freudian psychoanalysis contributed to new directions in European and North American psychiatry. Psychoanalysis tempered the strictly organic and medical approach to mental illness by emphasizing the role of subjective experience. Moreover, it expanded the concept of mental illness to include a wide range of *personality "neuroses" that manifested in personal experience and interpersonal relations* that were clearly distinguishable from the more profound forms of psychotic illness. Most importantly, for this discussion, psychoanalysis addressed and attempted to chart complex relationships across adult personalities, childhood experiences, and mental illness. By offering therapy for relatively mild forms of mental illness that were largely based in experience, psychoanalysis helped pave the way for the mental hygiene movement, community-based psychiatric therapy, and the child guidance movement. The social impetus for applying psychoanalysis and other psychologically oriented therapy resided in part in the social articulation of childhood delinquency as a public policy issue. Popularization of the environmental model of delinquency demanded a mode of therapeutic rehabilitation. And rehabilitation required early identification of children who exhibited incipient disturbances in their moral functions, social development, and "personality."

As the parameters of normality and abnormality in childhood "development" came under increased systematic scrutiny, school psychologists, social workers, and psychiatrists in the 1920s and 1930s encountered a new class of children who were "normal" in most regards but displayed problematic behaviors, interpersonal conflicts, neuroses, and personality attributes that (within the context of the new framework) demanded therapeutic rehabilitation (Jones 1999: 7). These "troublesome" children were as likely to be the sons and daughters of the middle class as they were to be the children of immigrants. Thus, by the mid-1920s, school screenings in North America sought to identify children of all economic classes who were viewed as "troublesome" and destined for criminality unless therapeutic interventions were administered to rehabilitate their maladaptive personalities.[5] Although it was the job of the psychologist, using newly developed screening profiles, to assess children's personalities, it was the psychiatrist's job to explain the origins of personality failure in either the family dynamics or in some organically based condition (Jones 1999). Thus, the psychic development of middle-class children thus came under the governance of psychiatric authority.

More systematic psychological evaluation of children in the schools led to the creation of more community-based clinics that offered therapeutic services for referred children (Jones 1999; Richardson 1989). As Richardson (1989: 107) points out, the institutionalization of these clinics contributed to the "medicalization of childhood" by disseminating psychiatric frameworks and vocabulary into popular culture as well as into the social services then directed toward children. So pervasive was this dissemination that one begins to find references to the child guidance literature in popular periodicals. For example, *Parents Magazine*, established in 1926, was a well-circulated outlet for child guidance precepts. Within such popular media, middle-class readers found that "the troublesome child acquired an 'everyday' face, one that looked remarkably like the reader's daughter or son" (Jones 1999: 97).

The new classes of child experts—pediatricians, child psychologists, and child psychiatrists—played an active role in the creation and dissemination of professional knowledge about normal and abnormal stages and processes of child development. For example, by 1924, the "normal" stages of childhood cognition were articulated by Jean Piaget in his *Judgment and Reasoning in the Child*, thereby enabling the identification of "abnormal" or delayed cognitive development. In 1935 Leo Kanner, working at Johns Hopkins Hospital, published the first child psychiatry textbook in English, *Child Psychiatry*, which was designed to acquaint pediatricians "with the principles of unbiased and practical common-sense work with the personality problems of their little patients" (Kanner 1935: xvii). Appel and Strecker's (1936) *Practical Examination of Personality and Behavioral Disorders: Adults and Children* illustrates the systematic and "scientific" approach to studying and diagnosing multiplying forms of social pathology. Much of this early-twentieth-century work focused not simply on cognitive norms of development but also on the *development of normal affect and interpersonal relations in the context of family dynamics* and school relationships (see Jones 1999).

The role of the mother, in particular, was highlighted within the models of child development influenced by the psychodynamic framework that finally came into vogue in North American psychiatry in the early 1930s. In particular, the experts agreed, mothers needed to be educated on the most appropriate ways whereby they could facilitate their children's "normal" development. Nineteenth-century reform efforts that attempted to educate mothers on proper feeding and hygiene practices may have prepared mothers in the early twentieth century to accept the expert advice of the new child guidance and mental hygiene movements. Although early American behaviorism had addressed maternal influences, it had largely focused on the mother's role in the child's acquisition of routines and appropriate behavioral responses. However, as the work of psychodynamic theorists such as Anna Freud (1895–1982) and Melanie Klein (1882–1960) slowly infused child psychiatry, the role of parenting—particularly mothering—was seen as vital to the child's psychic development and personality, the latter of which was primarily defined in relation to an ability to initiate and maintain social relations.

The psychodynamic emphasis on mothering was consistent with and easily adapted to the environmental explanatory framework and medical rhetoric of the mental hygiene movement generally and the child guidance movement specifically. Given the purported fragility of child development here conceived, mothering took on new import and increasingly required the input of experts. The development of the well-adjusted child could not be presupposed; rather, it became an accomplishment in itself.

In this early-twentieth-century focus on identifying and formalizing normal and pathological behavior, cognition, and affect in children we see contradictory forces at work. On the one hand, psychological and psychiatric efforts to distinguish the characteristics of the normal and abnormal child, in the absence of mania or retardation, further developed the nineteenth-century project of dividing populations. On the other hand, this effort to differentiate between normal and abnormal populations using the idea of the neurosis and its relation to personality development had the effect of problematizing the very idea of normality as more and more behavioral and social idiosyncracies came to be regarded as deviant or abnormal. The early-nineteenth-century molar distinction between sanity and insanity had been replaced by a continuum of abnormal states, ranging from the psychological neurosis of childhood deviance such as truancy or shoplifting to the outright delusions and hallucinations of the psychotic. Indeed, by 1935, the idea of a childhood "personality disorder" had become expansive enough that it included timidity, unresponsiveness, weak-willed and delinquency (Jones 1999). As public knowledge about child "development" grew through publications and institutional apparatuses linked to the schools, the parents of the middle class were more likely to bring their "troublesome" children to the psychiatric clinic for evaluation and therapy. Mental hygiene was for everybody's child and "outpatient" psychiatric treatment was available for conditions that heretofore would have been unrecognizable.

Identifying niche conditions

This chapter has addressed the specific, historically embedded niche conditions that enabled the identification and emergence of autism as a personality disorder specific to childhood characterized by defects in affect and interpersonal relations. It is important to keep in mind that prior to the early twentieth century, the conceptual and institutional apparatuses for diagnosing infantile autism (in the absence of outright psychosis) and Asperger's syndrome simply did not exist. Children who nowadays would be labeled with those disorders would have been regarded throughout most of the nineteenth century as "feebleminded" or, when their conditions were less extreme, would have escaped the medical gaze altogether. Accordingly, the matrix of institutions and practices that engendered the identification and exploration of autism in the works of Leo Kanner and Hans Asperger in the 1940s was dependent upon the emergence of an early-twentieth-century model of the medical subject that centered childhood, personality, and interpersonal dynamics. That model, here articulated in relation to the child guidance movement, sought to ensure healthy, productive adults by engineering childhood conditions. At an institutional level, this movement engendered community-based clinics that were staffed by growing cadres of child experts including social workers, educational psychologists, and child psychiatrists. As schools increasingly utilized psychological testing, the focus of these clinics was expanded beyond a psychopathology of delinquency to investigate childhood neuroses and personality disorders. The popularization of these clinics and the creation of special schools simultaneously heightened public awareness of mental health issues in childhood and reduced the stigma associated with them. The sheer number of child experts coupled with changing understanding about and valuation of mental health resulted in an explosion of psychiatric diagnoses. While many of these diagnostic cases were handled by the clinics, cases in which patients exhibited more severe symptoms of psychosis were addressed by the psychiatric wards attached to the community hospitals. And so, by the 1930s, in North America and in Europe the mental hygiene and child guidance movements had created the conditions of possibility for psychiatric diagnoses of both severe and mild forms of "deviant" behavior, particularly social behavior, in children. It was in this context that Leo Kanner and Asperger identified and described autism and (what has come to be called) Asperger's syndrome.

In the 1930s, Leo Kanner was working as a child psychiatrist at Johns Hopkins Hospital where he treated patients in the psychiatric clinic and served as a liaison between the hospital's psychiatric and pediatric services. In an effort to familiarize the hospital's pediatric staff with psychiatric vocabulary and diagnoses, Kanner wrote a text in 1935 titled *Child Psychiatry*, which became one of the definitive texts on the subject and by 1979 had gone through four editions and seventeen printings (Jones 1999). In the earliest version of this text, Kanner addressed "autistic" symptoms in relation to childhood schizophrenia, which had been formally recognized in pre-pubertal children in the United States by Potter in 1933 (Bender 1991). However, as described in Chapter 2, Kanner (1943) went against prevailing psychiatric research in the United States that regarded autistic symptoms as expressions of childhood schizophrenia and identified "autism" as a unique communication and affect based disorder, as illustrated in his description:

> The combination of extreme autism, obsessiveness, stereotypy, and echolalia brings the total picture into relationship with some of the basic schizophrenic phenomena. Some of the children have indeed been

diagnosed as of this type at one time or another. But in spite of the remarkable similarities, the condition differs in many respects from all other known instances of childhood schizophrenia.

First of all, even in cases with the earliest recorded onset of schizophrenia, including those of De Sanctis' dementia praecocissima and of Heller's dementia infantilis, the first observable manifestations were preceded by at least two years of essentially average development; the histories specifically emphasize a more or less gradual *change* in the children's behavior. The children of our group have all shown their extreme aloneness from the very beginning of life. . . .

Second, our children are able to establish and maintain an excellent, purposeful, and "intelligent" relation to objects that do not threaten to interfere with their aloneness, but are from the start anxiously and tensely impervious to people, with whom for a long time they do not have any kind of direct affect contact.

(Kanner 1943: 48–49)

Kanner also noted that unlike children with schizophrenia, autistic children tended to show improvement in their social skills and some normalization of their behavior as they grew older. Kanner summarized the difference between the schizophrenic and the autistic in this way:

While the schizophrenic tries to solve his problem by stepping out of a world of which he has been a part and with which he has been in touch, our children gradually *compromise* by extending cautious feelers into a world in which they have been total strangers from the beginning.

(Kanner 1943: 49)

Although Kanner was careful to distinguish the disorders in terms of concrete diagnostic criteria, observers point out that Kanner's own ability to differentiate autistic and psychotic children was suspect since the latter also exhibited "autistic" symptoms (by definition). This confusion no doubt stemmed from Kanner's implicit formulation of both disorders as disease entities, characterized by deficiencies of social (Bleuler's autistic contact) contact whose development was influenced by environmental (constitutional and psychodynamic) factors.[6]

Kanner's efforts to explain the source of the affective "autistic" disturbances were influenced by the work of his mentor, Adolph Meyer (1866–1950). As noted previously, Meyer took a community-based orientation to preventive psychiatry and advocated that psychiatrists specializing in child psychology be attached to public schools (Wardle 1991). In developing his therapeutic approach, Meyer took a *psychobiological* view that incorporated both psychoanalytic and biological frameworks in understanding the "longitudinal" development of patients over their lifetime (Stone 1997: 153). Meyer's approach to schizophrenia as a "reaction type" caused by both hereditary and environmental (constitutional and psycho-dynamic) influences no doubt influenced Kanner's formulation of infantile autism as influenced by individual-specific "constitutional" factors and by the social dynamics of parental influences. Accordingly, Kanner's observation that "there are very few really warmhearted fathers and mothers" among the parents of his patients was combined with his summary of the disorder as "*inborn autistic disturbances of affective content*" (Kanner 1943: 50). Like Meyer, Kanner also stressed the "developmental" progression of autism among his patients, a framework that had become popularized in the child studies literature as well.

Unfortunately, in the United States Kanner's insight that autistic symptoms were caused by a variety of environmental, constitutional, and hereditary factors was overshadowed by the idea that both childhood autism and childhood schizophrenia were most significantly affected by the social dynamics of parental influences, particularly maternal influences (Bender 1991). In her retrospective account, Lauretta Bender suggests that Frieda Fromm-Reichmann's (1948) idea of the *schizophrenogenic mother*, coupled with the work of others such as Bettelheim, Szurek, Blau, and Despart, led to the ascendancy of a purely psychodynamic approach to studying most forms of childhood neuroses, psychoses, and schizophrenia, including autism. More biologically informed approaches such as the one endorsed by Bender, who took a more biological approach to studying autistic symptoms in children as expressions of childhood schizophrenia and/or psychosis, tended to be marginalized by the 1940s (Bender 1991). Because the relationship between autism and the psychodynamic model will be taken up in Chapter 5, I will now turn to Asperger's work in Vienna.

While Kanner worked in the United States, Hans Asperger, a pediatrician, worked at the University Paediatric Clinic in Vienna, Austria. Asperger was particularly interested in the area of "remedial pedagogy," a therapeutic approach to remediating the behavior of difficult children that had been instituted at the clinic in 1918 (Frith 1991). This clinical approach should be contextualized within the European study and remediation of childhood "deficiencies" that was popularized around the beginning of the twentieth century (Dekker 2001). As with the American approach, the study of childhood deficiencies in Europe was first motivated by fears of future criminality and heritable degeneracy but was later expanded to address the role of sociological and psychodynamic factors in affecting childhood deviance (Dekker 2001; Wetzell 2000). Out of this context emerged the field of "pedagogical pathology" in Germany and the Netherlands, which sought to apply pedagogical practices therapeutically in the remediation of childhood deviance. As Dekker points out, the close relationship between medical pathology and pedagogical pathology in children demanded close collaboration between doctors and "pedagogues" in the diagnostic differentiation between physical illnesses and mental "deficiencies" (Dekker 2001: 124). Although such distinctions between physical/psychiatric illness and personality deficiencies were attempted, the boundaries between them were often unclear and the medicalization of childhood deviance throughout Europe and North America in the early 1900s led to a degree of synthesis in the approach of "remedial pedagogy" that involved the collaborative efforts of doctors, nurses, teachers, and therapists in addressing the biopsychological deficiencies of troublesome children (Frith 1991). Throughout the early 1900s, various institutions emerged dedicated to the practice of remedial pedagogy, of which Asperger's clinic was but one.

In his practice at University Paediatric Clinic in Austria, Asperger focused on a group of children who he believed suffered from an inherited personality disorder that led to their "troublesome" behavior (Frith 1991). Although Asperger believed that the ultimate source of the children's differences was heritable, he described their "autistic psychopathy" using a psychological framework that was indebted to Bleuler's formulation of autism as one of the four primary symptoms of schizophrenia (see Chapters 2 and 3). As with Bleuler's schizophrenics, Asperger (1991) felt that autism in his patients "totally colours affect, intellect, will and action" (39) and that this coloring also leads to disharmony "between affect and intellect" (79).

Accordingly, Asperger wrote of the reasons for choosing Bleuler's idea of autism to capture the quality of his patients' psychopathy:

> I have chosen the label autism in an effort to define the basic disorder that generates the abnormal personality structure of the children we are concerned with here. The name derives from the concept of autism in schizophrenia. Autism in this sense refers to a fundamental disturbance of contact that is manifest in an extreme form of schizophrenic patients.
> (Asperger 1991: 37–38)

Like Kanner, Asperger distinguished schizophrenic's gradual and progressive loss of contact with the autistic child's inborn difficulty with social contact. Moreover, Asperger (1991: 39) stressed that "unlike schizophrenic patients, our children do not show a disintegration of personality. They are therefore not psychotic." Asperger claimed that his patients with "autistic psychopathy" did not suffer from a disease entity insomuch as they suffered from a personality disorder that was free from the secondary psychotic expressions (e.g., delusions and hallucinations) described by Bleuler. And from Asperger's point of view, this personality disorder engendered certain intellectual strengths as well as weaknesses, including peculiar interests and a "paucity" of "expressive movements," including deficiencies in eye contact and expressive gestures (69).

In retrospect, it is difficult to discern the diverse philosophical and historical influences that impacted Asperger's approach to, and naming of, his patients' autistic psychopathy. Few published analyses of Asperger's work are available in English. However, it is clear that Asperger framed his disorder using Bleuler's psychological understanding of autism, which was partially indebted to Freud's ideas about auto-eroticism. Asperger observed that his patients' personalities did not threaten disintegration; therefore, they did not suffer from full autistic psychosis so much as they suffered from a pervasive but limited form of autistic withdrawal. In Asperger's times, personality disorders were the available alternatives for classifying individuals with socially designated forms of psychopathology in the absence of psychosis. Most then extant formulations of personality disorders remained directly tied to the neurosis (e.g., such as "childhood neuroses of character" (Berrios 1993: 22)) while still others blended organic psychiatry with elements of psychoanalysis to describe the pre-schizophrenic or schizophrenic-like personality disorder of the "schizoid." Asperger would surely have been familiar with both frameworks and yet neither would have enabled him to save his patients from Nazi eugenics surveillance (see Frith for Asperger's concerns on this matter). However, an alternative framework was available in the form of Schneider's personality theories.

Close consideration of the parallels between Schneider's formulation of the psychopathic personalities and Asperger's formulation of autistic psychopathy suggest that Asperger had Schneider's work in mind when he attempted to classify his patients. Like Schneider, Asperger felt that his patients did not suffer from a developmental syndrome; rather he believed that they suffered from an inherent affliction of personality. Also like Schneider, Asperger felt that this affliction stemmed from a disharmonious integration of the psyche. And yet, Asperger like Schneider felt that this disintegration was qualitatively different from psychosis and that it was not symptomatic of a disease entity, in the sense of Kraepelin psychiatry. Also, like Schneider, Asperger felt that this disharmony potentially enabled special skills or aptitudes. Finally, like Schneider, Asperger described the sources of his patients' differences in a phenomenological vein. This descriptive frame is particularly evident in Asperger's comments about his patients' patterns of perception.

Asperger was particularly intrigued by the unique manner of perception specific to his more intelligent patients. Although he may have stressed his patients' special skills to save them from eugenics policies, his accounts stress sincere interest in the form and expression of their "autistic strengths." Specifically, Asperger commented on his patient's "originality of experience," by which he meant that, "Autistic children have the ability to see things and events around them from a new point of view, which often shows surprising maturity" (1991: 71). Asperger felt that this originality of experience, coupled with specialized interests in science or art, could lead to professional achievement in adulthood.

Asperger did not theorize elaborately on the source of his pupils' particular originality but his brief account stresses his patients' relationship between bodily functions and consciousness. Accordingly, Asperger observed that with his autistic patients, bodily functions that in other children remain unconscious are brought to consciousness, registered and "disturbed" (Asperger 1991: 73). Asperger believed that the bringing to consciousness of bodily and social functions led to the peculiar deficiencies and strengths of his patients. On the one hand, it led to a disturbance in "normal" relations to objects and people but on the other hand it could lead to a degree of conceptual "abstraction" necessary for "exceptional achievements":

> The normal child, especially the young one, who stands in a proper relation to the environment, instinctively swims with the tide. Conscious judgment does not come into this and in fact can occur only when one has some distance from the world of concrete objects. Distance from the object is the prerequisite of abstraction of consciousness, and of concept formation. Increased personal distance which characterises autistic individuals and which is also at the heart of their disturbed instinctive affective reactions, is, in a sense, responsible for their good intellectual grasp of the world. This is why we can speak of "psychopathic clarity of vision" in these children, since it is seen only in them.
>
> (Asperger 1991: 74)

Although Asperger's formulation of "psychopathic clarity of vision" invokes the quality of autism Bleuler associated with daydreams and fantasy it also invokes another framework of interpretation, one rooted in early-twentieth-century German phenomenology.

Early-twentieth-century German phenomenology emphasized "suspending" the everyday attitude (i.e., "natural attitude") in order to gain privileged access into the structure of experience. Asperger may have believed that his patients lacked the natural attitude that constitutes the socially shared lifeworld, as understood phenomenologically. Certainly, this lack of fit was emphasized in relation to the autism of the schizoid and schizophrenic in the works of other German psychiatrists, as illustrated by Hans Gruhle, who described the schizophrenic as "not fitting into the world, of standing outside of it" (cited in Gundel and Rudolf 1993: 297). However, rather than regarding his patients purely in terms of their deficiencies, Asperger may have used phenomenology to address the intellectual strengths afforded by this lack of fit (see Chapter 5 for further discussion).

In conclusion, in summarizing the contributions of Kanner and Asperger in the 1940s, it is important to stress the social conditions that made possible the identification of the disorders that have come to be known as autism and Asperger's syndrome. In identifying the "niche conditions" that enabled the disorders' identifications, and differentiation from childhood schizophrenia, I do not mean to suggest that the syndromes are purely social in nature. Rather, the existence of a biological dimension to autism and Asperger's syndrome is not being disputed. Instead, my intent has been to identify the nexus of institutional practices and vocabularies that gave rise to the possibility of psychiatric identification. These conditions identified by Asperger were outlined briefly in Chapter 2 and include: (1) the emergence of the child as a research focus, (2) the emergence of personality as a research focus and clinical locus, and (3) the emergence of interpersonal dynamics as a research focus and clinical locus as a source point for individual pathologies.

First, as Asperger pointed out, the emergence of autism as a distinct disorder required that childhood be brought into focus, a project that began in the early nineteenth century but did not reach its peak until the twentieth century. The expansion of public schooling throughout the nineteenth century led to the identification of troublesome children who, by the late nineteenth century, were linked with biological degeneracy and criminality. These historical circumstances played important roles in setting up the conditions of possibility for the early-twentieth-century mental hygiene, child guidance, and remedial pedagogy movements. Contributing to these conditions of possibility was the emergent recognition within psychiatry and pediatrics that children could be afflicted with psychosis and neurosis and that childhood-based ailments, both biological and psychological in origin, affected adult well-being. These factors contributed to the medicalization of childhood deviance early in the twentieth century and to the concomitant proliferation of professions—child psychologists and psychiatrists and social workers—dedicated to identifying and remediating troublesome children. In effect, the early-twentieth-century child guidance and mental hygiene movements were direct outcomes of nineteenth-century efforts to govern and divide populations through increasingly "expert" forms of knowledge.

Second, Asperger observed that the identification of autism as a distinct disorder was fundamentally linked with the study of affective and communication-based disorders. As discussed in Chapter 3, throughout much of the nineteenth century, psychosis was predominately linked with intellectual disturbances—delusions—and perceptional disturbances and hallucinations. Indeed, Kraepelin psychiatry inherited the empiricist idea that madness stemmed from or involved disturbances in thought associations, although Kraepelin attributed those disturbances to biological causes. However, when Bleuler refigured Kraepelin's dementia praecox as schizophrenia using "autism"—or withdrawal of affective contact—as a primary symptom, he set the stage for increased medical and psychiatric focus on affective/social contact in the development of psychiatric illness. Bleuler's interest in, and focus on, affective responses and relationships was, no doubt, influenced heavily by his relationship to Freudian psychoanalysis: indeed, the semantic context for his formulation of autism includes Freud's auto-eroticism. And yet, Bleuler blended and reconfigured psychoanalysis within the framework of biological psychiatry opening the door, with Jung and Meyers, for more and more psychological psychiatry.

Third, as Asperger rightly points out, autism awaited the emergence of personality as a distinct field of psychiatric inquiry. The legacy of Freud and the psychodynamic theorists was critical for the formulation and development of childhood-based character neuroses. Inquiry into the nature of these neuroses coupled with increased social surveillance of children facilitated development of the various mental hygiene clinics available to screen and serve the growing number of problem children. Character and personality were not, however, restricted to psychodynamic psychiatry. Increased social surveillance of "preschizophrenics" in the 1920s and 1930s engendered interest in the schizoid and/or schizophrenic "personality" type, a type autistic in character but lacking the symptoms of psychosis. Additional formulations that sought to reframe personality types outside the parameters of medicalized vocabularies and character neurosis were indebted to Jung, Jaspers, and Schneider, whom all broke with the Freudian tradition but retained an interest in psychological psychiatry. They integrated aspects of psychoanalysis, phenomenology, and Gestalt psychology into new formulations of personality, formulations that no doubt significantly influenced Asperger's ideas about autistic psychopathy.

Accordingly, ideas about personality influenced Kanner and Asperger in distinct ways. In the case of Kanner, the role of personality was emphasized in the psychodynamic effects of parental influence on the constitutionally affected child. For Kanner, autism was not purely a function of frigid mothering, but the biologically susceptible autistic child's developmental progression was fundamentally affected by the personality quirks and character neuroses of the parental environment. Although ambiguity and ambivalence can be found across Kanner's writings, it seems fair to say that he regarded autism as a disease entity—in terms of its commonality with schizophrenia—but whose manifestations and developmental course were largely subject to environmental influences.

In contrast, although Asperger adopted Bleuler's vocabulary of autism to describe his patients' affective and communication-based defects, he appears to have rejected the disease-entity, schizophrenic-linked framework for describing his patients' deficiencies. Instead, Asperger appropriated the idea of a personality disorder, most probably Schneider's theory of psychopathic personalities. Perhaps the idea of autism as a "type" of personality disorder—as opposed to a *disease entity* or *developmental syndrome*—was important for Asperger because he wanted to stress what he saw as the unique attributes of the autistic personality. Schneider's contention that psychopathic personality types were innate forms of being potentially capable of unique capacities would have appealed to Asperger in this respect. The political exigencies of Nazism would certainly have contributed to Asperger's desire to valorize his students' special abilities.

In conclusion, having recognized the niche conditions that enabled the identification of autism and Asperger's syndrome in the early twentieth century, the time has come to investigate the evolution of the disorder within psychiatric and public discourses across the twentieth century.

Notes

1 Not all historical commentators share Aries' conclusions about the absence of childhood in medieval society. See for example Linda Pollock's (1983) *Forgotten Children: Parent–Child Relations from 1500–1900*, Hugh Cunningham's *Children and Childhood in Western Society since 1500*, and Shulamith Shahar's (1990) *Childhood in the Middle Ages*.

2 Alternative approaches to child development and educational psychology were being developed by John Dewey, who stressed the interrelationship between mind and environment as mediated by education and by Lightner Witmer, who took a clinical approach to therapeutic interventions for children who exhibited learning disabilities (Jones and Elcock 2001).

3 Galton published *Hereditary Genius* in 1869 in which he adapted Darwin's idea of natural selection to explain what he saw as hereditary aspects of intelligence. Galton wished to discourage reproduction among people he regarded as unfit.

4 Kanner (1972: 13) argues that Wickman's studies, published in 1928, were particularly instrumental in the shift toward a focus on the "psychology of the social development of children."

5 It is important to note that present-day diagnostic guides such as the DSM-IV advise against diagnosis of a personality disorder for children in the absence of sustained symptoms.

6 My argument that Kanner regarded autism as a disease entity is supported by the fact that Adolph Meyer, Kanner's mentor, explicitly regarded psychosis as a "disease entity" (cited in Beer 1995: 193). Moreover, in his 1972 edition of *Child Psychiatry* Kanner approvingly cites Margaret Mahler's division of childhood psychosis into two groups, "one representing cases of early infantile autism and the other comprising the cases of symbiotic infantile psychosis" (Kanner 1972: 703). Although Mahler's work is situated within the psychoanalytic movement, she did recognize that biological factors affect psychopathology (Stone 1997). Thus, the evidence supports an interpretation of Kanner's formulation of autism as a disease entity despite his willingness to incorporate psychodynamic influences.

5   Psychological discourses construct autism

What niche conditions are implicated in the articulation of autism as the most common "developmental disorder" of the twentieth century? Analysis of these conditions must extend beyond the forms of institutional analysis found in Chapters 3 and 4 to encompass the professional discourses (i.e., vocabularies and conceptual constructs) constituting twentieth-century psychological paradigms because the idea of autism depended then and now upon the language and practices used in its naming, identification, and therapeutic remediation. However, the role that psychological knowledge and practices play in twentieth-century child guidance extends beyond identifying and naming "developmental disorders" in children. As Graham Richards put it, "Psychology has clearly acquired a role as the site where society's concerns and anxieties regarding children and childrearing are most systematically and authoritatively debated" (1996: 137). Put otherwise, psychology possesses perhaps the most "authoritative" voice on twentieth-century childhood: psychological knowledge, institutional practices, and the dissemination of "pop" psychology together serve as *the* hegemonic framework for knowing and acting upon those people we regard as children.[1] In particular, psychological knowledge and practices function to delineate for parents, educators, and medical professionals the character and behavior of children identified as "normal" and those "others" whose apparent psychological deviance led to their identification as "delinquent," "neurotic," or more recently, "developmentally delayed."

The two psychological paradigms most directly involved in delineating children in terms of standards of psychic and behavioral normality are psychoanalysis and cognitive psychology. Accordingly, how these paradigms served as the primary conceptual and material apparatuses engendering ideas about autism in the twentieth century requires explanation. The influence of these paradigms was (and is) not restricted to the texts and clinical practices of psychological and psychiatric experts. The vocabulary and practices for knowing children derived from these paradigms find expression in educational psychology, developmental pediatrics, and popular cultural artifacts such as childrearing manuals and developmental inventories and guidelines. From the baby book, to the women's journal, to the pediatric developmental screening device, psychoanalytic and cognitive psycho-psychiatric knowledge narrated the story of children's "normal" and "superior" intellectual and emotional development throughout the twentieth century. Contextualized as such, the early-twentieth-century mental hygiene movement and child guidance literature stand as merely incipient forms of what transformed into the full-scale "medicalization" of childhood as constituted by psychological expertise. This increasing medicalization of childhood combined with parents' growing familiarity with these representational frames, subtly changed parenting and pediatric practices, leading to historically unprecedented forms of surveillance and social engineering.

The willingness of parents, pediatricians, and school educators to embrace expert psychological constructs of childhood requires contextualization within the social and economic institutions of the times. For the psychoanalytic paradigm in North America and Great Britain, the characteristics and features of the post-World War II terrain contributed to and, in turn, were affected by psychoanalytic principles including the emphases on "normal" processes of ego development in childhood and the role of maternal behavior in mediating that development. For the cognitive paradigm, the information revolution and the subsequent transformations in workplace roles and expectations in North America no doubt contributed to that model's growth, which in turn increased parents', among others, receptivity to its forms of expert knowledge about children. However, the twentieth century's willingness to embrace expert knowledge had significant consequences for parents and children alike. The explosion of research about children's emotional and cognitive development and the concomitant extension of surveillance over children's youngest years led to the problematization of old boundaries between normality and pathology. Just as turn-of-the-century discourses and practices extended the idea of pathology to include the idea of delinquent and troublesome children, so too did late-twentieth-century cognitive vocabularies and practices alter the boundaries of normality by including within its other—pathology—behaviors and personality profiles previously escaping the medical, scientific gaze.

This chapter addresses the twentieth-century psychological terrain by focusing first on the rise of psychoanalysis in the post-war period before moving to address its replacement by the cognitive paradigm starting in the mid-1960s. Each paradigm will be contextualized within the Zeitgeist of its times before the discussion turns to a detailed look at how each paradigm constructs and treats autism. The chapter concludes with a discussion about the impact of psychological expertise on the identification of normality and pathology in twentieth-century childhood.

The rise of psychoanalysis 1940–1960: the Zeitgeist of the times

Although the psychological paradigm of psychoanalysis vied for supremacy with behaviorism in North America throughout the early to mid-twentieth century, the former approach monopolized clinical approaches to understanding and treating autism in the 1940s through the early 1960s. The reasons for the ascendancy of the psychoanalytic paradigm and its monopoly over many forms of child psychopathology are complex and rooted in a variety of historical contingencies specific to the post-World War II era. This section provides a brief overview of psychoanalytic assumptions about mental health and discusses historical contingencies leading to popular dissemination of these principles in the post-war era. Thus contextualized, the discussion turns to a more detailed account of psychoanalytic formulations of autism developed during this period.

Framed within a psychoanalytic perspective, most forms of psychopathology—including both psychoses and neuroses—are psychological in origin. Consequently, mental disorders are not typically viewed as disease entities; rather, disturbances in the development of the ego are seen as causing mental disorders. In particular, psychoanalysis locates many forms of psychological disorders in the infant's failure to develop a differentiated sense of his- or herself, through "normal" relations with external reality. The infant's failure to differentiate her/himself from the mother, to develop a coherent ego, theoretically results in defense mechanisms that impinge against the infant's awareness of and access to the social world. A variety of "object relations" approaches, which largely dominated American and British psychoanalysis in the post-war period, articulated and rearticulated this complex formulation. Psychoanalysis' alliance with the medical community in the post-World War II period furthered its claim of expertise over childhood mental health and mental disorders, particularly infantile autism and schizophrenia (Jones 1999: 217).

However, the influence of psychoanalysis was not limited to professionals and academics. In the 1940s and 1950s, psychoanalytic principles disseminated through popular culture in advice columns, baby books, and other expressions of child guidance (Jones 1999; Rose 1989). Consequently, psychoanalysis provided the dominant metaphor for viewing child "development" in the post-war period. This metaphor constructed the infant as engaged, from the moment of its birth, in a fierce struggle for consciousness: for the development of its "ego." The infant's mother was seen as the determinant force in the infant's environment that either enabled or impinged against the infant's success in mastering the forces of psychosis in its quest for ego development and "normal" relations with its external environment (i.e., normal "object relations"). The ego's apparent fragility, and its susceptibility to psychological injury, thus dictated that mothers intensively attend and respond to their infants' needs. Maternal failure due to absence, negligence, or ignorance theoretically engendered psychoses at worst and neurosis at best. Consequently, the psychoanalytic metaphor for understanding child development necessitated that mothers seek out expert advice to maximize their children's potential for developing "normal personalities."

The psychoanalytic metaphor for understanding child development and its approach to remediating child psychotherapy must be contextualized and explained in relation to the Zeitgeist of the times, particularly in relation to the era spanning the 1940s through the 1960s. In the post-World War II era, psychology emerged as a professionalized and respected discipline applying itself vigorously to "solving" the problems of adjustment in modern society (Napoli 1981). The problems of child adjustment in the contexts of the family and the home were constructed in this era as vital to social stability and the preservation of democracy and were thereby taken up in the project of social engineering, a project viewing psychologists as "expert authorities" (Richardson 1989; Rose 1989). Psychoanalysis, in particular, gained heightened visibility and legitimacy during this period as the body of knowledge with the cadre of experts capable of diagnosing and remediating social and individual pathology (Hale 1995). Children turned into the objects of psychoanalytic inquiry during a period in which social, political, and economic stability were increasingly linked to developmental outcomes. Situated at the crux of developmental outcomes in this period was the figure of the mother, whose real or imagined behavior determined the infant's success at ego differentiation.

A variety of factors produced the psychoanalytic emphasis on motherhood as the supreme mediator of child development and social stability. Although it would be impossible to address all of these factors, pre-eminent among them were the heightened import afforded childhood in relation to the larger project of social engineering, the push to remove women from the workforce after World War II, and the proliferation of psychoanalytically informed child guidance literatures specifically addressing mothers, whose increasingly isolated existence in their homes and suburbs may have made them particularly susceptible to "expert" knowledge emphasizing their importance in child "development."

Although efforts to popularize children's needs occurred prior to World War II, the post-war period witnessed increasing efforts by government and various mental health agencies to sensitize the public to the mental hygiene of child development (Richardson 1989). This push was international, as evidenced by the foundation in 1948 of the World Federation of Mental Health (Richardson 1989). Children were an important focus of this agency, and in pursuing this interest British child psychiatrist John Bowlby was employed as a consultant to prepare a monograph on child development and mental health. Published in 1952, Bowlby's monograph, *Maternal Care and Mental Health*, blended psychoanalytic and ethological principles to argue for consistent, full-time maternal care as the ultimate predictor of successful developmental outcomes. Specifically, Bowlby appropriated the idea from object relations that the maternal figure mediates the infant's ego development, which he blended with the ethological principle of "sensitive periods" of development. This blend led Bowlby to argue that lack of maternal care during sensitive periods of development led the infant to develop an "affectionless character" vulnerable to psychopathology (cited in Hunt 1993: 367). Not surprisingly, maternal deprivation and "normal" infant attachment became important research foci during the 1950s and all categories of social ailments, including "delinquency" and "pre-delinquency," were linked to both phenomena (see Grant 1998; Jones 1999; Richardson 1989; Rose 1989).

Public receptivity to Bowlby's (1952) work was, no doubt, conditioned by earlier child guidance material published in the 1930s and 1940s. In 1938, Mary and C. Andrews Aldrich published *Babies are Human Beings,* a text that used simplified psychoanalytic principles to counter the behaviorist-informed childrearing approach of Watson (West 1996). In the immediate post-war period, Dr. Benjamin Spock was commissioned in the United States to write a guidebook on childcare precisely because he had training in psychoanalysis (Grant 1998). Spock's friendship with Margaret Mahler (Hale 1995), a prominent psychoanalyst in the post-war period, no doubt reinforced his (at least initial) commitments to the psychoanalytic frame of reference for child development. Dr. Spock's retrospective comments about his 1946 text, *Common Sense Book of Baby and Child Care*, illustrate these early commitments: "I was trying to take the psychoanalytic concepts I was studying and somehow fit them together with what mothers were telling me about their babies" (cited in West 1996: 237). These early texts disseminated psychoanalytic interpretive frameworks and vocabularies into the popular conscience and facilitated subsequent public acceptance of Bowlby's works, and later, Bruno Bettelheim's.

Accordingly, by the 1950s, many American, Canadian, and European middle-class mothers stood primed for psychoanalytically informed guides directing them on the principles and practices of infant care (Grant 1998). Pushed out of the workforce and exhorted to stay at home and care for their children, intensive mothering became the occupation of most middle-class North American (and western European) women. The project of intensive mothering, linked as it was to economic and political stability, required expert advice and intervention. As explained by Grant (1998) in her *Raising Baby by the Book: The Education of American Mothers*, by the 1950s American women, at least, willingly sought that expert advice. The desire of middle-class mothers to raise *"perfect* children—with unblemished bodies, high intelligence, and 'normal' personalities" (Harvey cited in Grant 1998: 202) coupled with their relative isolation in the newly emerging suburbs enhanced this need to solicit expert advice. The widespread availability of psychoanalytically informed guidance literature responded to this desire, and helped fuel it.

The desire of middle-class parents to raise children with "normal personalities" points to the emphasis on psychological "adjustment" dominating mid-twentieth-century thinking about children (Rose 1989). As explained in Chapter 4, the early-twentieth-century molar conception of psychological adjustment in children, first linked to outright delinquency, expanded to incorporate a continuum of levels of adjustment as more and more behavioral idiosyncrasies were subject to the medical gaze of pediatricians, school psychologists, child guidance clinics, and the increasingly "medicalized" gaze of parents. By the mid-1940s, society viewed the project of producing an "adjusted" child as fraught with complications across all socio-economic strata. As Rose (1989) explained:

> In the new psychology the impulse to social adjustment was inscribed in the individual at the psychic level. . . . And maladjustment, from bed-wetting to delinquency, had become a sign of something wrong in the emotional economy of the family. . . . If families produced normal children, this was itself an accomplishment, not a given; it was because they regulated their emotional economy correctly. The production of normality now appeared to be a process fraught with pitfalls. . . . A constant scrutiny of the emotional interchanges of family life was required, in the name of the mental hygiene of the individual and society.
>
> (Rose 1989: 159)

Not only experts trained in psychological principles, but also mothers mobilized to search out psychological expertise accomplished the "constant scrutiny of the emotional interchanges of family life." Failure to produce a "normal" child pointed directly to the psychological failures of the maternal environment. The mother's feelings, wishes, and anxieties all required scrutiny in order that they not undermine her children's normal development (Rose 1989).

Thus, the desire and imperative to produce children with "normal" personalities required mothers to attend most carefully to every stage of their child's development. Gesell's developmental scales, popularized in pediatric charts and baby books, provided the developmental continuum to evaluate each child's development.[2] Failure to reach developmental "milestones" required immediate attention and intervention. Explaining and remediating every possible childhood ailment or expression of deviance from asthma to bedwetting required psychological expertise. And, given Rose's (1989: 140) observation that during this period personality differences were "receding into the interiority of the soul," it was appropriate that psychoanalysis was particularly suited for rendering "legible" the unconscious and subconscious processes articulated as a threat to children's normal development.

Thus, the heightened attention afforded mothering and its articulation as mediating both individual ego development and the security of the state effectively problematized former boundaries between normalcy and abnormality in child development. The two-year-old child evidencing "developmental" delays as measured against Gesell's scales might merely be a "late bloomer" or, increasingly, seen as suffering anxiety from a neurotic, fractured and/or undifferentiated ego brought upon by maternal dysfunction. Likewise, the mild neurosis of a seven year old was increasingly seen as portending future mental illness, perhaps schizophrenia. Even more, the "naughty" ten year old was more and more seen as a "pre-delinquent." Only clinical evaluation and, if necessary, therapeutic remediation by psychological expertise could determine the developmental impact of such anomalies and act, if necessary, to avert or ameliorate them. And so, as children came under increased surveillance by their parent's medicalized, psychiatric gaze, their "problems" multiplied. Thus the state and the professional fields of psychology, psychiatry, pediatrics, social work, and education found their responsibilities in fostering and ensuring mental hygiene expanded (see Rose 1989).

Although psychoanalytically inspired ideas persist in popular culture today and therapists still practice psychoanalysis, the paradigm lost its hegemonic hold over psychiatry and psychology in English-speaking languages. The psychoanalytic era largely came to an end in the early 1970s with the construction of new metaphors for understanding the emergence of consciousness and the development and treatment of psychopathology. In the early 1970s, the classical dualism between (1) approaches stressing biology and genetics in understanding humanity, as evidenced by Kraepelin's psychiatry, and (2) those approaches stressing consciousness and perception, as illustrated by psychoanalysis, emerged cloaked in new vocabularies and new interpretive frameworks as the disciplines of psychiatry and psychology parted ways. Psychiatry directed its inquiry on bodily processes by incorporating ideas generated from the fields of evolutionary biology and ethology (Stone 1997). Psychology, on the other hand, claimed the mind as its terrain, as cognitive psychology soon dominated the discipline. The rise of the cognitive paradigm in psychology and its implications for understanding autism will be discussed later in this chapter, while Chapter 6 addresses the bio-genetic approach.

Looking back upon that era, gauging the effects of the psychoanalysis and its therapeutic interventions is a tricky business. Moves to pathologize relatively mild forms of childhood "deviance" led to the expansion of governmental scrutiny over private life. The effects of this expansion may have been most problematic for women and mothers, whose needs were subordinated to the production of "future citizens" and whose maternal acts and attitudes came under increasing scrutiny. On the other hand, the import afforded children and the securing of their value in relation to state security, ensured at least some level of state and professional attention directed at their happiness and well-being, even if love was subordinated to the ideals of adjustment. Likewise, although psychoanalysis pathologized mothers, its optimism about its own therapeutic powers in the post-war period enabled more systematic attention to, and help for, children's mental health. The ambivalence of these effects is demonstrated in the case of autism.

In the nineteenth century a child born with severe autism would very likely have been abandoned, neglected, or institutionalized. The biological psychiatry of Kraepelin had no interests in, or solutions for, such children. The "mildly" autistic child would have been regarded as "eccentric," if regarded at all. Such a child might or might not have mastered the rudimentary arts of living enabling him or her to survive independently in adulthood. But by the 1940s, psychoanalysis wrought significant changes. Parents became more attuned to their children's "development" and were more likely to seek expert advice, if financially able. A psychiatric diagnosis of autism, then regarded as one form of child psychosis, led simultaneously to "mother blaming" and, perhaps, psychoanalytic intervention. Although it is difficult to know in retrospect how helpful psychoanalytic treatment actually was, one finds assertions of success with autistic children across the writings of psychoanalytic thinkers such as Melanie Klein, Margaret Mahler, and Frances Tustin. Certainly, psychoanalytic treatment by a caring "expert" would have been more productive in helping the autistic child than the nineteenth century's practices of neglect or institutionalization. Moreover, as noted in Chapter 4, even Kanner and his mentor Meyer had exposure to psychoanalytic therapeutic principles and used them, albeit in modified form, in their treatment of autistic patients. Thus, the effects of the psychoanalytic era are complex and multifaceted. Although much of the original theoretical formulations for the etiology of psychopathology stand rejected, some of the original therapeutic treatment devices are still employed. The discussion turns now to explore these psychoanalytic formulations and trace them to their current expression in the autism literature.

Psychoanalysis and autism in English-speaking countries: ego psychology and the mother–infant relationship

The popular imagination often perceives psychoanalysis as a school of thought unified by the lasting legacy of Freudian theory. This homogenized representation of psychoanalytic theory glosses over and elides the divergent theoretical perspectives and therapeutic approaches that have, in fact, characterized psychoanalytic developments over the past one hundred years. For example, Hale (1995), in his comprehensive approach to psychoanalytic thought in the United States, argued that by the end of the 1930s, psychoanalytic approaches already began diverging sharply in terms of their underlying assumptions about whether innate conflicts, as argued by Freud, or environmental factors such as early mothering or repressive capitalism generated psychic conflict. By the mid-1930s, the logic of psychoanalytic character theory, which rooted adult character types in early libidinal eroticism (both oral and anal), was slowly giving way to the ego psychology of Anna Freud and the object relations approach of Melanie Klein, and the focus on mothering and ego development developed by Margaret Mahler (Hale 1995). Indeed, in his 1972 edition of *Child Psychiatry*, Leo Kanner described Anna Freud's work as significantly influencing the development of child psychiatry in the early 1940s:

> Child psychiatrists, looking around for similar means of giving their patients opportunities for self expression [as adults were given], were directed by Anna Freud toward the utilization of *play* as the most natural and promising instrument. Children were afforded a chance to playfully reveal and work out their insecurity, anxiety, and hostility. This method, free from third-degree rudeness and from disturbing verbalization of filial disloyalty, gave the observer significant knowledge of a child's feelings and at the same time provided curative emotional releases for the child himself, who thus learned how best to reshuffle his own attitudes and relationships.
>
> (Kanner 1972: 15)

Framed from a psychoanalytic perspective, children's psychopathology was viewed as rooted in anxiety, largely traceable to the forms of intrapsychic conflict described by Freud and elaborated upon and revised by subsequent psychoanalytic figures such as Anna Freud, Melanie Klein, and Alfred Adler (see Treffers and Silverman 2001).

Up until late in the twentieth century, the idea of childhood autism in North America and Great Britain was inextricably linked with schizophrenia and psychosis, forms of psychopathology typically constructed within a psychoanalytic framework until the 1970s. For example, relatively late versions of the *International Classification of Disease* published by the World Health Organization identified autism (referred to as *infantile autism*) in relation to schizophrenia (1967) and psychosis (1977) (Wing 1997). Although researchers such as Bender (1947) rejected the psychological origins of childhood psychosis in favor of organic causes, she like many others persisted in viewing autism as an expression of childhood schizophrenia. Even Leo Kanner's work, as illustrated in the various editions of his *Child Psychiatry*, evidences ambivalence about the relationship between autism and psychosis, and the relative impact of psychodynamic versus biological factors in the etiology of the disorder. In effect, within the context of mid-twentieth-century culture, the psychoanalytic framework achieved hegemony, although not totally, in its influence, particularly in the area of research on childhood disorders generally and autism specifically.

The works of Anna Freud, Melanie Klein, D. W. Winnicott, and Margaret Mahler eventually influenced, both directly and indirectly, attempts to explain autism in terms of the psychoanalytic framework. Moreover, these thinkers provided the groundwork for the influential psychoanalytic approaches to autism developed by Bruno Bettelheim and Frances Tustin. Although academic and medical psychoanalytic formulations often fell short of "blaming" the mother for her child's autistic distress, the popularization of simplified renditions of complex psychiatric formulations engendered in the United States, at least, a tendency to see mothers as directly responsible for their children's psychiatric distress. The discussion now turns briefly to the theoretical contributions of key figures.

Anna Freud and the pyschoanalytic relationship between mothering and psychopathology

Anna Freud (1895–1982) extended and refined the ideas of her father, Sigmund Freud, particularly in the area of child psychiatry. Her main contributions to psychoanalysis concerned her emphasis on ego development in pre-Oedipal children, her analysis of ego "defense mechanisms" in young children subject to psychological stress, and her use of "play therapy" in the process of child psychoanalysis. Her varied experiences with childcare, especially those experiences with children separated from their mothers during World War II in England, probably exerted the most direct influence on her adaptations of Freudian theory. These experiences led her to emphasize the role the mother plays in the infant and child's processes of ego differentiation.

Like her father, Anna believed the psychic differentiation of the ego, id, and superego was accomplished primarily in relation to the Oedipal complex. However, unlike her father, Anna stressed the mother's role in the child's mastery of the id by the ego, as Anna believed it was *for the mother* that infants suppressed and redirected instinctual aggression (Sayers 1991). Child development, Anna argued, was less dependent on instinctual repression than on attachments with adults, primarily the mother (Sayers 1991).

Accordingly, Anna Freud believed the development of consciousness and identity is contingent upon intrapsychic differentiation of the "ego" (the "I") from the "id," defined as the repository of instinctual drives, and from the "superego," defined as the fear of parental threat and admonitions. The infant develops the ego, or sense of I, by internalizing parental images and as a coping device for mediating the competing demands of the id (instinctual drives) and the (internalized) superego. Consequently, the goal and satisfaction of the ego derive from the ego's ability to "appease the forces that impinge upon it from above, from below, and from outside" (Freud and Sandler 1985: 170). Anna posited a variety of "defense" mechanisms whereby the ego could satisfy or repress challenges posed by the id and the superego including repression, regression, reaction formation, isolation, undoing, projection, introjection, turning against the self, and reversal (Freud and Sandler 1985: 108). For Anna Freud, the infant's ability to negotiate the terrain of the id and the superego largely, although not exclusively, depends upon its relationship with its first love fixation, the mother (196).

Anna stressed the mother's role in the process of ego differentiation after observing the effects of maternal separation on children at her nursery during World War II. Often times, young children reacted to maternal separation with overt forms of violence or by severe withdrawal, leading Anna Freud to hypothesize that the presence of the mother is necessary for children, who lack object constancy, to inhibit their expression of instinctual aggression. Moreover, as the first love object, the mother facilitates the child's relationship with the world, the world of others and of objects. Consequently, Freud believed maternal absence complicates the development of the ego and can lead to anxiety and neurosis as a consequence of the young child's efforts at compensation. Thus, although Anna Freud stressed that mechanisms of defense are intrinsic to the process of ego differentiation, these mechanisms can also indicate and lead to symptoms of psychopathology:

> The structural development of the individual neurosis begins with the arousal of danger and the anxiety, and as a consequence, the wish to get rid of the anxiety. This then arouses the defense and the regression that occurs to avoid the new conflict on the new level; and in turn there is the compromise formation, which leads to symptoms. That is what I mean by the development of the neurosis, the Neurosenbildung. For that process the existence of the anxiety is the main starting point, not where it comes from.
>
> (Freud and Sandler 1985: 275)

The particular anxiety and its source affect the content of the neurosis and the particular defenses implemented. Anna identified three sources for anxiety including anxiety emanating from the id, anxiety emanating from a perceived inability to meet the demands of the superego, and anxiety emanating from *Realangst,* or justified fear (Britzman 1998). Although the idea of *Realangst* seems problematic at an ontological level, one must remember the context within and about which Anna Freud was writing—war-stricken England in which children were faced directly with the very intrusive and material facts of war.

Although neurosis acquired in childhood could carry over into adult life, Anna Freud was optimistic about therapeutic interventions. For example, her experiences with children led her to believe that a variety of therapeutic practices proved helpful in assisting young children in coping and adapting, even in the event of maternal separations. Unlike her father, Anna Freud did not use free association, as she believed this method unsuitable for young children. Instead, she facilitated and studied children's play activities as a means for understanding and developing successful ego differentiation. However, she did not view therapeutic play as equivalent with adult free association: Anna held it was difficult for the analyst to differentiate between play activities that signified to unconscious conflicts and those activities that merely signified to real events in the child's life (Likierman 1995).

Anna Freud's work legitimized psychoanalytic treatment for children and provided a diagnostic and treatment regime—play therapy—still used today to treat a variety of forms of childhood psychopathology, trauma, and distress. Although contemporary psychoanalysts might reject Anna Feud's tripartite model of the id-ego-superego, her description of ego defense mechanisms still holds relevance today and can play a role in the treatment of children with "high-functioning" forms of autism. For example, characteristically "autistic" behavior such as perseveration can be explained psychoanalytically as a form of ego defense against psychic anxiety produced by sensory overload, in contrast to a cognitive explanation that views perseveration in terms of an "executive functions" dysfunction (see Zelazo et al. 2001 for the latter account).

The following abstract illustrates the role of ego defense in psychoanalytically informed approaches to understanding and treating "autistic" behavior:

> This paper focuses on defense mechanisms employed by children with autistic spectrum disorders, and Asperger's syndrome in particular, as a means of warding off intense anxiety, including the fear of annihilation. This fear arises when the child with an autistic spectrum disorder is faced with the demands of everyday reality. Forced from their private worlds, their defensive responses include delusional fantasy, obsessions, and projective identification. These processes are often manifest in dramatic terms within the form and content of their art. The symbolization of annihilation fantasy allows the art therapist a dramatic glimpse into the inner mental life of children on the autistic spectrum.
>
> (Henley 2001: 113)

Art therapy functions akin to Freud's play therapy within this psychoanalytic approach to identifying and treating the sources of the autistic child's ego defenses.

Despite the continued relevance of Anna Freud's legacy for the identification and treatment of psychiatric distress in children, her role in the history of child psychiatry tends to be overshadowed by the legacy of her main intellectual adversary, Melanie Klein.

Melanie Klein and the development of object relations approaches for explaining psychopathology in children

Like Anna Freud, Melanie Klein (1882–1960) was instrumental in centering the mother in her object relations approach to psychoanalysis. Following the Freudian tradition, Klein incorporated the idea of instinctual drives and the tripartite system of the psyche, the superego, ego, and id.

Klein's major innovations included her detailed analysis of pre-Oedipal conflicts and their impact on the development of a balanced ego. Her work
directly influenced the theorizing of D. W. Winnicott, who in turn influenced Frances Tustin's ideas about psychogenic forms of autism. However,
Klein's theory of object relations underwent significant revisions with each
appropriation by subsequent generations of psychoanalytic theorists
(Doane and Hodges 1992). Thus, the discussion begins with a brief
overview of her approach before moving to a more narrowly focused discussion of Klein's analysis of the development of schizophrenia, which
influenced subsequent formulations of autism as a form of child psychosis.

Klein (1946/2000) oriented her analysis of ego development in relation to
the infant's conflicted approach to the mother, particularly as expressed in
the infant's relation to the nursing mother's breast. According to Klein, the
nursing infant experiences both pleasure and aggressive anxiety in relation
to the breast, the source of pleasure and frustration. Klein believed the new-
born infant represents these experiences of the breast to itself—through
introjection—as "good" and "bad" objects. Klein described this representational process as "phantasy." Over time, the infant acquires the capacity
to integrate these episodically based (phantasy) representations into a
coherent image of the mother. This integration signals a transition from the
infant's "pre-objective" phase of life—the "paranoid-schizoid position"—
to the phase of object relations Klein termed, the "depressive position."
Klein described this phase as depressive because the infant's newly developed integrative skills lead to its realization that the object it loves and the
object it hates are one and the same, embodied in the form and image of the
mother. Klein argued that this synthesis between the "loved and hated
aspects of the complete object gives rise to feelings of mourning and guilt
which imply vital advances in the infant's emotional and intellectual life"
(Klein 2000: 131). These depressive feelings actually function to integrate
the ego because they enable better understanding of "psychic reality" and
the "external world," as well as their synthesis (139). Ultimately, the emotions driving integration in the depressive position are guilt and love for the
mother. As shall be explained, the infant's abilities to successfully transcend
the anxieties specific to both of these phases, particularly the former one,
during the first few years of childhood predict the presence or absence of
psychopathology in later childhood and adulthood.

Accordingly, Klein believed the infant's abilities to develop a balanced
ego through its successful negotiation first of the paranoid-schizoid position
and subsequently the depressive position depend on the infant's mastery of
anxiety rooted in instinctual drives and traumatic experiences:

> I hold that anxiety arises from the operation of the death instinct within
> the organism, is felt as fear of annihilation (death) and takes the form
> of fear of persecution. The fear of the destructive impulse seems to
> attach itself at once to an object—or rather it is experienced as the fear

of an uncontrollable over-powering object. Other important sources of primary anxiety are the trauma of birth (separation anxiety) and frustration of bodily needs; and these experiences too are from the beginning felt as being caused by objects. Even if these objects are felt to be external, they become through introjection internal persecutors and thus reinforce the fear of the destructive impulse within.

(Klein 2000: 132)

In attempting to deal with these anxieties, the infant develops "fundamental mechanisms and defences," particularly projection and introjection (Klein 2000: 132). The destructive impulse is projected outwards in the form of one conception of the mother's breast as a bad object. The infant represents the "bad" object engendered by this splitting and projection (internally) as persecutory and engenders the infant's paranoia. Conversely, a "good" image of the mother's breast also exists in this process of splitting. Introjection of the idealized good object, the good breast, serves as the "focal point in the ego" (133). According to Klein, as the object is split in phantasy, so is the ego. The infant's ability to master the experience of disintegration accompanying these processes depends upon, among other factors, the "external good object"; that is, the mother who serves as the bases for introjection and synthesis. However, as Klein cautioned: "If states of splitting and therefore of disintegration, which the ego is unable to overcome, occur too frequently and go on for too long, then in my view they must be regarded as a sign of schizophrenic illness in the infant" (136). Klein felt that inability to adequately deal with anxiety in the paranoid-schizoid phase caused regression or lack of progression in the depressive phase, within which the split images are integrated. Likewise, the infant could not proceed to the Oedipal phase if she/he were unable to master the anxiety specific to the depressive phase.[3]

In essence, Klein's complex framework can be most concisely summarized in relation to the processes of splitting, introjection, and projection: for Klein (2000), the course of ego development hinges upon an "optimal balance between introjection and projection in the early stages of development" (136) and disturbances in this balance, implied by excessive splitting of the ego, disturb the relationship between internal and external worlds, leading to some forms of schizophrenia. Indeed, Klein explicated psychosis in terms of "violent splitting of the self and excessive projection" (137). Likewise, the less impaired neurotic impulses find explanation in relation to problematic projections such as in obsessional neurosis, wherein the root of the desire to control others/objects is grounded at least in part in "a deflected drive to control parts of the self" (138). Another symptom of the obsessional-neurosis, the desire to collect and accumulate objects, can be explained in terms of "impoverishment" in the development of the ego (Klein 1931: 264). In essence, Klein felt the precursors to adult psychotic illness are present in the infant's early psychic life, or phantasy (Likierman 1995).

In her effort to legitimize child psychoanalysis, Klein argued that play therapy could be used to identify and treat children manifesting psychoses or obsessional neuroses (Likierman 1995). Klein believed the phantasy elements of children's play signified directly to unresolved pre-Oedipal or Oedipal conflicts. This approach is evident in a 1931 publication wherein Klein described a boy whose "neurosis consisted partly of neurotic symptoms, partly of character-difficulties, and also of quite severe intellectual functioning" (Klein 1931: 254). One important way in which the boy's neurosis manifested was in his desire to collect objects, a desire Klein explained in terms of a deeply rooted anxiety pertaining to (infantile) splitting of dangerous and good substances. Klein reported her successful analysis of the boy's underlying problem in object relations led to "remarkable improvement where his intellectual inhibitions were concerned" (254). Today, the boy's behaviors would very likely lead to an autistic spectrum diagnosis.

An example of application of Klein's framework to the study of autism in children is in Emilio Rodrigue's (1955) essay, "The analysis of a three-year-old mute schizophrenic," whom Rodrigue described as "autistic" because the child appeared locked in phantasy:

> The autistic child is an omnipotent creature. . . . Melanie Klein's theories regarding the mechanism of projection identification are essential for an understanding of the way in which the autistic child comes to feel that he omnipotently controls the world. By projecting parts of his self into the object he feels that he controls it, for he identifies the object with projected part of the self.
>
> (Rodrigue 1955: 176)

Accordingly, the autistic child's amplified pattern of projective identification leads to the narcissistic belief (in the child's phantasy life) in the external world as part of him- or herself. However, when the external world surprises the child with its resistance it shatters the child's phantasy of omnipotence, leading the child to fear his own annihilation: "This forceful re-entry of the persecutors seems to be the main anxiety-situation in infantile autism" (Rodrigue 1955: 177). From Rodrigue's point of view, autism manifests as an ego defense mechanism for a child whose confusion over the differentiation of an "inner good" world and "outer bad" world, over the differentiation between "me" and "not-me," leads to persecutory impulses. Consequently, the child relates to an "ideal internal object" (178), whose presence in the child's phantasy Rodrigue used to explain "the beauty, the talent for music, and the graceful movements of such children" (178). This ideal internal object is the Kleinian "good object": an idealized and internalized representation of the good external object—that is, the good breast satisfying desires in contrast to the internalized bad object, the bad breast, rendered bad by the infant's projections of frustration and subsequently internalized.

In focusing on the phantasy form of intrapsychic conflicts specific to early infancy, Klein and her direct followers tended to de-emphasize environmental factors, including the actual behaviors of mothers or fathers, which might (or might not) have contributed to the psychic distress in "psychotic" children. Moreover, although Klein did not preclude the possibility that a child's vulnerability to psychosis or neurosis might be influenced by "constitutional" or biological factors, these considerations were basically irrelevant to her therapeutic approach and theoretical framework. Klein's steadfast adherence to the importance of the child's phantasy life—their internalized representations and externalized projections—was regarded as somewhat problematic by *later object relations theorists* who eclipsed discussion of the infant's phantasy life with a *new emphasis on the "maternal environment" produced by real behaviors of mothers*. This move is particularly associated with D. W. Winnicott and Margaret Mahler whose extensions of psychoanalytic theory influenced the development of the semiotic linkage between "autism" and "frigid mothering."

Psychoanalysis and autism: Winnicott, Mahler, Bettelheim, and Tustin

D. W. Winnicott simultaneously domesticated Klein's theoretical framework and popularized it in his radio programs that advised women on the proper care of their infants (Doane and Hodges 1992). Winnicott domesticated Klein's framework by de-emphasizing the conflicted and violent aspects of the infant's phantasy life and focusing instead on the role of the actual mother in creating an environment enabling the emergence of the infant's ego. Winnicott claimed that through her purportedly instinctual drive toward "good enough mothering" the mother's nurturing care assists the infant to traverse the pitfalls of the "stage of concern," a stage Winnicott coined to replace Klein's depressive position. In particular, the mother assists the infant by acting as a "mirror" that ideally reflects back the infant. The "good enough" mother fundamentally subsumes herself to her infant (Doane and Hodges 1992). Should the mother neglect this form of mirroring due to her own preoccupations, then serious "consequences" can occur, threatening the infant's ego development (Winnicott 1967/2000: 145).

For Winnicott, a "transitional object that stands for the breast, or the object of the first relationship assists the infant's process of ego development" (Winnicott 1951/2000: 155). The transitional object functions to mediate phantasy and reality, enabling the infant to develop a differentiated sense of itself from its earliest stage of "unintegration" (cited in Hughes 1989: 136). First, the "good" mother who adapts to the infant enables the infant's primary illusion that her breast is part of the infant and under its control. This adaptation and the illusion it fosters give the infant the idea that "there is an external reality corresponding to the infant's own capacity to create" (Winnicott 1951/2000: 157). Second comes the process of "disillusionment" whereupon the infant accepts (although this acceptance is never complete) gradually through the mediation of the transitional object the existence of an external reality. The good mother's initial complicity in fostering the illusion of the infant's control through her mirroring and in relation to the transitional object is absolutely vital for the infant's ability to develop a differentiated ego, to a state of being "in relation to the mother as something outside and separate" (159). Winnicott claimed that bad mothering, including the separation of mother and child during critical phases, led to psychopathology, and the development of a "false self" based on pathological defenses (cited in Hughes 1989: 137). Although Winnicott did not make the association between "frigid mothering" and autism, his theoretical framework enabled it in the work of Bruno Bettelheim, who will be discussed presently.

Another contemporary of Winnicott, Margaret Mahler (1897–1985), also played an important role in emphasizing the role of the actual behavior of mothers in contributing to ego differentiation and psychopathology. Mahler's main contribution in this regard involved her idea of "symbiosis," defined as "hallucinatory or delusional omnipotent somatopsychic fusion with the representation of the mother and, in particular, the delusion of a common boundary between two physically separate individuals" (cited in Kirschner 1996: 196). In Mahler's framework, the emergence of the ego, or self-consciousness, emerges out of an early infantile state of "normal autism" characteristic of this state of symbiosis. However, Mahler believed the infant is driven to individuate itself from this delusionary state of fusion. Success at individuation is in large part seen as contingent upon the mother's initial empathic support for the delusion of symbiotic fusion. The mother's work in fostering this delusion of fusion—the "social symbiosis"—while the infant builds up its representations of the mother is seen as vital for enabling the infant to gradually differentiate self by incrementally engaging with the external world of objects (Mahler 1952: 286). Mahler described four sub-phases of separation-individuation wherein the growing infant's psychological independence is developmentally contingent upon the mother's emotional availability and support.

In a seminal 1952 essay, Mahler described autism as a form of psychosis emerging when this process of ego differentiation, hinging upon the symbiotic process, goes awry. Mahler's description of "autistic infantile psychosis" focuses on extreme forms of autistic affliction wherein "there are no signs of affective awareness of other human beings" (Mahler 1952: 290). In an attempt to explain this lack of affective awareness, Mahler argued that it was indicative of "scattered ego functions" and a "lack of peripheral cathexis" in which the libido and aggression "exist in an unneutralized form, due to the absence of the synthetic function of the ego" (291). In contrast to autistic infantile psychosis, Mahler also identified "symbiotic infantile psychosis" which she believed occurred when the child's ego fails to move beyond the "delusion of oneness with the mother" (293). Mahler contrasted these views by describing the autistic child as resisting a parental embrace whereas the child afflicted with the symbiotic psychosis melts into the embrace. Later, in a 1965 essay, Mahler elaborated upon the role of the "living maternal object world" in fostering or impinging upon the infant's ego differentiation, based on the degree to which the maternal environment satisfied or frustrated the infant during the symbiotic stage of development. As is later explained, Frances Tustin (1969, 1991), in her early and later works on autism, appropriated Mahler's works on symbiosis, ego-differentiation, and the maternal environment. Moreover, as a close friend of Dr. Benjamin Spock, Mahler's ideas may have been indirectly popularized in the form of his baby books.

Out of Winnicott's and Mahler's appropriations of Klein, emerged two ideas extending object relations approaches to studying psychopathology, particularly autism, in children. First, the object relations tradition subsequent to Winnicott held that the infant manages the difficult transgression between phantasy and reality by creating and holding the illusory idea that it is part of the mother. The mother's role in enabling or frustrating ego differentiation becomes the focus of the second important idea dominating post-Kleinian object relations. Accordingly, the second important idea that follows from Winnicott and Mahler involves the mother's work in enabling the infant's differentiation between self and other. The territory of post-Kleinian object relations theories celebrates the therapeutic work of the "good enough" mother as the means and measure of the infant's capacity to develop a balanced, differentiated ego. Poor mothering and maternal absence were regarded from the late 1940s until the mid-1970s as the primary origin of psychopathology, particularly, but not exclusively, in children. One of the most widely popularized accounts of the relationship between parenting—particularly mothering—and autism can be found in the work of Bruno Bettelheim.

In 1967 Bruno Bettelheim published *The Empty Fortress: Infantile Autism and the Birth of the Self*. At that time, Bettelheim's work was generally well received in North America because of his reputation as one of the most respected experts on child psychopathology, a status in part due to his tenure as head of the Sonia Shankman Orthogenic School for disturbed children from 1944 to 1978. Bettelheim's status as "expert" popularized in the form of an advice column that he wrote for ten years in *The Ladies Home Journal* (Gardner 2000) may have bolstered his fame within the wider American culture. Bettelheim's "expert" standing and access to popular culture contributed to the popularization of his ideas about autism in professional and popular social discourses. His ideas about the origins and course of autism simplified and/or adapted psychoanalytic ideas articulated by Winnicott and Margaret Mahler while blending them with ethological research and principles such as "critical periods" of development (Bettelheim 1967: 39). Nowadays, Bettelheim's equation between mothering style and autism has been widely critiqued for directly blaming mothers for their children's condition.

Perhaps the most damaging aspect of Bettelheim's account was his rejection of the idea that inborn organic disturbances possibly engendered the autistic defenses described in psychoanalytic approaches. What is more, like Winnicott, Bettelheim was less interested in the infant's phantasies of the mother than he was in the role of *actual* maternal behavior in engendering psychopathology. The emphasis afforded the maternal environment was widespread at the time of Bettelheim's writings due to its popularization by Rene Spitz's (1945) studies of institutionalized infants and Bowlby's (then regarded as) authoritative texts (1952, 1953) on infant development. Bettelheim approvingly cited both figures, particularly Spitz, whose research conclusions pepper Bettelheim's text. However, while the last chapter of *The Empty Fortress* pursues forceful and explicit efforts to link poor mothering with autism, earlier chapters use a more remote style in describing autistic withdrawal in relation to a failure in ego differentiation due to infantile frustrations.

Accordingly, Bettelheim's (1967) blend of psychoanalysis and ethological research constructed autism in relation to a frustration of the autistic child's "strivings" for individuation (i.e., sense of autonomy) and object relations. For Bettelheim these frustrations led to a complete lack of development if experienced in early critical periods or a lack of complete individuation if experienced during the second year of life. Thus, Bettelheim wrote:

> Infantile autism . . . stems from the original conviction that there is nothing at all one can do about a world that offers some satisfactions, though not those one desires, and only in frustrating ways. As more is expected of such a child, and as he tries to find some satisfactions on his own he meets even greater frustration: because he neither gains satisfaction nor can he do as his parents expect. So he withdraws to the autistic position. If this happens, the world which until then seemed only insensitive now appears to be utterly destructive, as it did from the start to the child who succumbs to marasmus.
>
> (Bettelheim 1967: 46)

Bettelheim's reference to "marasmus" refers to the condition used by Spitz to describe the failure to thrive in institutional infants. Accordingly, Bettelheim appropriated and adapted the Kleinian idea of the paranoid-schizoid position as a "fortress" created by the autistic child as defense against frustrations brought on by lack of appropriate care at critical stages of development and/or by "oversensitivity to the mother's emotions" during critical periods (Bettelheim 1967: 398).

It seems probable that Bettelheim's account of the origins of autism in relation to maternal behavior was so devastating in its effects, in its promotion of the refrigerator mother thesis, precisely because of its readable simplicity. What is more, Bettelheim blended his psychoanalytic appropriations with "scientific" findings from ethological theories very much in vogue in the 1950s and 1960s. Because ethological approaches used the empirical methods of the natural sciences to establish parallels between animal behavior and human behavior, they no doubt added legitimacy to Bettelheim's ideas during a period in which positivism was dominant in the social sciences. Thus, although Bettelheim's text can be faulted for its gross simplifications, distortions, and eclectic appropriations, his "mother blaming" occurred in a popular and scientific environment already receptive to such arguments. The discussion returns to the social environment's role after introducing the psychoanalytic work of Frances Tustin, which is still widely referenced in the autism literature.

The work of Frances Tustin appropriates much of the same psychoanalytic sources used by Bettelheim but does so in a markedly different way. Whereas Bettelheim blended his psychoanalysis with ethology, Tustin was and is more of a psychoanalytical purist in her descriptions of "psychogenic" autism, which she distinguishes from organically induced forms of autism. This difference in theoretical leanings manifests in Tustin's work in relation to a greater focus on the infant's phantasies and less emphasis on actual maternal behavior, other than maternal absence. Moreover, unlike Bettelheim's more accessible writings for a popular audience, Tustin's works are not particularly readable for audiences unfamiliar with basic premises of the object relations approach. Finally, over the course of her research and therapy, Tustin remains relatively open to research advances in the area of autism and adapts her theorizing to better incorporate these advances. This discussion primarily addresses her most recent accounts of autism.

Frances Tustin's (1991, 1992) work arguably constitutes the most significant psychoanalytic research on autism today. Tustin adapted ideas from Klein, Winnicott, and Mahler to explain, diagnose, and treat forms of autism she believed are primarily psychological in origins, which she distinguished from primarily organically induced forms of autism. In her 1991 essay, "Revised understandings of psychogenic autism," Tustin concisely summarized her view of psychogenic autism: "The crux of these revised understandings is that autism is an early developmental deviation in the service of dealing with unmitigated terror" (Tustin 1991: 585). Following the tradition of object relations, Tustin described autism in relation to a disruption of "normal" ego development occurring in early infancy. Tustin located the source of this disruption in the infant's failure to develop normal object relations due to a pathological failure on the part of the infant to differentiate itself from its illusion of symbiotic unity with the mother (symbiosis), or due to the infant's pathological response to its experience of maternal separation. The following passages articulate Tustin's (1992) approach to understanding autism as a defense mechanism stimulated by the infant's unbearably traumatic experience of bodily separation from the mother:

> In these terms, autism can be seen as a massive "not-knowing: and "not-hearing" provoked by traumatic awareness of bodily separateness. As

such, it would seem to be an intensification and entrenched exaggeration of an in-built set of reactions which are specific to trauma. It is of the nature of a post-traumatic stress disorder. It is also a survival mechanism.

... the traumatic stress which had provoked the autistic reactions had been experiences of unbearably sudden and painful awareness of bodily separateness from a mother with whose body they had previously felt fused and equated. Prior to the alarmingly unexpected awareness of bodily separateness they had not been aware of a mothering person, as such. They had taken her bodily presence for granted. They only realized that "it" had been there when they felt that "it" had gone. . . .

Autism became an impenetrable protection which shut out the frustrating and terrifying awareness of bodily separateness. But this prevented the development of a sense of individual identity, since awareness of bodily separateness is a necessary precursor for that development.

(Tustin 1992: 11–12)

In early accounts of this process (e.g., Tustin 1969), Tustin believed autism to be a lack of progression from, or regression to, a state of symbiosis normal in early infancy. She later (1991, 1992) revised her claim that this state of symbiosis is characteristic of "normal" infancy and argued instead it was pathological and specific to infants experiencing disturbances in the typical processes of object relations. For Tustin, pathological symbiosis impinges against ego differentiation and can engender autistic defenses, in the form of auto-stimulation, in response to the infant's cataclysmic experience of awareness of bodily separation, should such experience occur. The auto-stimulation involves what Tustin described as "autistic objects" functioning for the child to block the experience of threatening "holes" engendered by the bodily separation (Tustin 1992: 145–146). Autistic objects replace the normal "transitional objects" used by children in their development of object relations:

The frustration of unbearable disappointment means that instead of the creation of healthy illusions and hallucinations which lead on to dreams, fantasies and ideas, the infant begins to manipulate autistic objects in an excessive way. These, being tangible, sensation-dominated and ever-present, keep the child stuck at a primitive level of over-concretised mental functioning.

(Tustin 1992: 119)

Unlike the normal transitional objects, autistic objects do not foster the development of the child's imagination; instead, they lock the child into a sensation-dominated and concrete level of cognition. Moreover, autistic objects, used as a form of auto-stimulation, prevent the child from reaching out and establishing the forms of human contact that would help them through their "disillusionment" (Tustin 1992: 117): hence, Tustin claimed: "Autistic objects are the result of primary creativity having gone wrong" (118) but for the autistic child they fend off the fear of "annihilation" (119). Autistic objects explain the "impulse-ridden, uncontrollable, stereotyped and excessive" behavior often associated with autistic children (119).

In describing the development of the autistic child and other forms of child psychosis, and the various forms of "objects" associated with these forms of psychopathology, Tustin did address the role of maternal responses in impacting the child's developmental potential. For example, she approvingly cited a mother whose "confident and skillful" manner probably prevented her child from becoming an "extremely disturbed child" due to her child's inborn potential for psychopathology (Tustin 1992: 131). However, unlike Bettelheim, Tustin often emphasized the child's experiences, rather than the mother's actual behaviors. Moreover, throughout her 1992 text, Tustin implicitly acknowledged that biological factors may lead autistic children to be particularly susceptible to the processes of psychopathology. In this regard, Tustin remained open to the possibility that autism is not purely a result of psychological factors. Tustin also was/is more open to the possibility of "recovery" than her predecessors or successors who construct(ed) autism as a purely bio-genetic phenomenon.

End of an era: rise of organic psychiatry and cognitive psychology

Although Tustin's work stands as the most prominent psychoanalytic approach to autism at the dawn of the twenty-first century, it is not well known outside of psychoanalytic circles and is not frequently cited in what is now "mainstream" autism research. The psychoanalytic paradigm holding sway from the 1940s through the 1960s lost favor in psychology, psychiatry, and in popular culture at large. And so, the psychoanalytic metaphor of autism—an ego shipwrecked in the storm of object relations—sits replaced by new metaphors, new ways of constructing autism. Volkmar (2000), a professor of psychiatry, psychology and pediatrics at Yale University, underscored the apparent irrelevance of psychoanalysis for understanding autism in an essay that commented, "The utility of psychoanalysis for therapeutic management of autism is highly limited" (Volkmar 2000: 661). Although some therapists and researchers continue to advocate that psychoanalysis has merit for aiding autistic children, particularly more high-functioning children (e.g., Bromfield 2000), the paradigm lacks wide support as an exclusive therapeutic approach in North America or Great Britain. More often, scholars in English-speaking countries adopt psychoanalytic principles such as "play therapy" eclectically in their efforts to develop therapeutic regimes blending cognitive psychology with strands of psychoanalytic techniques.[4] Volkmar's essay reflects this tendency toward eclectic appropriations by acknowledging that Mahler's insight that autistic children are "unable to use the auxiliary ego functions of the mother" holds relevance for autism research while simultaneously discrediting Mahler's idea of "normal autism" as a typical developmental stage (Volkmar 2000: 669).

Perhaps the psychoanalytic approach to autism was doomed because its therapeutic methods resist quantification and are therefore untestable within the framework of "scientific" inquiry increasingly dominating research on autism. Perhaps the forces involved in the marginalization of this paradigm are more specific to the Zeitgeist of the 1970s and the re-emergence of organic psychiatry. And perhaps it was the popularization of Lovaas' behavioral-cognitive management of autistic symptoms by parents of autistic children that signaled the final demise of the widespread psychoanalytic treatment of autism (see for example Maurice 1993).

Behavioral approaches to managing autism were used in clinical settings from the 1950s to 1970s but their popularity increased in the late 1970s with the application of applied behavioral analysis (ABA) to autism by O. Ivar Lovaas (1977). ABA adopts the Skinnerian technique for modifying behavior to help autistic children "unlearn" dysfunctional behaviors while learning more adaptive ones. ABA therapy is relatively simple to describe and apply, although its execution is exceedingly time consuming and emotionally exhausting for all parties. The simplicity of the approach and its potential application in the home environment by non-experts no doubt enhanced its popularity among parents who were (and continue to be) desperate to help their autistic children.

Despite its widespread popularization, ABA-based therapy was discounted by many professional psychologists for its failure to explain the core autistic deficits. Moreover, successes with ABA therapy were extremely uneven and the regime's overall effectiveness appeared greatest with children who were highest functioning. As summarized by Uta Frith, a cognitive psychologist: "It turned out, however, that behavior modification—the practical application of behavioral principles—involved heroic effort, and often the effort did not justify the limited results. Specific learning did not lead to the hoped-for generalization" (Frith 1991: 16). ABA is still used in clinical and home settings to help eliminate particularly problematic behaviors associated with autism or other developmental delays (such as self-injurious behavior) but is not a dominant paradigm in autism research.

However, teasing out the various forces involved in the marginalization of psychoanalysis lies beyond the scope of this project. For the moment let it suffice to say that by the late 1960s the psychoanalytic paradigm slowly ceded ground to new paradigms, new constructs and new therapeutic practices. The rise of biological psychiatry and the rise of cognitive psychology heralded the move away from psychoanalysis in the study of autism. And so an organic metaphor, within which autism is constructed metaphorically as a "disease" specific to bodily processes, dominates prevailing general understanding of psychopathology today. Gone is the psychoanalytic focus on an ego, which in its abstraction was represented as (almost) lacking embodiment. Gone are the role of the maternal environment and its role in fostering ego development. The pendulum swung away from consciousness and towards bodily processes. Philosophical psychiatry and psychology have been largely replaced by biological psychiatry in the area of autism research. Chapter 6 explores this shift and the matrix of practices, vocabularies, and niche conditions involved in its production.

Before turning to explore this new biological psychiatry and its role in autism research there remains a paradigm left for exploration. Although secondary to biological psychiatry in the therapeutic treatment of autism, cognitive psychology stands today as the dominant psychological paradigm in the social sciences, and most of the non-biogenetic research on autism originates in this paradigm. Moreover, perhaps motivated by the desire for legitimacy, some cognitive psychologists attempted to bridge the mind–body dualism by synthesizing cognitively framed constructs with neural anatomy and neural processes engendering the specialized field of cognitive neuropsychology. What follows introduces the cognitive paradigm and contextualizes it within the niche conditions involved in its emergence as the dominant psychological paradigm today. The discussion then turns to explore more specifically how autism is constructed and researched within the matrix of practices and vocabularies that constitutes the paradigm.

The rise of the cognitive paradigm: 1970–2004

The cognitive approach stands as the dominant non-biogenetic paradigm within the field of psychology today. Before describing how cognitive psychologists study autism, the discussion introduces and describes the cognitive paradigm and locates the socio-historical niche conditions involved in its popularization, in both the academic community and popular culture. The popularization of the cognitive paradigm contributed to increased social surveillance of very young children's development, leading to greater knowledge about and scrutiny over children's intellectual and emotional growth. However, the import of the cognitive paradigm extends beyond child development and autism research because its metaphor of the mind has become the dominant interpretive framework from which academics, scientists, and the public perceive human intelligence. What follows introduces the paradigm, its historical assumptions and current theoretical vocabularies, before moving to explore the cultural context within which the paradigm flourished and continues to find relevance today. The paradigm's relevance for contemporary autism research follows these discussions.

The cognitive "computer" metaphor: cognitive modules, information processing, CPUs, and connectivity

Emerging in the 1970s against the backdrop of the competing theoretical frameworks of psychoanalysis, behaviorism, and humanistic psychology, cognitive psychology appropriated from these frameworks as it carved out its theoretical terrain and research methodologies. Like psychoanalysis and humanistic psychology, cognitive psychology focuses on the mind. Like American behaviorism, cognitive psychology tests its theoretical constructs and hypotheses using the methods of the natural sciences. However, although cognitive psychology is eclectic in its appropriations, its metaphor for mind/consciousness is unique. As described by Schultz and Schultz (1987), cognitive psychology takes the computer as its primary metaphor for the mind and its goal is to discover the "library of programs the human has stored away in memory—programs that enabled the person to understand and produce sentences, to commit experiences and rules to memory, and to solve novel problems" (Howard (1983) cited in Schultz and Schultz 1987: 374). Undergirding most cognitive approaches is the "central argument that human behavior can best be understood in terms of the nesting and clustering of 'plans'—programs of action through which the organism runs to order to reach its goals" (Richards 1996: 72). The "library of programs" and "plans of action" are the mental representations cognitive psychology believes the mind implements in "processing" information. In essence, the cognitive paradigm takes an "information processing" approach to studying the mind focusing on the mental processes purportedly linking perception, cognition, and behavior or attitudes.[5]

Theoretical foundations and contemporary vocabularies

Although cognitive psychology's computer metaphor of mind is distinctly late twentieth century, its theoretical foundations can be traced to historical philosophical debates about the role of experience and the existence of innate or transcendental structures of mind. Early-twentieth-century efforts to synthesize *a priori* structures of mind with experience led to the development of Gestalt psychology, phenomenological philosophy, and developmental psychology, among other approaches that ultimately influenced cognitive theories developed in the 1970s. For example, Piaget's (1923, 1924) early theories of child development (popularized in the American context in the 1970s) blended experiential knowledge (i.e., sensory experience) with the child's (purported) *a priori* mental organizing capacities to create the various stages of development Piaget coined. Popularization of cognitive psychology in the 1970s in the United States occurred in large part through Chomsky's (1968) model of transformational grammar, which stipulated that the capacity to learn language is hard-wired into the species, although that process is believed to be impacted by experience. Both

Chomsky and Piaget believed in the existence of *a priori* forms/structures that enable development and learning through experience. Although cognitive psychology has moved well beyond these important foundational approaches, it still remains committed to the existence of formal structures of mind.

Piaget's legacy for cognitive psychology was particularly evident in the cognitive research conducted in the United States in the 1960s and 1970s. This research addressed the developmental acquisition of specific cognitive skill capacities or formal mental constructs including memory in infants, language acquisition, intellectual development, and the development of self-concept (Hunt 1993). These lines of research continue today but are modified and/or expanded to include other cognitive constructs including, for example, the idea of cognitive scripts, which are used to describe the internalization and externalization of behavioral repertoires.

However, between the 1970s and 1980s cognitive psychology began to rely extensively on a computer metaphor to frame discussion of *a priori* cognitive structures. Moreover, research emphasized formal processes whereby cognitive structures were believed to function in processing thought and experience. Increasingly, cognitive psychology viewed human cognition as functioning akin to artificial intelligence.

The cognitive paradigm's adaptation of the computer metaphor influenced the way the paradigm understood mind, reason and rationality, and human intentionality. Accordingly, many cognitive approaches assume that human cognition is *programmed* and that people reason and act on the basis of these programs. Viewed from this framework, people are represented as implicitly rational agents who assimilate "bits" of information, process that information in relation to mental programs (e.g., language) and/or scripts, and then act on the basis of this programming to fulfill their goals (Phillips 1999: 260). Articulated as such, cognition is often viewed as a "computational" process in which "mental processes are computations on formal, syntactical symbols" (Jones and Elcock 2001: 218).[6]

Many contemporary cognitive researchers believe it possible to model (at least some aspects of) human cognition by identifying the various mental "modules" involved in the reception and processing of information (see Fodor 1983). Cognitive modules are viewed as "autonomous, functionally intact" psychic entities within which higher-order cognitive functions are metaphorically localized as with the computer central processing unit (CPU) (Jones and Elcock 2001: 218).

Since the early 1980s, ideas about the nature and operations of cognitive modules have undergone revisions, reflecting innovations in the theory and practice of artificial intelligence applications. Early cognitive accounts stressed the isolation and domain specificity of each cognitive module whereas more recent accounts focus on the interrelations across modules (Uttal 2001). Moreover, some cognitive researchers, particularly in the area of cognitive neuroscience, now reject modular approaches in favor of more distributed models attempting to represent human cognition through "connectionist" networks of information processing (Hardcastle 1995; Jackson and Georges 1998; McLaughlin 1998). However, efforts toward more distributed models of cognition tend to smuggle in modular constructs, particularly when researchers attempt to link cognition with neural anatomy (Uttal 2001). I turn briefly to distinguish the more modular approaches to cognition associated with *cognitive neuropsychology* from the more connectionist ones associated with *cognitive neuroscience*.

Cognitive neuropsychology

Cognitive neuropsychology is situated within the more mainstream paradigm of cognitive psychology and thereby extends the tradition initiated by Piaget and Chomsky of identifying universal cognitive structures of the mind. Traditionally, cognitivists focused on the formal characteristics of these structures and ceded their content to environmental experience. Cognitive *neuropsychology* innovates on this tradition by directly linking the cognitive structures—or modules—of "mind" to neural-anatomical brain structures. Accordingly, researchers in the area of cognitive neuropsychology attempt to link cognitive modules of information processing (i.e., mind) to localized areas of the brain, often by studying the specific cognitive deficits of individuals with specific brain injuries using magnetic resonance imaging (MRI or fMRI). As will be discussed later, cognitive neuropsychology informs much of the newest psychological research on autism (e.g., research on theory of mind and its relevance for the amygdala).

Cognitive neuropsychology is best distinguished from cognitive neuroscience by the former's top-down approach to human cognition. As described by Loveland (2001: 17–18), *top-down explanations* theorize the formal structure/module of cognition and then attempt to link the structure or module to a specific brain center. More emphasis tends to be placed on the mental processes of mind—construction, processing, and manipulation of mental content—than of the brain per se (Loveland 2001). Efforts to link cognitive modules of mind to the brain can be either *functional* or *direct*. Functional accounts for linking mental constructs with brain constructs suggest that a particular mental content (e.g., depression) can be linked to a particular brain operation or content (e.g., serotonin) but functionalist accounts caution that all instances of that mental content (depression) cannot necessarily be linked directly to *a* (singular) *specific type* of brain content/operation (see Jackson and Georges 1998). In contrast, direct accounts, or identity theory accounts, of the relationship between mental and brain content argue that a particular type of mental state (depression) is *necessarily* linked with a particular type of brain state (Jackson and Georges 1998). Cognitive neuropsychologists are more likely to take a functional account, whereas cognitive neuroscience is more likely to take a direct account.

Cognitive neuroscience

Since the 1980s, cognitive psychology borrowed directly and explicitly from "connectionist" research on artificial intelligence (Hardcastle 1995) to create mentalist models of how the brain creates and maintains neural networks, seen as responsible for perception, information processing, and the linking of intention with action. This connectionist research often uses brain-scanning devices such as positron emission tomography (PET) or MRI technologies to try and relate neurological processes back to mental operations or specific behaviors. These efforts are primarily pursued by researchers in the area of *cognitive neuroscience*, which takes an information-processing view stressing the "materialist" source of cognitive functions by reducing mind (e.g., consciousness) to brain (i.e., neural-anatomy) and stresses the *connectionist* nature of cognition.

Cognitive neuroscience tends to take a "bottom-up" explanatory approach that establishes relatively direct and unilinear linkages between the brain and behavior (Loveland 2001). Cognitive neuroscience therefore often adopts the "identity theory" that stipulates that brain states are roughly equivalent with mental states such that a particular mental state (e.g., happiness) is seen as deriving directly from a particular brain state (e.g., norepinephrine and dopamine). The "brain science" of emotion and cognition has been popularized in texts such as *Why We Love: The Nature and Chemistry of Romantic Love* (Fisher 2004) and *Mind Wide Open: Your Brain and the Neuroscience of Everyday Life* (Johnson 2004). As suggested by the titles of these popular texts, neuroscience often explains the characteristics and capacities of mind as derivative of brain. Often times, although not necessarily, the relationship is seen as one way such that mind becomes mere effect, or epiphenomenon, of brain.

Cognitive neuroscience and neuropsychology, often collectively described as "brain science," have captured the interest of academics as well as the popular imagination. The reasons for the paradigm's popularity are complex but paramount among them are the "information revolution" accomplished by the computer and cultural changes in attitudes about intellectual and emotional development in children. In the following section, the cognitive paradigm is contextualized within its cultural milieu. This contextualization will ultimately be relevant for understanding academic and popular interest in and research about high-functioning forms of autism such as Asperger's syndrome.

Cognitive psychology: the Zeitgeist of the times

As noted above, the reasons for the ascendancy of the cognitive paradigm, and its eclipse of behaviorism and psychoanalysis, are complex and historically entangled. Although unable to do full justice to these reasons, the discussion address two forces contributing to the establishment and popularization of the cognitive paradigm. The first force is implied by the paradigm's organizing metaphor of the mind as the computer. The development of the cybernetics model of information processing and its application in computing technologies engendered the late twentieth century's love affair with the "computer." It is therefore hardly surprising that humanity's innovation was appropriated to mirror its maker. The second force contributing to the popularization of the cognitive paradigm stems from its perceived relevance for aspiring and anxious parents who sought to apply "scientific" findings on child development to their own offspring in their personal projects of social engineering. The cognitive paradigm's metaphor of the mind as computer appealed to parents who sought to program their children with just the right skills and aptitudes required in an increasingly competitive and technical workplace. Moreover, this appeal was enhanced by the marriage of cognitive psychology and "brain science" in the specialized but soon popularized fields of cognitive neuropsychology and neuroscience. Parental and educational interest in the specifics of children's cognitive development led ultimately to more forms of social surveillance over children's youngest years and contributed to the emergence of new forms of cognitive "difference" and psychopathology, including the newly coined "Asperger's syndrome" by Lorna Wing in 1981.

Graham Richards (1996) in his text *Putting Psychology in its Place* chronicles the development of the cognitive paradigm's computer metaphor. He observes that technological innovations made during the 1930s and early 1940s, including innovations in radio, television, aerospace engineering, and the Manhattan project, required more sophisticated methods for engaging in mathematical calculation and for integrating complex technical systems. Efforts to solve for problems of coordination and control led to the creation of the earliest computers in the 1940s. These early computers drew on the advances in mathematical logic achieved by Post (1936), Church (1936), and Turing (1936) (Hardcastle 1995). Shannon and Weaver's (1949) efforts to articulate information in relation to the uncertainty it eliminates enabled further refinement in the quantification of information and communication, and helped pave the way for more efficient computational systems (Richards 1996). Norbert Weiner's model of cybernetics, using the idea of feedback to explain how a system maintains or changes a state of homeostasis, enabled newly developed computing systems to be combined with robotics (Richards 1996). The idea of self-regulating machines capable of advanced problem-solving had obvious economic and military applications, and captured the public's imagination as well, as clearly evidenced by the fascination with robots in the 1950s popular media (e.g., *Lost in Space*). Moreover, from the development in the 1960s of sociologist Talcott Parsons' (1963) cybernetic model of society to Allen Newell and Herbert Simon's (1972) information processing model of decision-making, to the cybernetic idea of the learning organization that emerged in the 1980s, the idea that social and individual processes can be represented using cybernetic, computational models has found expression in a wide range of academic specializations.

By appropriating the computer as the metaphor for the mind, the discipline of psychology persuaded the academic world and the public of its legitimacy and relevance for late-twentieth-century life. Within the discipline of psychology, even behaviorism appropriated aspects of cognitive psychology and ethological and maturational approaches to development now typically incorporate cognitive constructs. The blend of neurology with the cognitive framework afforded the latter legitimacy while providing the former a coherent representational framework for modeling the brain–mind relationship. Finally, the cognitive metaphor of the mind as computer disseminated throughout popular culture, and now frames popular dialogue and policy debates in a wide range of areas, particularly with respect to issues affecting children and their "cognitive development."

The second force involved in the ascendancy of the cognitive model stems from its perceived relevance within the purview of the needs and anxieties of middle-class life. In the contexts of childrearing and education, the cognitive model was adopted to explain and predict early learning at home and learning styles in the classroom. In the context of the workplace, the cognitive model was used to explain decision-making (Simon 1957), decision-making biases (Tversky and Kahneman 1974), and models of control and compliance. By the late 1980s, the purported needs of the workplace and childrearing conjoined in such a way to employ the cognitive model in the project of engineering future knowledge workers from the earliest moments of life (Nadesan 2002). The idea of understanding the human brain and human social organization using the computer model of information processing supports all these examples of the dissemination of cognitive psychology. I will briefly unpack some examples of the way the cognitive metaphor, with its computer metaphor, has influenced and been influenced by the Zeitgeist of the late twentieth century.

The development and expansion of computer technology in the workplace, coupled with Cold War tensions, led to a profound shift in the cultural Zeitgeist of the 1960s, away from an emphasis on the psychological "adjustment" of personality and toward an emphasis on "cognitive" fitness of intellect (Rose 1989). From the 1960s onward in the industrialized countries, the demands of the global economy and the late-modern workplace required intellectual agility, and increasing technological adeptness in middle-class workers (Nadesan 2002). Additionally, in the American context, fears of the Soviets "winning" the race to space, evidenced by their accomplishments with Sputnik, fueled the public's interest in educating a technically and/or scientifically skilled workforce (Ehrenreich and English 1978). Rising entrance scores for college dismayed aspiring middle-class parents, who saw their children's futures linked to technical skills that required a credential in higher education (Ehrenreich 1989; Ehrenreich and English 1978). In an effort to ensure their children's future success, middle-class parents anxiously sought expert advice on how to provide for their children's intellectual success.

As explained by Rose (1989) in *Governing the Soul: The Shaping of the Private Self*, the experts' answers to the problem of engineering intellectual excellence were largely generated in relation to a different project of social engineering, the project of "compensatory education" aimed at breaking "the cycle of poverty" (Rose 1989: 194). Expert research into and prescriptions for compensatory education increasingly targeted children's preschool years as the temporal "critical" site for the development of intellectual and linguistic proficiencies. This research into children's intellectual development blended insights from developmental theories (e.g. Gesell's studies) with models of cognitive development (e.g. Piaget's works), with the ethological idea of "critical periods" of development. Although the early longitudinal results of intervention efforts at compensatory education were somewhat disappointing, the researchers who advocated this theoretical blend stood undeterred and their numbers grew as government funding in North America and Great Britain expanded (Rose 1989). Moreover, the possibility of engineering intellectual and linguistic skills during the preschool years through proper cognitive stimulation appealed to the aspirations and anxieties of middle-class parents.

By the late 1960s, ensuring one's offspring's success came to require that middle-class parents, particularly mothers, familiarize themselves with expert research on cognitive development in young children (Rose 1989). A new body of literature seeking to instruct mothers in the project of building their child's intellect helped translate the esoteric wisdom of academic researchers. This literature included books directed at parents such as Joan Beck's (1986/1967) *How to Raise a Brighter Child* (Rose 1989), advice columns in women's magazines, and brochures on child development published by government agencies. The effects of these literatures, in conjunction with parental anxieties and aspirations, were profound in that a metaphor of the child as a site of intellectual potential whose realization requires familiarization with the expert literatures on early learning and brain development slowly replaced the psychoanalytic metaphor of the child focusing primarily on the drama of the child's emotional development (Rose 1989). Although psychoanalytic principles still informed research in child development—e.g., the research on the *Strange Situation Test* conducted by Mary Ainsworth in the 1970s—the emphasis on information processing slowly eclipsed the emphasis on maternal attachment.

By the early 1970s, the relentless search for the earliest flowerings of the intellect pushed research into child development back further into infancy. As observed by one text on infant development in 1971: "Infant research is exciting, informative, challenging, and exacting. It is still *new*, however, and its research tools are tentative" (my italics, Caplan 1971: 13). Of course, research on infant development was not really "new" since psychoanalytic and ethological researchers had pursued it in the 1940s and 1950s; rather, what *was* "new" was the paradigm used in the study of infant development. Framed from the perspective of the emergent cognitive paradigm, infant development was not defined in terms of the development of the ego and emotional adjustment; rather, infant development was viewed in relation to the development of specific cognitive and social skills.

In the 1980s the mainstream American media began popularizing cognitive neuropsychology and neuroscience, particularly as they pertained to infant and early childhood development. And as the twentieth century waned, the use of the computer metaphor to model brain and mind became ever more explicit. Media efforts to explain the principles of cognitive neuroscience dramatized the parallels between human cognition and artificial intelligence, particularly in media efforts to describe the "irreparable" effects of "early programming." For example, a 1996 article in *Newsweek* magazine claimed that:

> It is the experiences of childhood, determining which neurons are used, that wire the circuits of the brain as surely as a programmer at a keyboard reconfigures the circuits in a computer. Which keys are typed—which experiences a child has—determines whether the child grows up to be intelligent or dull, fearful or self-assured, articulate or tongue-tied.
> (Begley 1996: 56)

The use of the computer analogy reinforces the implied immutability of early brain formation. The article implies that after the first few years, a young child's brain is irrevocably "wired." In contrast to mental rigidity after age three, late-twentieth-century American media promote the *infant's* brain as "neuralplastic," as illustrated in a *Newsweek* article, "How to build a baby's brain" (Begley 1997: 30). The emphasis on early programming is not restricted to the development of intellectual skills but is also used to explain emotional development, framed either in terms of the stimulation and maturation of "specific neural circuits" or to social learning of emotional behaviors and their displays (Hunt 1993: 371).

The ascendancy of the cognitive metaphor for the brain, coupled with the popularization of "brain science" research in the media, increased parental surveillance of infant development, particularly in middle-class families. Facilitating informed parental surveillance was a new version of the baby book that helped parents track and stimulate their children's acquisition of physical, social, and cognitive skills (Nadesan 2002). Books such as Murkoff, Hathaway and Eisenberg's (1989) *What to Expect the First Year* and Eisenberg, Murkoff and Hathaway's *What to Expect the Toddler Years* (1996), advise parents to consult with their pediatrician if their child fails to meet developmental guidelines outlined on a monthly basis. Parents, enjoined to be responsible for engineering their child's intellectual and emotional development, became increasingly sensitive to any "delays" in their children's cognitive and social development.

The ascendancy of the cognitive paradigm with its computer metaphor and emphasis on early programming further problematized old boundaries between normalcy and abnormality in child development. Whereas the psychoanalytic paradigm focused on the development of an adjusted personality, whose measure of normalcy was defined primarily in relation to the presence or absence of neuroses and delinquency, the cognitive paradigm complicated and fragmented the possibilities for evaluating child development. The idea of a complicated system of neural circuitry in which programs are hard-wired (neural development) or soft-wired (scripts) replaced the idea of a more or less adjusted ego. Patterns of cognitive development are not evaluated in relation to ego adjustment; rather, these patterns of development are evaluated in relation to very specific skills objectified and measured as discrete capacities (e.g., perspective taking) and/or modeled in terms of neuropsychological processes. The purported potential for "hardwiring" either cognitive skills or neuropsychological structures/pathways during the first years of life demands the implementation of expert knowledge in the surveillance and remediation of cognitive deficiencies even before the developing child reaches preschool.

As the cognitive paradigm proliferated forms of cognitive differences it also created new ways of regarding children's "delays" in intellectual and social development. Aylward's (1997) neural-anatomical description of the development of cognitive impairments illustrates the nuanced way in which developmental disabilities are regarded within the neuropsychological paradigm:

> [neural] functions are processed through many neuronal pathways that are parallel in distribution; complex faculties are constructed from serial and parallel connections among several brain regions. Therefore, early damage to a single area does not necessarily result in the disappearance or maldevelopment of a specific later mental function. Partial return may occur by continued development or reorganization of undamaged parts of the brain. It is not the individual function, but the integration of functional units that is critical to efficient neuropsychological operations.
>
> (Aylward 1997: 33)

Aylward's invocation of the computer metaphor through word choices such as "serial and parallel," "connection" and "distribution" not only engenders a disembodied, machine-like understanding of the person, but also encourages a move away from molar assessments of disability by recognizing that localized brain "damage" does not necessarily impair all, or even most, cognitive processes. This "localized" formulation of a disability encourages efforts to help people with disabilities overcome or compensate for their specific limitations by developing alternative forms of cognition.

The ascendancy of the cognitive paradigm thereby produced significant effects for the study of "abnormal" child psychology. As delineated above, it led to more interest in, research about, and surveillance over very early processes of cognitive development in infants. The paradigm both tele-scopes for scrutiny and fragments the mind as it seeks to identify the vari-ous components of cognitive development, from scripts, to cognitive capacities, to synaptic development. Accordingly, I believe it has con-tributed to the increased rate of diagnoses of high-functioning forms of autism including PDD, Asperger's syndrome, as well as partially explaining the increased diagnoses of ADD and ADHD (Croen et al. 2002). On the other hand, it has also destigmatized, to a certain degree, a psychological diagnosis because it replaced molar categories of normalcy and pathology with a multitude of developmental continua used to describe the acquisition of a considerable range of intellectual and social skills and abilities. When used to assess children's developmental progress, the cognitive paradigm leads to a more nuanced and less molar approach to assessing each child's intellectual strengths and weaknesses. Framed from this perspective, the old molar categories of mental disability such as "retardation" are not always intelligible unless applied to a specific developmental dimension. Even whole-scale diagnostic categories such as Pervasive Developmental Disorder frame the expression of the disorder in terms of *specific* cognitive and social "delays." Moreover, although cognitive research on autism typ-ically stresses specific cognitive impairments (and sometimes links those impairments to neural topography), there is also a move in the literature to address cognitive strengths—skills and aptitudes—seen as expressed by "autistic" individuals.

The move to recognize cognitive strengths in people with autism, partic-ularly high-functioning people, actually precedes the cognitive paradigm as it finds expression in the work of Hans Asperger. However, for almost forty years Asperger's work was relatively unknown in English-speaking coun-tries. When Lorna Wing translated it in 1981, the English-speaking world of academic psychology stood ensconced in the cognitive paradigm. Within the cognitive interpretive framework, Asperger's work was sure to fasci-nate. Asperger's careful, detailed description of children who evidenced very specific cognitive deficits in their social skills and imaginative play, despite displaying normal to high intelligence, was sure to interest researchers seek-ing new territory for the discovery and application of the principles of cognition. Moreover, the "special achievements" observed by Asperger, including "independence in thought, experience, and speech" (1991: 50) coupled with specialized interests in mathematics, technology, and art cap-tured the interest of psychologists in an era valuing "independence" and, increasingly, technical facilities. This disorder fascinated because it pointed to the possibility for specific cognitive deficiencies to coincide with specific cognitive strengths, strengths which were in the 1980s increasingly tied to economic success. Additionally, Asperger's strongly stated belief that the children he observed suffered from a hereditary disorder suggested the possibility of linking cognition to genetics and/or neurology. Finally, Asperger's claim that the "autistic personality is an extreme variant of male intelligence," which he defined in relation to a "logical ability, abstraction, precise thinking and formulating, and for independent scientific investigation" (1991: 85) (in contrast to the feminine "concrete and practical" orientation and "tidy methodical" work) held relevance in an era during which research on "sex differences" exploded. Asperger's claim that "In the autistic person abstraction is so highly developed that the relationship to the concrete, to objects and to people has largely been lost" (85) had defined the popularized image of the high-functioning autistic person by the end of the twentieth century, although the academic community quickly rejected the idea that autistic people excel at abstract thinking. Thus, although Asperger's work predates the cognitive paradigm, its vivid description of cognitive deficiencies, no doubt, captivated the interest of cognitive researchers in a later era.

Autism and cognitive psychology

As mentioned previously, by the early 1990s, cognitive psychology emerged as the dominant (strictly) non-biological approach to studying and treating autism. For example, Uta Frith (1991), a prominent autism researcher, wrote that "The cognitive explanation of autism provides the most complete understanding of the cause of this disorder so far" (Frith 1991: 16). Frith's description of the cognitive paradigm clearly invokes the computer metaphor in its description of *mind* and lays open the possibility for linkages between cognitive psychology and neurology:

> The cognitive view, to put it simply, maintains that between behavior and the brain there is a legitimate level of description: the *mind* . . . the cognitive approach attempts to explain behavior by a set of mental processes and mechanisms. These mechanisms need to be specified eventually in computational form, so that they can be mapped on to brain processes. . . . The image I prefer [of the mind] is that of a wondrously complex machine. . . . For a start, we assume that the mind is made up of components which are innately programmed to process information, to produce knowledge and abilities, thoughts and feelings. Secondly, we know that great changes take place during development. If one of the innate components is faulty the whole course of development will be affected.
>
> (Frith 1991: 16–17)

Frith's description implies that autism and other such disabilities result from problems "innately" hard-wired into the brain. Framed from this perspective, the goal of cognitive research on autism is to identify the specific cognitive deficiencies in people with autism and, ultimately, link those deficiencies to the specific problems in the neural-anatomy of autistic people. As described by Loveland (2001: 17–18), some of this autism research takes a *top-down explanation* that first identifies the specific cognitive deficiency, and then links it to a specific brain center or function believed impaired; for example, cognitive "theory of mind deficits" are linked to brain abnormalities of the amygdala. Other research takes a *bottom-up explanation* that studies how impaired brain structures impact behavioral functioning; for example, impairments in the parietal lobe could be linked with deficits in visual-spatial attention. As explained previously, top-down approaches typically represent cognitive neuropsychology whereas bottom-up explanations are more typically representative of cognitive neuroscience.[7] Material covered in this section represents more top-down research as the bottom-up research will be addressed further in the next chapter.

Three distinct research foci addressing the three aspects of cognition—perception, information processing, and goal adaptation in social situations—organize the more established lines of cognitive research on autism (e.g., see Burack et al. 2001). These three foci reflect the various components of the machine metaphor for cognition including inputs, throughputs, and outputs. Although beyond the scope of this chapter to provide a comprehensive state of the art examination of the research trends within these foci, the discussion provides a very brief introduction to the research on (1) perception and autism and (2) information processing models including the theory of mind hypothesis, the executive functioning hypothesis, and the central coherence hypothesis. Research on "output" phenomena such as communication and adaptive behaviors will be included under "inputs" (i.e., perception) and processing.

After addressing the research on perception and processing, discussion in this section turns to explore the model of consciousness implied by cognitive models of information processing. This model of consciousness will be critically explored in the last section of this chapter dealing with cognitive psychology and autism.

Perception and autism

Speculation upon how perception occurs is not restricted to cognitive psychology. The processes whereby humans sense and interpret stimuli from the "external" world intrigued philosophers for hundreds, if not thousands, of years. However, from its inception the field of psychology claimed perception as its special interest. Although twentieth-century behaviorism rejected theorizing on perception as mere speculation, the rise of cognitive psychology in the late twentieth century returned the issue of perception to its former glory as a pre-eminent research focus, particularly in the area of autism research. However, interest in the relationship between autism and perception predates the cognitive paradigm. In his writings, Hans Asperger emphasized the peculiar pattern of perception he believed characteristic of the boys under his care. Before addressing contemporary cognitive research on autism and research, it will be helpful to briefly reintroduce Asperger's views on the subject since his ideas still influence some approaches to studying "autistic" patterns of perception and may have influenced popularized ideas about autistic savants.

As described at the end of Chapter 3, Asperger observed what he believed to be a unique pattern of perception in the children under his care. Asperger felt his patients experienced a unique consciousness of bodily processes that in "normal" people remains unconscious. This unusual pattern of perception, Asperger believed, led to disturbances in his patients' "normal" relations to objects and people. These disturbances impaired social interaction but also engendered a "clarity of vision" Asperger believed reflected a more direct, or unmediated form of perception:

> The normal child, especially the young one, who stands in a proper relation to the environment, instinctively swims with the tide. Conscious judgment does not come into this and in fact can occur only when one has some distance from the world of concrete objects. Distance from the object is the prerequisite of abstraction of consciousness, and of concept formation. Increased personal distance which characterises autistic individuals and which is also at the heart of their disturbed instinctive affective reactions, is, in a sense, responsible for their good intellectual grasp of the world. This is why we can speak of "psychopathic clarity of vision" in these children, since it is seen only in them.
>
> (Asperger 1991: 74)

As suggested in Chapter 4, Asperger's belief that his patients had a particular clarity of vision, engendered by their personal distance, may reflect the influence of early-twentieth-century German phenomenology. Pre-1940s German phenomenology emphasized the importance of "suspending" natural beliefs, or the natural attitude, in order to engage in direct experience. Within Edmund Husserl's (1859–1938) work, the most pre-eminent phenomenologist, the simplest form of suspension is the eidetic reduction, which enables insight into *eidos* or essences of the natural world (Husserl 1913/1967). Although studied by the natural sciences, these essences are constituted in relation to consciousness, as Husserl rejected the idea that material objects could be known *in themselves*. The phenomenological method was appropriated by the early-twentieth-century German Gestalt psychologists who rejected particularistic accounts of sensory experience in favor of an account of perception that emphasized Gestalt relationships across organisms, their environments, and organisms' perceptions of their environments (Schultz and Schultz 1987). Asperger would surely have been familiar with Gestalt psychology and probably was conversant with the phenomenological method, particularly since, in 1921, Kurt Koffka published *The Growth of the Mind*, a gestalt text on developmental psychology, which was popular in both Germany and the United States (Schultz and Schultz 1987). Casting his students' eccentricities of perception within a positive frame, Asperger may have believed their "disturbed" relationships facilitated the kind of social detachment, or suspension that, within the phenomenological method, enables insight into the realm of *eidos*.

This idea that gifted autistic people have keen insight into non-social realms of experience finds expression to this day in some research on autism and perception, particularly that research attempting to explain the artistic giftedness of some autistic people who excel at representational art. For example, the *Autism Research Review International* ("Autistic savant artists" 1998: 6) reported research on autistic savant artists by Snyder and Thomas (1997) that employed this idea that autistic people have special perceptual insight:

> The researchers suggest that the normal brain has preexisting expectations about what is to be seen, and that these mental representations allow us to make quick judgments without actually analyzing everything in our environment. In effect, they say, our vision is "prejudiced" by internal concepts about our world . . . they [the researchers] suggest, autistic children "observe the world without interpretation."

Although the research cited in the *Autism Research Review International* reflects, perhaps, a naive realism that Husserl would have rejected, it incorporates the idea that autistic children are somehow "free" from the everyday assumptions that "distort" normal perception. Viewed from this perspective, autism leads to particular perspicuity in some aspects of perception.

However, in contrast to the position outlined above, most cognitive researchers today reject the idea that disturbed social relationships engender a special insight into the essence of experiences, although some cognitivists argue these disturbances may engender a particular cognitive style possibly leading to technical expertise. Notwithstanding this possibility for exceptional skills in some gifted people with autism, most of the research within the cognitive paradigm holds it is the autistic person's disturbances in perception that define their disability: thus, within the cognitive paradigm, *it is autistic person's failure to engage in the social world, as mediated by social patterns of perception, that explains or describes their cognitive deficiency*. Some researchers believe that autistic people's failure to acquire socially shared mental structures leads to sensory distortions and/or the inability to integrate sensory data meaningfully. This view contrasts with Asperger's idea that his patients had particularly objective acuity of perception. Discussion now turns to the cognitive paradigm's approach to the problem of perception and the development of autism.

Following the theoretical traditions outlined previously, most cognitive psychological research views all meaningful perception as being mediated by mental structures and/or mental representational frameworks and thereby differs from accounts that suggest the possibility for unmediated perception. Thus, cognitive psychologists see humans as making sense of their world through their acquired or innate cognitive structures. They view consciousness (and/or "mind") as dependent on these structures for the contents of its experiences. Following the Kantian philosophical tradition, some cognitive psychologists believe the mentalist structures organizing sensory data are *a priori*, or intrinsic, to the human mind and/or brain. Other cognitive psychologists are social constructionists, viewing most mental structures as acquired during the processes of socialization. Some cognitive psychologists try to blend both approaches in order to explain mental structures/ representations as both innate and acquired. Only a select few cognitive approaches—primarily those promoted by cognitive neuroscience—hold that the mind is free of mental structures that organize perception. The research on autism and perception tends to reflect the traditional cognitive belief in mental structures, although it varies in its assumptions about their source.

One challenge for cognitive psychologists who study the acquisition of cognitive structures is explaining the emergence of a social world shared across discrete individuals. This presents a problem because psychologists have historically studied perception as an individual, psychological phenomenon. How then does one explain how mental structures—believed to inhere in individual minds—are acquired and *shared*? Put otherwise, how do cognitive psychologists explain how people in a specific culture tend to share the same perceptions given the individual nature of perception? Psychologists who view cognitive structures as transcendental and innate to all humans, and those psychologists who view *sense*—meaningful patterns— as intrinsic in the natural world do not have the problem of explaining how sense is shared because it is viewed as being intrinsic to people or to nature or to both. However, if psychologists wish to explore the acquisition of shared cognitive structures, then perception, particularly in early childhood, becomes a pivotal process.

One interesting approach to studying the emergence of a shared social world through attentional processes focused on the development of "joint attention" in typical children and in children with various forms of developmental delays. Leekam and Moore (2001) provide a concise statement of what is meant by joint attention:

> Joint attention is a term that refers to a complex of interactional behaviors including gaze following, in which the child turns to look where another person is looking and other prelinguistic communicative acts such as pointing and showing objects to others. The characteristic components of these interactional episodes are a sharing of experience

(i.e., *joint*ness) and *attention* to some third object or even apart from the two participants in the interaction.

(Leekam and Moore 2001: 106)

By sharing the same perceptual focus with others in their social environment, very young children learn to associate sounds with objects and, eventually, build up a concept of the object that is generalizable and applicable to other contexts. Thus, the very young child learns the sound of the word "bird" associates with a particular object, and over time learns this sound can be applied in other contexts, to other similar objects. Hypothetically, the child eventually abstracts the idea or meaning of "birdness" from this process and thereby establishes a link between a sound, an object, and a concept.[8] In this fashion, through the process of joint attention the child acquires mental structures and/or relational interaction patterns enabling it to inhabit a shared social world constituted by shared perceptual and interpretive schemes and by shared behavioral conduct.[9]

One of the striking aspects of children diagnosed with autism is that many or most of them exhibit disturbances in their ability to engage in joint attention (Baron-Cohen 1989; Leekam and Moore 2001). The following example illustrates this disturbance in joint attention: in order to determine whether a two-year-old boy had autism I attempted to direct his attention to a very interesting "bug"—an object many young children find interesting. All of the other children in our immediate environment immediately scanned for the bug and gave it their undivided attention for a few minutes, as it was a very interesting-looking beetle. Although other two year olds focused on the beetle, the boy with autism would or could not direct his attention to the phenomenon capturing the attention of all others in his environment. For some reason, this child either was unable to share experiences with others in his environment or failed to recognize the others attending to an object. Over time, the inability to share attention can stymie language acquisition and significantly impact acquisition of the non-verbal routines and practices that constitute "normal" comportment in the social world.

New research publicized in *U.S. News and World Report* ("(Not) all talk" 2003) supports the importance of joint attention in the development of speech. Meredith West, at Indiana University, found that infants "change how they vocalize in reaction to social responses—not sounds but sights" (cited in "(Not) all talk" 2003: 14). According to West's findings, caretakers' reactions motivate infants to alter their vocalizations by observing, suggesting babies who fail to monitor social others would have more difficulty acquiring speech. Although tentative and its implications (e.g. for blind children) appear untested, this research reinforces the importance of joint attention in the acquisition of language. It also points to possibilities for therapeutic intervention in children with autism. Following up early diagnoses of autism with intensive therapeutic treatments encouraging joint attention may alter the developmental progression of autistic symptoms by helping to enable the autistic child to acquire language. Since language acquisition is often cited as the most important outcome predictor for childhood autistics, this form of therapeutic intervention holds promise.

Ideas about the role of joint attention in the development of autism play important roles in the development of other research trends about the specific deficiencies in cognition—that is, information processing—associated with autistic spectrum disorders. Some researchers believe the lack of joint attention impinges on autistic children's abilities to develop a "theory of mind," an implicit theory of the emotional states, responses, and intentionalities of relational others (e.g. see Baron-Cohen 1995). Other researchers believe the perceptual oddities in people with autism lead to, or indicate, a unique cognitive style characterized by an emphasis on parts, rather than wholes (Happé 1999). Other researchers believe the perceptual oddities and lack of joint attention evidenced in people with autism together constitute merely two dimensions of a more general set of "executive functions" cognitive deficiencies. In what follows, the discussion addresses these approaches to studying information processing in people with autism.

Information processing

Cognitive approaches to studying autism express particular interest in the deficiencies, eccentricities, and irregularities characterizing the sense-making processes of autistic people. The underlying idea states people with autism *process information*, or at least some forms of information, differently than do *normal* people. The problem for the cognitive paradigm lies in identifying typical styles of cognition and differentiating them from atypical ones. More traditional cognitive efforts to understand typical styles of cognition generally involve the creation of theoretical models of how the mind works, and include models of the development of a sense of self, a sense of the idea that relational others experience consciousness, and a sense of the difference between "real" and imaginary phenomena. Researchers who study cognition also acknowledge a variety of "cognitive styles" for making sense of the world—for example, analytic and synthetic—and that individuals differ in their proclivities. However, efforts to acknowledge the existence of a wide spectrum of cognitive styles complicate the ability to make evaluative judgments about the normality or abnormality, adaptability or maladaptability of these various styles. In order to introduce these debates, discussion turns to describe three important approaches to studying cognition in people with autism: (1) theory of mind, (2) theory of executive functions, and (3) theory of weak central coherence.

Cognitive research addressing "self-identity" and "conceptions of others" in people with autism contends that a diagnosis of autism often implies a deficient or underdeveloped "theory of mind." In short, a theory of mind is a mental picture, held in a person's mind, of the feeling states and intentions of other people. A theory of mind enables us to impute attributions to others and to respond empathically to their emotions. It also enables us to suspect deception. A theory of mind may be what enables young children to differentiate between imaginary/pretend thoughts and play and actual events, events for which socially agreed upon meanings resonate as social facts. Research by Baron-Cohen (1988) demonstrated that children with autism have a hard time accomplishing tasks requiring a developed theory of mind and, in particular, have a difficult time making attributions about others' intentions and deceptions, even when they possess a basic knowledge of the difference between self and others and are familiar with common social roles such as mother/father/child (Baron-Cohen 1993). Researchers believe the irregularities in eye-gaze found in children with autism either cause, or are related to, a cognitive deficit in the autistic person's ability to develop a fully functioning "theory of mind" characterized most specifically by a deficiency in their understanding of "false belief" (Tager-Flusberg et al. 1993: 6).

The theory of mind hypothesis is one account of the "modalized" (see Baron-Cohen 1998) specific social deficiencies characterizing the behavior and communication of people with autism, even people who are otherwise "normal" in their intellectual functioning. Consequently, the idea of a theory of mind and its implications for autism have stimulated much interesting research and considerable debate about whether the phenomenon is innate—hard-wired into the human brain from birth—or acquired (albeit hard-wired in its acquisition), through social interaction and language development (Tager-Flusberg et al. 1993). Those neuropsychologists that believe that the theory of mind is innate often point to fMRI research on abnormal patterns of activity in the amygdala of autistic patients, thereby localizing the development of the theory of mind at least partially in that brain component. From this point of view, the irregularities of eye movement found in autistic children would be symptomatic of amygdala deficiencies. The possibility that the irregularities in eye contact might shape the development of the amygdala activity seems less interesting to those that hope to locate mental structures in brain structures. Despite the widespread appeal of theory of mind research, other cognitive lines of research dispute the idea of the theory of mind and attempt to replace it with an emphasis on the autistic person's development of self or social desire or with an emphasis on deficiencies in "executive functions" (Tager-Flusberg et al. 1993).

An important approach competing with the theory of mind hypothesis incorporates the computer metaphor more directly to describe autism as a deficiency in the mind–brain's "executive functions." This line of cognitive research focuses most directly on the deficiencies autistic people display in planning and in handling novelty (Houston and Frith 2000). However, it can also be expanded to include deficiencies in joint attention, theory of mind, and perception of emotion (Ozonoff 1995). Thus, the idea of executive function comprises an "umbrella term" used to cover a wide range of "higher cognitive processes" (Houston and Frith 2000: 196), often seen as emergent from neural operations. Theorists believe executive function deficiencies explain the obsessive routines and inflexibility of many, if not all people, with autism. According to this hypothesis, inflexibility and obsessiveness arise from the inability to generate novel responses and/or plans of actions, due to the deficiency in executive functions. The theory of executive functions appeals to those cognitive researchers who seek to link their cognitive models with the brain's neural anatomy; with the brain's frontal lobes and/or cerebellum typically cited as the source of executive function operations (Ozonoff 1995; Waterhouse and Fein, 1997). Cognitive neuroscience has also focused on executive functions deficits by presuming that such deficits are directly indicative of impaired neural circuits and topography.

The theory of weak central coherence is yet another approach to explaining the purportedly unique cognitive processing style associated with people with autism. According to this theory, people with autism lack or are deficient in their ability to process information contextually: that is, they lack the ability to synthesize information in order to achieve "higher-level meaning" (Hill & Frith 2003: 284). Consequently, people with autism tend to focus on parts through "piecemeal processing" (284) and have difficulty integrating information synthetically. At a neurological level, the theory of weak central coherence suggests "poor connectivity throughout the brain between more basic perceptual processes and top-down modulating processes, perhaps owing to failure of pruning" (284). Although "weak central coherence" of information processing engenders particular cognitive deficits, it is also seen as potentially affording particular savant abilities.

The research on information processing deficits in autism extends well beyond the primary theoretical explanations provided here and interested readers should look to comprehensive reviews of this literature in a variety of sources including Cohen and Volkmar's (1997), *Handbook of Autism and Pervasive Developmental Disorders* and Burack et al.'s (2001) *The Development of Autism: Perspectives from Theory and Research*. The cognitive research cited in these sources shares an underlying interest in identifying the specific cognitive impairments impinging and/or distorting the autistic person's patterns of information processing or processing of affective—emotional—content (see Waterhouse and Fein (1997) for review of affective accounts). Although the research cited in these sources approaches cognitive impairments from a variety of theoretical perspectives, the dominant meta-theoretical perspective holds that autistic people process information and emotion differently than do "normal" people. This presumed model of difference has implications for implied and explicit models of the consciousness of autistic people.

Characteristics of consciousness

How do cognitive models of information processing construct the consciousness of autistic people? Although cognitive psychology discarded the psychoanalytic vocabulary of the psyche, it shares with that paradigm an interest in the characteristics and operations of *mind*. And *mind* is a construct integrally tied to explicit and implicit models of consciousness. As shall be demonstrated here, cognitive formulations of the autistic mind imply a deficient or qualitatively different model of consciousness. Before directly exploring this issue, it is important to keep in mind that the ontology of mind and/or consciousness is not self-evident, and efforts to describe its nature and operation span thousands of years.

Across western history, consciousness has been represented as characterized by transcendental (i.e., universal) ideals or capacities dualistically divided from bodily processes and it has been materially reduced to the operation of the brain's organic processes in the form of mind–brain identity theory. *Phenomenological* accounts viewed consciousness dualistically (in relation to mind–brain) and defined consciousness in terms of the transcendental capacity for reflexivity (e.g., in terms of the capacity for consciousness itself to be the object of intentionality). In contrast, much contemporary *neuroscience* views consciousness in terms of the mind–brain identity theory wherein the mind emerges directly out of neural-anatomy: consequently, neuroscience tends to view consciousness as mere epiphenomenon of neurological operations. In opposition to these universalizing accounts, *social constructivist* accounts view consciousness as historically and culturally produced, and reject both the idea of transcendental structures or contents of consciousness and the hard materialism of the mind–brain identity: social constructivists endorse a culturally mediated and embodied view of consciousness. Cognitive psychology as a whole cannot be categorized in terms of the paradigm's ontology of consciousness: some cognitive accounts incorporate dualist accounts of consciousness rejecting the reduction of mind to brain, whereas other physicalist accounts often associated with cognitive neuroscience see mind and consciousness as emerging from, or as being reduced to, the brain's neural processes.

More traditional cognitive accounts, developed by thinkers such as Piaget and Chomsky, articulated the components of consciousness (e.g. cognitive reasoning or language) in terms of universalized and modalized mental structures described in terms of very specific content and/or capacities. These traditional accounts tend towards a more dualistic approach to the relationship between mind/consciousness and brain. But more recently, some cognitive psychologists and neuroscientists see themselves as mediating the mind–brain dualism by mapping mind—in the form of cognitive structures—directly and/or functionally onto the brain's anatomy. Within the cognitive framework, the modalized mental/neural structures identified as enabling consciousness—executive functions and/or theory of mind—are precisely those that are viewed as impaired in autism (this holds less for the theory of weak central coherence).

Although the research on *autism and executive functions* seems to have little to say on consciousness per se, other cognitive research studies on executive functions link this umbrella concept with precisely those modular "higher mental functions" associated with the emergence and operation of consciousness (see Hardcastle 1995). Even more distributed models rejecting the CPU metaphor for the (modular) source of consciousness locate its emergence in higher-order information processing networks associated with executive functions (Hardcastle 1995). Accordingly, if consciousness is defined in terms of the "higher-order cognitive abilities" to generate novel responses, to innovate, combined with the ability to make representational models of others' experiences (i.e., theory of mind), then people with autism must be regarded as lacking or being deficient in "consciousness."

Although it is difficult to find research on executive functions and consciousness in the autism literature, research pursuing the theory of mind hypothesis addressed its implications for the *self*-consciousness of people with autism (Frith and Happé 1999). Before describing this research, let me remind the reader that if consciousness is enigmatic then the nature of *self-consciousness* remains more so (see Lormand 1998). In their article, "Theory of mind and self-consciousness: what is it like to be autistic," Frith and Happé (1999) define self-consciousness in terms of the capacity for introspective awareness of personalized subjective states.[10] Using this definition, Frith and Happé speculate that autistic people's deficits in their theory of mind—i.e., in their capacity to make attributions about the mental states of others—also impacts autistic people's ability to model their own mental states. According to this logic, many autistic people lack the capacity of personal introspection—defined by Frith and Happé in terms of self-consciousness—and high-functioning autistic people who develop this capacity do so in an atypical manner. Frith and Happé emphasize that people with autism do not lack mental states (i.e., what might be referred to as phenomenal consciousness); rather, these researchers speculate they lack the capacity to reflect or reflect normally on those mental states, or self-consciousness (i.e., what might be referred to as introspective consciousness).

However, cognitive speculations, including those forwarded by Frith and Happé, presume a whole framework of assumptions about the nature and operation of consciousness and self-consciousness. Since it is beyond the scope of this chapter to present the metaphysical debates surrounding views of consciousness (see Flew 1979 and Lormand 1998 for summary), I will merely raise some pragmatic considerations about the assumptions implied in Frith and Happé's approach to defining consciousness primarily or most importantly in terms of introspective consciousness. First, their approach assumes consciousness can be defined *universally,* in such a way that its nature and operation (i.e., introspection) are presumed the same for all people across all time. Second, they imply consciousness is *representational*, in that it is assumed that consciousness can accurately and transparently represent or *re-presence* to itself external events and the subjective states of self and others, which are themselves viewed *atomistically* in terms of discrete mental contents (see Phillips 1999). Finally, consciousness is represented in a modalized manner seeing mental capacities as localized in distinct mental modules. Many cognitive psychologists view the modular model as desirable because it enables them to talk about specific cognitive deficiencies existing in relative isolation from other cognitive capacities and to speculate about the direct equation of mind and brain as cognitive constructs graphed quite directly (or functionally) on localized parts of the brain (see Uttal 2001). However, *all of these assumptions are speculative and subject to considerable criticism* (see Heil 1981; Phillips 1999; Richards 1996; Uttal 2001). What is important for this discussion is the view of the autistic person implied by these assumptions.

Accordingly, cognitive accounts of the nature and operation of consciousness articulate autistic people—even high-functioning autistic people—as having a *distinct, generalizable, and qualitatively deficient and/or alien form of consciousness*, or at least self-consciousness, that is markedly and (empirically) measurably different from "ordinary" people's.

However, since many aspirational models of humanity locate the quintessential essence of what it means to be human in consciousness, theoretical approaches defining the phenomenon in terms of narrowly defined and universalized introspective functions may unintentionally dehumanize people with developmental disabilities, particularly autism. This is indeed an ironic effect given that most cognitive researchers see themselves as preserving the humanity/value of people with developmental disabilities by focusing on discrete and modalized disabilities. In sum, the philosophical implications surrounding debates about the nature of mind, consciousness, and its relevance for people with autism certainly beg further discussion than what exists in the literature.

Cognitive constructions: problematic assumptions and alien models

Every theoretical paradigm, including cognitive psychology, possesses strengths and weaknesses specific to its ability to describe and understand the nature of reality. Most scholars in the "hard" sciences, the social sciences, and in the humanities reject the idea that a theory can explain everything. Given the inherent limitations of our efforts to exhaust reality with our accounts, it is imperative that researchers be reflexive about the implicit operating assumptions and methodological biases of their theoretical frames. Whereas it is often easy to identify the limitations of theoretical paradigms that have lost their luster—such as psychoanalysis—it is more difficult to identify and evaluate the limitations of extant models as they often appear "commonsensical" since they appeal to and draw upon cultural themes specific to their times.

What are the overarching implications of the cognitive framework for our understanding and treatment of autism? In what follows, the discussion briefly identifies some problematic assumptions specific to the cognitive paradigm and outlines potential drawbacks in cognitive approaches to autism research. In particular, I will suggest the cognitive framework's assumptions of modularity coupled with its computational, representational, and rational model of decision-making may lead to particular research biases. The research biases that may follow from these assumptions include a variety of effects including (1) the potential for researchers to overstate the introspective capacity and/or cognitive rationality of "normal" people, (2) the potential for researchers to make problematic assumptions about the relationship between cognitive constructs and neurological processes, and (3) the potential for researchers to inadvertently reify and dehumanize "autistic" intelligence. There are two primary detrimental effects of these assumptions: autistic people are represented as lacking "normal" consciousness and are therefore viewed implicitly as deficient, and autistic people, particularly "intelligent" high-functioning autistics, are viewed as possessing an alien, machine-like form of intelligence.

Problematic assumptions

The cognitive framework's assumptions of modularity coupled with its computational, representational, and rational model of decision-making may lead researchers to view people with autism as devoid of "normal" consciousness thereby dehumanizing them and their contribution to humanity. This effect derives from a tendency to reify and universalize theoretically derived cognitive modules.

The idea of dividing the human thought processes and experience of consciousness (i.e., "mind") into discrete and transcendental modules is a metaphysical representational system open to considerable criticism. Even Jerry Fodor (2000), one of the most influential computational psychologists, argues that although the computational framework outperforms the classical psychological model of associationistic empiricism (discussed in Chapter 3) in its ability to explain mental processes, it is "nonetheless quite plausible that computational nativism is, in large part, not true" (Fodor 2000: 3). One criticism holds that cognitive constructs such as "intelligence" or "theory of mind" are not universal or *a priori* categories of mind, but are historically and culturally specific representational models generated by researchers attempting to (artificially) delimit and categorize aspects of human experience/cognition, *that are themselves culturally and historically specific* (see Kagan 1989; Richards 1996). Although many (functionalist) cognitive psychologists would agree in principle with the idea of theoretically derived cognitive constructs as representational frames that should not be taken too literally, research practices that inadvertently end up reifying and universalizing representational constructs tend to implicitly *forget* this recognition. In the late 1990s, efforts to localize cognitive constructs such as theory of mind in terms of specific areas of the brain added to the dangers of reification.[11]

Although many interesting aspects about, and practical applications for, the theory of mind hypothesis exist, this representational construct can illustrate the dangers of reification. First, the construct implicitly holds a rational, transparent view of human agency by assuming we respond to others rationally based on our internal representations of others' conscious motivations. That is, it assumes my communication and actions toward another person are rationally calculated in relation to attributions I make about their internal motivations and feeling states. However, if we reject the idea that *conscious* intentions that can be *directly represented* by self or others motivate much or most human behavior then the viability of the theory of mind hypothesis begins to break down. At least, the idea breaks down as applied in a generalized way to explain the basis of most or all forms of social interaction. If much of human behavior is not, in fact, directly and transparently motivated by conscious intentions and representations then it simply makes no sense to say autistic people are deficient primarily because they cannot accurately or predictably model other people's intentions and regulate their behavior in relation to those intentions.

Moreover, even if we accept the theory of mind hypothesis and all it entails, the question of the boundary between normalcy and psychopathology arises. How do we differentiate people with strong and/or accurate theories of mind from people with weak or inaccurate theories of mind, and where lie the boundaries for the determination of autism? How do we know when and in what conditions theories of mind guide behavior? How do we account for "irrational" social interactions characterized by lack of interest in others' intentions and/or misunderstandings about the intentions of others? Methodologically, can we rely on research subjects to provide accurate retrospective accounts of their intentions and their attributions about others and do those accounts have any real connection to the unraveling of observed events? Finally, can we generalize from laboratory tests of theory of mind to people's everyday social interaction?

Efforts to link cognitive constructs to specific areas in the brain perpetuate and exacerbate the dangers of reification and the (potentially) untoward universalization of culturally specific constructs. In *The New Phrenology: The Limits of Localizing Cognitive Processes in the Brain*, William Uttal (2001) provides a comprehensive and articulate critique of the efforts by cognitive neuropsychologists to map mental constructs on neural anatomy.[12] In addition to presuming mental states can be directly identified with physical states, efforts to localize mental constructs in neural anatomy also assume the brain itself operates in a linear computational and modular manner when, in fact, it is very likely the more complex the psychological process, the less likely it becomes that "a narrowly circumscribed region uniquely associated with this process will be found" (Uttal 2001: 13). Even "connectionist," distributed accounts of mental processes face insurmountable challenges when faced with the inevitable task of explaining how neural "networks "represent, encode, or instantiate cognitive" processes (2). Uttal argues persuasively that even seemingly uncomplicated constructs such as "attention" are, in fact, reified modalized constructs that cannot be directly linked to localized brain centers, even using imaging devices such as MRI and PET scans (see Chapter 6 for critique). Although Uttal's critique primarily addresses cognitive neuropsychology, his arguments also have relevance for the *bottom-up*, materialist linkages between behavior and neural processes offered by cognitive neuroscience, whose strong materialism reduces the person with autism to a bundle of chemical states and deficient brain centers devoid of mind and cultural environment.

Although the literature on autism voices some criticism of the limitations of cognitive neuropsychology and cognitive neuroscience (e.g. Loveland 2001), these criticisms fail to stimulate the level of debate one would hope to find in such an important research area. Moreover, media efforts to translate and popularize findings on "brain science" are uniformly uncritical of the reaches of the technologies' abilities, the researchers' theoretical assumptions, and the research implications. Consequently, in the popular imagination at least, autism is increasingly reified as a thing unto itself whose secrets will ultimately be unveiled by the ceaseless and effortlessly coordinated efforts of cognitive psychology and/or neuroscience.

Alien autistic intelligence: Asperger's as cyborgs

The tendency to reify the idea of autism is particularly pronounced in cognitive accounts focusing primarily on the intellectual strengths associated with "high-functioning" people with autism. Both in the popular media and in the academic journals, research addressing the purported nature of "autistic intelligence" tends toward simplification and reification. This research takes a more traditional cognitive approach, and does not always make direct linkages across mental constructs and neural anatomical ones. However, although not always in line with the hard materialism of much of the popular "brain science," this cognitive research on autistic intelligence captured the imagination of the public and increasingly defines its ideas about high-functioning autism in the context of contemporary life in the "advanced-capitalist" nations.

The cognitive research on autistic intelligence establishes linkages across gender, technical facility, and autism, and, in so doing, constructs an image of high-functioning people with autism as possessing an alien form of intelligence that is simultaneously seductive and threatening. The following remarks introduce this research, discuss the image deriving from, and informing it.

Perhaps following Asperger's suggestion that high-functioning people with autism tend to be skilled in the "masculine" areas of technology and science, some cognitive researchers today suggest autism is an extreme form of "male" intelligence (e.g., Baron-Cohen 2002; Fitzgerald 2000, 2002, 2004) and the benefits of this form of intelligence are technical/scientific proclivities, while the cost is social ineptness. Certainly autism appears three to five times more often in boys than in girls. However, that is not the primary logic implied in the idea of autism as stemming from an extreme male brain. Rather, the logic here implies socially understood gender differences and stereotypes are in fact rooted in neural-anatomy. Moreover, gendered neural-anatomical differences are not thought to result from different gendered experiences, but are believed to be "hard-wired" into the brain at birth. Often time, this hard-wiring is attributed to the effects of prenatal hormones, which are believed to influence brain lateralization and the development of the corpus callosum. However, as is the case with much neuropsychology, the relationship between brain and mind remains unclear. In the case of gender differences, the relationship even between sex hormones and brain development remains unclarified, is hotly contested, and is, thus, still speculative (see Halpern 2000). Moreover, these descriptions of autism as an extreme male brain harken back to Asperger's 1940s-era stereotyped description of male and female styles of cognition in which men are technical and analytical and women are synthetic and empathic (and, according to Asperger, "tidy" and "practical").

Given the difficulty in proving the underlying assumptions across gender, cognitive style, and neural anatomy, it seems probable that this speculative line of research is at least partially indebted to some cultural anxieties about masculinity in a time in which early-twentieth-century constructions of masculinity invoking a "warrior" ethic are increasingly inappropriate. The "crisis" of masculinity has found popular expression in the American media, at least, in which commentators ruminate that many of the traditional characteristics of masculinity are increasingly irrelevant in the contemporary workplace (see Allen 2003; Conlin 2003). Given the irrelevance of "machismo" in corporate life, alternate "masculine" characteristics such as "rationality" take on added importance. According to this line of thought, the construction of equations across "innate" masculinity, technical/analytical facility (particularly engineering), and autism render autism the cost men must pay for their inherent technical/analytical superiority.

The symbolic equation between high-functioning autism and technical/scientific prowess plays out in the popular and academic imagination in a variety of forms. As mentioned previously, researchers have elevated the purported intellectual strengths of autistic people since the time of Asperger and media images have stereotyped autistic people as gifted mathematically; exemplified by Dustin Hoffman's portrayal of an autistic savant in Barry Levinson's *Rain Man* (1998), and as implied in the characterization of the mathematical genius in Darren Aronofsky's avant-garde film π (*Pi*) (1998).

However, a new approach now supplements these portrayals of autistic intelligence. Increasingly, scientific and musical geniuses are subject to the cognitive gaze as researchers ponder whether or not they display signs of autism. For example, a news release by Reuters cited research by Baron-Cohen and Ioan James that speculated retroactively that both Albert Einstein and Isaac Newton may have had Asperger's syndrome. Bill Gates has also been subject to this kind of scrutiny and popular gossip suggests he may have Asperger's syndrome. Framed from this perspective, high-functioning autism becomes inexplicably and, perhaps, inescapably linked with scientific and/or technical genius. Accordingly, Baron-Cohen et al. (2001) conducted research finding that *male* students in science and mathematics obtained higher scores on an instrument designed to measure autistic traits than did most students in the humanities and social sciences. Additionally, an article titled "The geek syndrome," published in *Wired* magazine, asks whether "math and tech genes" are to blame for the recent upsurge in diagnoses of autism and Asperger's syndrome in Silicone Valley (Silberman 2001).

Linkages across autism and technical/scientific genius have received tangential support from cognitive psychologists who describe the information processing style of people with autism as characterized by "weak central coherence" due to an unusual preoccupation with details or parts of the whole (Frith 1989; Houston and Frith 2000). Extrapolating from the idea that autistic people exhibit weak central coherence, one might infer the tendency for autistic people to emphasize parts, rather than wholes, might engender a particular strength in reductionistic and/or analytic thinking. Moreover, the potential for people with autism to be alienated from social interaction due to their social difficulties may incline them toward occupations and interests dealing with objects, particularly machines, as opposed to occupations dealing with people. From this perspective, the cognitive deficit engendering autistic characteristics in social interaction can engender, in the absence of mental retardation, unusually advanced analytical and technical capacities due to a tendency to focus on details coupled with an inclination towards non-social interests. Accordingly, autism in the absence of mental retardation could be reframed away from a form of psychopathology towards an eccentric but potentially productive cognitive style, a cognitive style most often found in men.

Although Chapter 7 readdresses fascination with the potential relationship between autism and technical/analytic skills, I would like to remark here about the social meanings and implications implied in this purported relationship, particularly in the context of the Zeitgeist of the late twentieth century. In a cultural milieu in which technology reigns supreme in the industrialized nations as the pre-eminent form of professional expertise, it is intriguing that those people who excel in this area are increasingly targeted for personal surveillance in order to detect deviancies in their social skills. Once detected, social deficiencies "prove" autistic psychopathology in such people. On the other hand, it is interesting that people who bear the label of autism are increasingly studied and/or celebrated in terms of their purportedly unique intellectual strengths in the areas of science, technology, math, and music.

The inadvertent effect of these linkages across autism and scientific/technical proclivities is that autism, in its high-functioning variants, has become symbolically equated with an affinity toward, and/or resemblance to, *artificial intelligence*. That is, the assumption that there exists a distinct computational model of cognition that often co-occurs with autistic symptoms and/or is engendered by the underlying form of autistic cognition enables the semiotic equations across autism, technology/science, and social awkwardness. Although the cognitive framework actually applies a computational model of cognition to all people, its application appears (on the surface) most strikingly appropriate for people with either high-functioning autism and/or who exhibit technical/scientific expertise, or both. Therefore when popular and academic representations of autism stress (purportedly) autistic people's "deficiencies" in "humanistic" areas and emphasize their "computational" intelligence, these representations implicitly stereotype and reify autistic intelligence in the mold of artificial intelligence: with the unstated implication that the genius of Einstein, Newton and Bill Gates stems from an inhuman form of intelligence more specific to computers than to people. In effect, a dehumanized form of cyborg intelligence is born from the semiotic marriage of scientific aptitude and social skills deficits.

This tendency to link or equate autism with artificial intelligence holds troubling implications. Despite the tendency to use the computer to make sense of human cognition, there remains a recognized *gap* between artificial and human intelligence. The irremediable gap between actual computers and human brains typically situates in the fundamentally human capacities of sociality (love, desire, sympathy, empathy) and spontaneous imagination (play, aspirations, fantasy), and in reflexive "self-consciousness" (whose nature remains ambiguous). The general public and academics are well aware of this gap, which is the subject of much interest in the science fiction genre, despite publicized efforts to create ever more sophisticated models of artificial intelligence. Consequently, the semiotic equations across autism, technology/science, social deficiencies, and lack of personal reflexivity contain the potential to dehumanize autism and the people associated with this label. They are dehumanized in their rendering as cyborgs.

Again, I would like to stress the question of whether or not a specific ontology of autistic intelligence exists, and whether it includes technical proclivities may remain forever unanswered. Rather than engaging in this debate, I would like to suggest the real or imagined facility of autistic people in the area of technology holds less importance than the popular fascination with it. The ontological question of whether or not "autistic intelligence" exists may never be answered, but the social implications of this metaphor for understanding people labeled with autism can be directly studied. Accordingly, I suggest the tendency to link autism with technical/analytical facility may have more to do with cultural anxieties about technology than it does with the fundamental ontology of autism and/or the real or imagined psychopathology of technical savants. From this point of view, anxieties about technology drive some forms of interest in and speculation about autism.

Frighteningly, representations of autism invoking computational models of "autistic intelligence" draw upon, and exacerbate, social anxieties surrounding technology as a force unto itself, devoid of concern about the human condition. Films such as Stanley Kubrick's *2001: A Space Odyssey* (1968) and James Cameron's *The Terminator* (1984) imagine totalitarian control by artificial intelligence, but in these instances technology represents an externalization of human praxis in the form of produced and self-replicating machines, whereas in the case of Asperger's syndrome the threat of technical domination rests *internally* within the human population. Therefore Asperger's syndrome is constructed as the sublimation of humanity by technology, cloaked in the guise of human genius. While these extrapolations may seem wild at first, careful investigation of the qualitative nature of popularized accounts of Asperger's syndrome in particular point to the public's simultaneous fascination and repulsion with a stereotyped and reified form of "autistic genius."

In conclusion, this line of speculation about the social equation between autism and technical giftedness does not exclude the possibility of autistic savants as somehow technically gifted; rather, it points to the interesting fact that only now, in the Zeitgeist of the late twentieth century, in technically advanced countries, have we pathologized people who, in former times, would have been regarded as eccentric at worst and were unremarked at at best. Although increased social surveillance explains the identification of these people as "eccentric," it alone cannot explain the qualitative nature of the cultural reaction to autism.

Conclusions on psychological constructions of autism: looking back at the twentieth century

Cognitive metaphors for articulating the nature and characteristics of autism have replaced the psychoanalytic paradigm's articulation of autism as an ego shipwrecked on the shores of object relations. While the psychoanalytic approaches tended toward a more homogeneous and unitary set of representations for describing and understanding autism, the cognitive framework offers many different articulations united primarily by their undergirding assumptions about the nature of the mind and its relationship to the brain. The idea of the computer, complete with modular and computational forms of intelligence, serves as the foundation for most cognitive assumptions about how the mind perceives and processes information and (purportedly) enables linkages between cognitive constructs and neural anatomy. As with the psychoanalytic paradigm, the effects of the cognitive paradigm are multifaceted and ambivalent.

One important implication of the ascendancy of the cognitive paradigm is the increasingly nuanced manner in which we differentiate normality from pathology. By focusing on discrete (and often modalized) cognitive aptitudes, this line of research essentially pathologizes people who bear very specific disabilities. Of course, the disabilities of many people with autism are more global in nature, particularly when accompanied by other disabilities. But for those individuals who exhibit very uneven developmental patterns, particularly those who do not exhibit clear mental retardation, these increasingly nuanced "scientific" measures effectively pathologize behaviors and personality characteristics that would have, in times past, been regarded as eccentricities.

The question about boundaries is particularly relevant for high-functioning people with autism. When is a speech delay a "communication disorder"? Where does one draw the boundary between a "late bloomer" and a person "developmentally disabled"? When is a person merely "socially" inept? When is a person afflicted with a "personality disorder"? When does a person suffer from a developmental syndrome such as Asperger's syndrome? Should one regard autism in the absence of mental retardation as psychopathology or "cognitive style" (Baron-Cohen 2000; Happé 1999)? These questions are not merely rhetorical but have significant social implications. Nowadays, educated parents anxious about their infants' development are likely to seek professional expertise on perceived "abnormalities" in cognition, speech, and social comportment considered unremarkable in days past. Anxious parents familiar with formalized developmental guidelines, coupled with a cadre of professionals equipped with an ever-expanding repertoire of diagnostic classifications, surely contribute to the increased rate of diagnoses of high-functioning forms of autism, within which diagnostic rates have swelled.

The effects of labeling are complex and multifaceted because many people with autism are, in fact, crippled by their social disabilities, even when they evidence other cognitive strengths. Thus, the medical pathologizing of their specific disabilities enables them to receive assistance perhaps invaluable in their development and well-being. However, the effects of labeling an individual with uneven skills and or "odd" personalities can also be detrimental, as decades of research on labeling reveals.

However, conversely, perhaps the debate about whether or not labeling should occur is misdirected. We live in an era subjecting children to such high degrees of social surveillance that developmental "irregularities," especially among the economic elites in the developed world, *will* be subject to early identification. These "irregularities" or "eccentricities" *will* be constructed within a medical and/or psychological framework and potentially pathologized. And, in a time in which the overall expectations for social conduct are becoming increasingly regimented, early identification and remediation of "eccentricities" may actually be necessary for the individual's social and economic success. Thus, given the inevitability of labeling in the contemporary context, perhaps the debate should focus more on the meanings implied by the labels used.

As observed by Lorna Wing (1997), successive editions of the World Health Organization's *International Classification of Diseases* and the American Psychiatric Association's *Diagnostic and Statistical Manual of Mental Disorders* "have reflected changing ideas of autism and related disorders" (Wing 1997: 148). Although Wing is optimistic in that she believes these changes reflect "advances in understanding" I caution that the transformation of metaphors from psychoanalytic to cognitive ones need not necessarily indicate a *truer* or *more authentic* understanding of autism. Questions about the nature and expression of autism involve deeply philosophical questions and issues about the nature of mind and consciousness, and their relationship to the human body and society. Also involved are questions about normalcy and difference within and across individuals, and within and across cultures. We attempt to answer these questions with socially constructed, philosophical ideas about what it means to be human, the nature of consciousness, the relationship between mind and brain, and the relationship between the individual and society. Over time these socially constructed ideas change in response to changes in institutional arrangements and changes in the forms and rhythms of everyday life. To argue we will definitely *know* autism elides the fact that our ways of knowing are always/already socially and historically situated. Thus, I suggest that although our ideas about autism have changed over time, they are not necessarily evolving toward its essential and transcendental essence. Chapter 7 addresses how social attitudes about autism have helped shape the experience and nature of autism while Chapter 8 concludes by addressing the implications of the new metaphors for understanding autism.

Notes

1 Although some might argue that consumer culture has taken over the role as the most hegemonic set of practices involved in the constitution of childhood, the battles over the legitimacy and effects of commercialized kids' culture are fought using the vocabulary and expertise of psychological authorities.

2 Gesell (Gesell and Amatruda 1941; Gesell 1952) was not a psychoanalytic thinker. Rather, he was a "maturationist" who believed that development is dictated genetically and emerges in patterned "developmental" sequences that are universal in form, although he recognized that each child has a unique developmental timetable.

3 According to Doane and Hodges (1992: 11), Klein identified the origins of the Oedipal conflict about the time of weaning. Framed as such, the Oedipal struggle is "subsumed and consequently redefined in terms of depressive anxiety and the attempt to restore the mother as a whole object." For Klein, depressive anxiety is more important than castration anxiety. Moreover, depressive anxiety is never fully reconciled in the Kleinian framework. Doane and Hodges (1992: 12)

claim that the work of symbol formation, including art and culture, are attempts to make reparation, "to regenerate the mother."

4 Greenspan's (Greenspan and Wieder 1998: 12) model of "floor time" blends the psychoanalytic approach to "play therapy" with an information processing model of cognition, derived from the cognitive paradigm:

> Traditional psychotherapeutic efforts tend to engage the child in a type of parallel play where he feels the clinician's warmth and support but is not mobilized into types of interaction likely to lead to growth in the critical areas of development. The floor time model, in contrast, mobilizes the child's emerging developmental capacities and is based on the thesis that affective interaction can harness cognitive and emotional growth.
>
> (Greenspan 2000: 685)

5 Cognitive psychology is part of the tradition engaged in explaining the source and forms of knowledge. Some forms of cognitive psychology can be considered "rationalist" and "nativist" in that they argue that there are *innate*, transcendental features of mind that are instrumental in the production of knowledge (e.g., Chomsky's transformational grammar). Cognitive psychology's tendency toward rationalism pits it against strict empiricism, which holds that the primary sources of knowledge acquisition involve association and conditioning (Samet 1998). However, within cognitive psychology, there are many ways of identifying, describing, and explaining the purportedly innate structures involved in knowledge production and there are therefore considerable theoretical discontinuities across the paradigm. Strictly nativist approaches, for example, conflict with "functionalist" ones that posit parallels between, rather than equivalences across, levels of analysis.

6 Jackson and Georges (1998) explain there are three forms of computational theories of the mind, all of which are functionalist, and model the functional states of the mind on the computational states of a computer. These three approaches include (1) the "classical theory" forwarded by Jerry Fodor (1983), which holds that computations take place in representations that have the logical, syntactical structure found in standard logical forms, (2) the view inspired by F. P. Ramsey (1931) that beliefs are maps steering reasoning via mental imagery; and (3) the more recent connectionist approach that rejects structured representations in favor of a view of the mind–brain as a network of nodes whose operations indicate learning (Jackson and Georges 1998). The first approach has dominated cognitive research on autism.

Jones and Elcock (2001: 216–217) provide a helpful summation of the assumptions of the first approach. According to their account, cognition within the classical approach is modeled on the idea of a "Physical Symbol System" (PSS) composed of "symbols (physical patterns corresponding to facts), expressions (structures of symbols), and processes (operations on symbols characterized by rules)." The PSS enables intelligent behavior by organizing and reorganizing symbol structures, making comparisons and then acting upon the basis of the results. Jones and Elcock (2001) explain that this form of PSS enables computers to operate but there exists considerable debate about whether or not human intelligence should be modeled on this system. Humans may not process information by a set of formal rules. The model is overly rational in its explanation for the grounds of human action. Moreover, the model of communication and thought invoked by the PSS system is "representational" and assumes the transparency of, and relative fixation of, symbolic meanings. The approach also evidences "methodological solipsism" in that it overemphasizes processing in the mind without adequately taking into account the environment and body, within which the mind resides. Finally, this approach evidences "computationalism," which holds that "mental processes are computations on formal, syntactical symbols" (Jones and Elcock 2001: 218).

7 In this chapter, I primarily make reference to the research that takes a *top-down* approach, which assumes that there are relatively universal patterns of cognition that can be related to neural-anatomy, either *functionally* or *directly*. However, within the literature on autism, both top-down and bottom-up approaches tend toward the identity theory account of a direct, *equivalent* relationship between mental types and brain types; although in the instances wherein functionalist accounts are pursued or implied, they would be more likely to be associated with top-down approaches. Importantly, across top-down and bottom-up approaches to autism, one finds computational metaphors for understanding the relationship between mind and brain that establishes metaphoric equivalences across artificial intelligence, mind–consciousness, and brain. The top-down approaches tend to be more modular in their framework, reflecting Fodor's (1983) "classical view of cognition," while the bottom-up approaches are increasingly, but not exclusively, employing the connectionist metaphor of computation.

8 Although there are many models of communication and/or semiotics explaining this process of language acquisition, the one just described can be regarded as the one most often implied.

9 Leekam and Moore (2001) claim that there are two explanations for impairments in joint attention, one cognitive and one affective. The *affective* explanation emphasizes the child's deficit in "intersubjective relatedness" or a deficit in regulation of the child's socio-emotional relatedness to others (cited in Leekam and Moore 2001: 107). The *cognitive* explanation emphasizes a deficiency in the child's internal representation of relational others. Despite variations in emphasis, all of these explanations describe autism in relation to a deficiency in the child's ability to engage in a shared social world through joint attentional processes. Although the affective approaches do not use the vocabulary of mental structures or representations, they too rely on the idea that patterns of social interaction and communication are acquired, or internalized in some fashion, from the coordination of attentional processes. Although, the affective approaches may be more likely to describe the *capacity* to coordinate social interaction as being intrinsically hard-wired (as opposed to the forms that are internalized).

10 For an excellent but concise discussion of consciousness and the problem of introspection see Lormand (1998). According to Lormand, there are several rival theories of introspective consciousness and all of them distinguish the characteristics of introspective consciousness from phenomenal consciousness, which concerns the qualitative nature of experience. Introspective consciousness is seen as entailing a form of mental reflexivity wherein the mind takes itself as a form of mental object open to inspection. Entailed in both forms of consciousness, phenomenal and introspective, are complex and unresolved questions about the relationship between mind–consciousness and brain. Flew (1979), in *A Dictionary of Philosophy*, itemizes some of the problems associated with introspective models of consciousness, including the philosophical issues surrounding the ways in which it is believed possible for "a subject to be made the object of their own awareness (how can introspection occur?)" and the necessity for consciousness to accompany every mental state (Flew 1979: 73). Flew points out that Freud demonstrated the inaccessibility of some forms of mental states and contends that introspective views of consciousness have been widely criticized, not just by Freud but also by the philosophers of language such as Wittgenstein who argue that the focus of mind is misplaced and should be replaced by a focus on the *expression* of mind in culturally determined forms including language and action and art.

11 It is important to again emphasize here that cognitive psychologists differ significantly in their underlying ontologies. The dangers of reification are more evident in works such as Steven Pinker's (1997) *How the Mind Works* and Henry Plotkin's (1997) *Evolution in Mind*, which both combine a computational theory of mind with psychological nativism and biological principles adapted from a neo-Darwinian account of evolution (Fodor 2000), leading to the slippery slope of the ontology of identity theory.

12 Uttal (2001: 2) argues that "localization" of mental constructs on neural anatomy is only one of three challenges facing psychobiology. The other challenges include "the issue of representation at the neuronal level" (how do neural networks represent, encode, or instantiate cognitive processes?) and also the challenge of learning, "how does our brain adapt to experience, what changes occur in its neural networks as a result of experience, and how do these changes correspond to externally observed behavior?" (Uttal 2001: 2). Although Uttal extends his critique to encompass all of these psychobiological foci, he explains that the localization approach has been more "amenable" to research for a variety of reasons and is therefore most prevalent.

6 Biogenetic approaches construct autism

> Variations among individuals within species are a unique consequence of both genes and the developmental environment in a constant interaction. Moreover, curiously enough, even if I knew the genes of a developing organism and the complete sequence of its environments, I could not specify the organism.
>
> (Lewontin 1993: 26)

Within our contemporary context, authority over the definition of mind and the meaning of human behavior are increasingly ceded to researchers working in the areas of genetics, evolutionary biology and neurology. Debates over the relevance, structure, and operation of consciousness are increasingly articulated in relation to approaches that establish direct equivalences across mental operations, neurological processes, and genetic profiles. Consequently, debates over the normality and/or pathology of individual behavior are increasingly cast in medicalized terms and/or are construed in relation to evolutionary fitness. For example, individual depression is articulated either in terms of neurochemistry gone awry due to faulty genes or is understood as a genetically coded evolutionary response entailing the internalization of aggression toward the self and away from social others. The role of social institutions and cultural practices in engendering both the definition and experience of depression has been pushed into the background by accounts that reify and universalize the construct of depression through its localization in neural-chemistry and/or the human genome. This also has occurred with contemporary representations of many forms of "mental disorders," particularly autism.

As with all representational frameworks, the current frameworks promoting neuroscience and/or evolutionary biology as providing the definitive answers to the nature of what it means to be human have complex and multifaceted effects for the study of autism and for those people labeled autistic. On the one hand, biogenetic accounts promise to identify the particular forms of brain chemistry, or neural-anatomy, or genes that give rise to the spectrum of disorders labeled autism. The hope is that identification of the etiology or etiologies of autism will enable researchers to find ways of "normalizing" autistic people through various possible interventions including, but not limited to, gene therapy, pharmaceuticals, and dietary interventions. On the other hand, biogenetic accounts face significant challenges in delivery for a variety of reasons that will be addressed in this chapter including the challenge associated with identifying distinct autistic phenotypes (i.e., characteristic mental and cognitive expressions of autism) and genotypes (i.e., characteristic genetic profiles). At first, this challenge of identifying and linking phenotypes with genotypes seems merely an "empirical" problem ultimately resolvable through careful, painstaking research and sophisticated computer-driven genomic analysis. However, closer inspection of this challenge reveals significant barriers that may prove insurmountable. Ultimately, the problem facing the successful identification of distinct autistic phenotypes and genotypes stems from the assumptions constructing autism. The problem, as it is typically articulated, rests on the assumption that there *are* distinct autistic phenotypes and genotypes that can be *reliably* identified and measured across populations. This assumption invokes a particular model of causal relations seen as weaving a tight web across manifestations of autistic behaviors and cognitive styles, the brain states of people with autism, and the genetic profile(s) of people with autism. However, this causal model—a model implying the existence of specific and generalizable unidirectional relations across phenomenal levels of analysis—may be misguided. The model's problematic assumptions addressed in this chapter include:

- The idea that genes and brains can be productively understood using a mechanistic and closed system approach characterized by reductionism and linear causality.
- The idea that "cognition," "mind," and "consciousness" can be reduced to localized brain states and/or gene alleles.
- The idea that brain states can be explained and/or predicted by gene states.

In critically assessing the assumptions of this causal model, this chapter explores the alternative possibility that autism is an umbrella term used to make sense of a complex array of behaviors and cognitive deficits that are themselves mediated by synergistic, non-summative relations only understandable within a non-deterministic, open systems model, a model stressing the brain's plasticity and rejecting the reductionistic equation of mind with brain.

What follows contextualizes the assumptions of recent biogenetic accounts of autism within the cultural Zeitgeist of the late twentieth century before moving to a specific discussion of some of the many biogenetic approaches to studying autism.

Biological psychiatry and geneticization: the cultural Zeitgeist

Sorting out the complex forces involved in the rise of biological psychiatry and the search for the genetic origins of human traits, particularly those labeled as "deviant," is a project well beyond the scope of this chapter. Given the complexity of these forces, I provide only a brief descriptive account of the ascendancy of the genetic model explaining mental disease and the concomitant rise in pharmaceutical psychiatry as the primary model for understanding and treating mental "diseases," whose neural-chemical manifestations are themselves believed to stem primarily from genetic factors.

The search for the hereditary bases of mental diseases and for "deviant" behaviors (particularly "criminality") can be traced back a hundred years. As explained in Chapter 4, the project of linking mental retardation and social deviance to heredity was of great interest to social reformers and eugenicists of the late nineteenth and early twentieth centuries. Moreover, the rise of Kraepelin's biological psychiatry contributed to the cultural belief that mental disease could be explained biologically and predicted through hereditary factors, despite the efforts of prominent psychiatrists such as Adolph Meyer who stressed the complex interaction of human biology and environmental factors.

Early-nineteenth-century efforts to link mental illness to hereditary factors understood hereditary in terms quite different from our contemporary genome-influenced understanding of the term. Although the tendency to view social inferiors as *intrinsically* inferior has a long and dark history, the idea of a systematic study of genetic inheritance of measurable traits is relatively new and is traceable to Gregor Mendel's studies on garden peas, published in 1865. Mendel did not invent the idea of the gene; rather, he was interested in the manifestation of patterns of difference across generations, and did not focus on the cause of those differences. Mendel's efforts to systematically describe and predict the *phenotypic* (outward characteristics) expression of traits such as pea color in successive generations were largely ignored until they were "rediscovered" in the early 1900s (Hubbard and Wald 1999; Lewontin 1993).

Early-twentieth-century efforts to study the inheritance of mental disease and retardation followed, although less systematically, the Mendelian approach to studying patterns of difference across generations. Thus, delinquency, mental retardation, and mental illness were "found" to group in families, reinforcing existing beliefs that degeneracy was a hereditary affair. For example, in 1916 Ernst Rudin published *On the Inheritance and Origin of Psychic Disorders* in which he studied the siblings of 701 patients with dementia praecox and concluded that the disorder was largely inherited (Stone 1997: 147). Up until the beginning of the twenty-first century, efforts to study the inheritance of mental disease have typically followed this approach of studying the frequency and severity of the symptoms of mental illness in family members across generations. This "Mendelian" model of gene transmission rests in the assumptions that the transmission of disease occurs via a single gene and that genetic diseases can be understood in terms of dominant, recessive, or X-linked patterns of inheritance (Insel and Collins 2003).

This kind of application of the Mendelian model of genetic inheritance to explain the etiology of mental disorders assumes that behavioral expressions of mental disease are grouped in families by virtue of direct and heritable influences rather than environmental ones (Lewontin 1993). That is, this approach holds that observable and measurable expressions of "mental illness" are directly caused in degree and form by the underlying organic disorder such that the observed expressions of the disorder are seen as mere epiphenomena of the "underlying" condition. Second, this way of applying the Mendelian model to the etiology of mental disorders assumes that the observers' constructs are fixed (i.e., universal) entities that are valid indicators of the underlying disorder and that the expression of said entities can be reliably measured. For example, efforts to examine the heritability of mental retardation typically presume that the observer's measure of intelligence is a valid indicator of the mental operations/capacities of his/her subjects and that the researcher can reliably measure intelligence across populations of individuals. In essence then, purportedly fixed constructs such as intelligence or "antisociality" are viewed as distinct and heritable traits that vary only in terms of the degree (or predetermined qualitative forms) of their expression, and are thus viewed as homologous to the expression of gene alleles that predict whether a sweet pea will be red or white. I will return later to these assumptions.

Although sociological and psychological studies on heredity and social pathology followed Mendel's approach, early-twentieth-century researchers in biology were intent on discovering the exact cause of the hereditary patterns observed by Mendel. Given the social and economic context of early-twentieth-century life, the issue of inheritance was seen as vital to explaining criminality and degeneracy and so the subject of explaining the cause of the mathematic variations described by Mendel was regarded as particularly important. The search for the ostensible kernels of heredity was on in both North American and Europe. Late-nineteenth-century successes in identifying structures (i.e., coined "chromosomes") visible in cells suggested the locus for investigation (Hubbard and Wald 1999). In 1909, the term "gene" was coined to denote the "particles" believed to inhere in the chromosomes. Although some scientists believed that these hypothetical genes were the locus for the material of inheritance, other scientists viewed the proteins, also constitutive of the cell's chromosomes, as a more likely site. This dispute was not resolved conclusively until 1953 when James D. Watson and Francis Crick offered their model of the structure of DNA, the double-helix, as the locus of hereditary material (Hubbard and Wald 1999).

Within this framework, the gene is a stretch of DNA that dictates the composition and synthesis of proteins, which mediate heritable traits. Accordingly, a gene "allele" is "one of several possible forms of a gene, found at the same location on a chromosome" that gives rise to phenotypic differences such as eye color (Hubbard and Wald 1999: 201). Consequently, it was not until the 1950s that it was even possible to begin efforts to link particular diseases to particular genetic variations (alleles) or to genetic errors.

The establishment of the purportedly definitive locus and form of genetic material fueled the geneticist program. The problem of genetic inheritance seemed, at first, a simple matter of mapping the specific genes and proteins constituting the chromosomes found in every cell of living organisms. If genes are discrete, functional units dictating in a one-to-one relationship the formation of the proteins constituting the building blocks of life, then the geneticist dream of explaining all expressions of life in terms of genetic building blocks could be realized. The discovery of gene alleles directly causing cystic fibrosis and Huntington's chorea bolstered the public's confidence in the new science of genetics. However, the story of the gene circulating throughout popular culture, particularly in media reports on the results of genetic science, involves simplifications so gross that they bear little resemblance to the science that they seek to describe (see Hubbard and Wald 1999; Keller 1995, 2000; Lewontin 1993).

Since the 1950s, genetic research on diseases believed to follow a Mendelian pattern of inheritance revealed the relationship between genes and disease is far from clear. It is very difficult to establish genetic linkages in disease because the same syndrome (e.g., Alzheimer's disease) can result either from different mutations of the same gene or from mutations of different genes (Insel and Collins 2003). Moreover, often the same mutation in the same gene can result in variable phenotypic manifestations (Insel and Collins 2003). Finally, the "extent of pathology, the location of pathology, or the age of onset can be influenced by modifier genes, by environmental factors, or by poorly understood effects that contribute to differences in severity" (Insel and Collins 2003: 617). In essence, the process of identifying a "susceptibility gene" represents only one step in the complex project of linking diseases directly with genes.

In an effort to demystify the ideology of the gene permeating popular culture, a number of scientists, particularly Evelyn Fox Keller (1995, 2000), Richard Lewontin (1993, 2000), and Ruth Hubbard (and Elijah Wald 1999), have provided accessible but technical accounts of what genes are and what they are not. Their accounts tell a story debunking the purported causal efficacy of the gene. It turns out the gene (i.e., a functional unit of DNA) is not a particle-like entity exerting direct action in a one-to-one fashion on proteins constituting the building blocks of life. First, the idea of the gene as a discrete functional unit is problematic because the operations of any one "gene" are always influenced by the operations of other chromosomal units and these influences are variable and almost impossible to predict in all cases. Consequently, genes do not produce proteins (through RNA) in a one-to-one fashion; indeed, Keller (2000) points out that a particular "gene" may be capable of producing a great number of proteins depending upon its interactions with other forms of DNA and RNA located on the same or other chromosomes and/or located in the cell's protoplasm, and/or located in the cell's membranes.[1] Insel and Collins (2003) observe that:

> By alternative arrangements of RNA following transcription of the DNA, 30,000 genes can code for 100,000 proteins. Adding posttranslational modifications (i.e., changes to the protein following translation from RNA) like proteolysis, phosporylation, and glycosylation may ultimately yield as many as 1,000,000 different human proteins.
>
> (Insel and Collins 2003: 617)

In effect, the more geneticists study the nature and operation of genes, the more holistic and variant their forms and operations appear. Thus, although geneticists may identify some genetic variations correlating with particular diseases, the real challenge is to explore the systemic processes occurring within and across various biological and cultural environments. This includes the genetic environment in which a particular "gene" is located, the cellular environment in which the chromosome is embedded, the biophysical environment in which the organism is embedded, and the cultural environment influencing all environmental models. Systemic frameworks must replace mechanistic ones when the challenge is to explain the relationship between genes and diseases or disorders.

However, the mechanistic and particle-like metaphor of the gene persists in the popular imagination (and in some science as well), still bolstered by what are now known to be the atypical cases of cystic fibrosis and Huntington's chorea. Today, the media bombard the public daily with news about the discovery of genes for cancer, for heart disease, for depression, for alcoholism and for aggression. Increasingly, science news features purported genetic links between behavior and/or abilities and specific genes. Typical headlines read: "Possible link of violence, gene found" (Cooke 2002), "Scientists link anxiety to specific gene" (Talan 2002), and "Researchers find stress, depression have genetic link" (Vedantam 2003). Such headlines lead the public to conclude that specific gene alleles hold the source of nearly all medical and social pathology, as well as the source for all human variation in skill and ability. That is, the assumptions underlying these articles are that particular genes function in specific and predictable ways to produce specific and predictable traits—traits seen as constituting the "phenotypic" expression of variations in human genotypes. These assumptions are, in fact, erroneous.

Although geneticists may be able, in some narrowly defined cases, to *correlate* genetic variations with physical and mental disease, the presence of a particular suspect allele fails to predict whether a person will develop the medical (autism) or psychological condition (depression) at issue. As stated previously, the relationships across DNA, RNA, and proteins are complex, systemic, and subject to variation depending upon a complex of synergistic "environmental" influences. Lewontin (1993) summarizes the inherent and probably insurmountable problems with the reduction of complex medical/psychological states to genetic ones:

> The problem of telling a coherent causal story, and of then designing a therapy based on knowledge of the DNA sequence in such a case, is that we don't know even in principle all of the functions of the different nucleotides in a gene, or how the specific context in which a nucleotide appears may affect the way in which the cell machinery interprets the DNA; nor do we have any but the most rudimentary understanding of how a whole functioning organism is put together from its protein bits and pieces.
>
> (Lewontin 1993: 156)

Although some might argue that Lewontin's argument against genetic determinism simply reflects inadequacies in our current knowledge base, this misses his point. As noted above, the cells that "house" our chromosomes are not closed systems; the cellular environment and the environment of the larger organism influence the very operation of cellular reproduction. Moreover, every person's chromosomes contain defective DNA sequences and since error is ubiquitous throughout the human gene pool, it is very difficult for scientists to identify which genetic errors and/or gene alleles, cause—either singly or in combination with other genes—disease and mental illness. As Lewontin (2000: 156) argues, "because there is no single, standard, 'normal' DNA sequence that we all share, observed sequence differences between sick and well people cannot, in themselves, reveal the genetic cause of disorder."

Given the now indisputable facts that "genes" "operate" in ways that are systemic, synergistic, and (often) unpredictable, why does the search for genetic answers dominate popular science and, increasingly, biological research? Many answers exist to this question and among them is the enduring desire for simplifying and controlling complex social and philosophical problems. Environmental influences include the air we breathe, the food we eat, the water we drink, the viruses and bacteria we share the planet with, the social/cultural environment within which we are and the sheer randomness of events characterizing existence right down to the level of cellular reproduction, if not further. The complexities, interdependencies, and sheer contingencies of our environment fundamentally affect our emergence as biological and psychological beings, at every level. Such environmental influences cannot be easily mapped and resist simple efforts at intervention. Thus, the idea of genetic determinism appeals to our desire for reducing complexity and hints at the possibility of future control. Consequently, complex biological and environmental processes are mistakenly collapsed into deterministic genetic agents localized in "susceptible" individuals.

The idea of genetic determinism also helps resolve the ancient problem described in Chapter 5 of linking mental states with brain states. The proponents of the various forms of identity theory, which holds that mental states can be linked directly to brain states, see genetic explanations of human behavior as confirming and/or extending their research assumptions. Using new imaging technologies such as fMRI (functional magnetic resonance imaging) and PET (positron emission tomography), scientists attempt to identify the particular brain sites and processes involved in regulating and/or producing specific cognitive skills and/or emotions. After identifying a particular brain site or brain process, scientists may then attempt to identify the particular gene alleles "responsible" for producing and regulating that brain site. In this fashion, complex and ambiguous phenomena such as intelligence are spatially localized in brain centers, which can then be subject to genetic analysis. A newspaper article titled, "Scientists claim to have pinpointed source of human IQ" (Suplee 2000) illustrates this type of reductionism. The article reports that European scientists claimed to have "located the precise subsections of the human brain involved in 'general intelligence,' the ability typically measured by IQ tests" (Suplee 2000: A26). Originally published in the journal *Science*, the study involved the use of PET, a process measuring which brain cells are using the most blood at a given moment, to identify what area of the brain activated in thirteen research subjects engaged in spatial and verbal puzzles. Although the newspaper account includes criticism that intelligence is not a unitary phenomenon and cellular blood use does not in itself indicate intelligence at work, the article's general message is that the mental operations of the subjects could be linked to specific brain centers in a universalizing equation.

The next step in the project of genetic determinism would require identifying the specific genes involved in producing and operating those specific brain cells activated by particular mental tasks. This type of research would attempt to plot out, step-by-step, the relationships across mental functions, brain states, and DNA sequences. For example, an article titled "Mapping genetic influences on human brain structure" (Thompson et al. 2002: 523) argues for the viability of modeling the complex interactions across mental states, brain states, and genetics. However, careful examination of the researchers' modeling techniques and assumptions calls into question the validity of their arguments due to questionable forms of data (e.g., twin registries) and questionable modeling techniques (e.g., "computational methods" synthesizing "algorithms from random field theory, anatomical modeling, and population genetics"). Despite the research's problems, it should be applauded for at least attempting to make explicit, in the form of a systemic model, what is often implicitly assumed by research that unreflectively reduces mental states (e.g., depression) to brain states, which are then seen as mechanistically affected by gene states.

Recent efforts to establish equivalences and/or direct linkages across mental states, brain states, and gene alleles have been particularly evident in the research on depression and anxiety. The rise of pharmaceutical medicine, particularly in the treatment of psychiatric medicine is particularly important in explaining the interest in and wide publication of these linkages. In the case of depression and anxiety, researchers have repeatedly cited genes implicated in the transmission of serotonin as "causing" these mental states. The logic here is enthymemic because the suppressed premise is that particular brain states involving the regulation of serotonin cause mental states of depression and anxiety. For example, the argument about depression follows this form:

- A specific gene *causes* depression by governing serotonin transporter (suppressed: serotonin regulation causes depression).
- Thus depression is a brain state governed by a defective gene or particular gene allele.

Since gene therapy is not yet (and may never be) a viable therapeutic option, the treatment for depression within the parameters of this configuration, requires manipulation of the brain state through some external, pharmaceutical, agent. The discovery of drugs that purportedly improved patients' reported levels of depression in the 1950s—particularly by affecting the regulation of serotonin and dopamine (Stone 1997)—opened the door to a rebirth of biological psychiatry and contributed to the medicalization of all forms of mental disorders.

For people who suffer from depression, anxiety, psychoses, and autism, the idea of genetic determinism and the promises of pharmaceutical medicine may seem promising. Their problems seem much more manageable when represented in the context of these interpretive frameworks and institutional practices. Their mental states derive from brain states, themselves caused by defective genes or deviant alleles. The solution to their suffering, particularly in the case of mental disorders, is now pharmaceutical and may some day be genetic. Some patients who suffer from depression or obsessive-compulsive disorder, for example, *do* seem to improve when treated with particular pharmaceutical agents such as the selective serotonin reuptake inhibitors (SSRIs), which affect the role of serotonin in the brain (McDougle et al. 2002). However, the exact relationship between the mental state (i.e., depression/anxiety) and the brain states involving neurotransmitters defies understanding (Valenstein 1998). Moreover, we do not fully understand the ways in which pharmaceutical agents (e.g., Prozac) affect brain states. Nor are the long-term neurological and/or systemic effects of these agents known. Finally, the degree to which patients' reports of their mental states are affected by factors other than the pharmaceutical agent (e.g., placebo effect) is also unknown.

This discussion is not to suggest that biological interventions produce no positive impact. Rather, I'm endeavoring to describe the ways in which very complex phenomena and relationships across mental states, brain states, and genes are being represented in ways that distort in their simplification. The case for gross simplification and distortion in biogenetic explanations is illustrated quite easily in the case of psychological conditions such as depression and anxiety but what about more complex phenomena such as schizophrenia and, as I will later discuss, autism?

As noted earlier, the search for the relationship between heredity and schizophrenia has persisted for almost one hundred years. Most research studies establishing a hereditary relationship for the disorder have simply studied its frequency (and that of manic-depressive disorder) in families. This kind of research is unable to separate out the influences of environment from genetics, even in the case of "twin" studies (Lewontin 1993). More recently, efforts have been made to find particular gene defects or gene alleles in individuals afflicted with the disorder. Although able to point to some successes, further research forced the retraction of claims to discovering the genetic basis of the disorder, and to this day the relationship between schizophrenia and genetics remains a mystery (Hubbard and Wald 1999). One reason, among many, that researchers have such difficulty establishing the genetic profile for mental disorders like schizophrenia is these disorders are characterized by complex phenotypes lacking reliable measurable traits, such as blood pressure or blood glucose (Insel and Collins 2003). However, it seems very clear that mental disorders such as schizophrenia and manic depression possess at least a partial biological dimension. Differentiating among distinct and replicable phenotypes and sorting out their distinct etiological influences—genetic, biological, environmental, social/cultural—remain Herculean tasks. And yet, even if it were possible to model the cataclysm of genetic, biological, and socio-cultural events resulting in the expression of mental disorders such as schizophrenia, how would that knowledge change treatment? Could it? These questions bear equal weight for the study of autism.

Research on autism increasingly focuses on studying the disorder's biological etiology, particularly in relation to genetic influences. The established facts that approximately 20 percent of people diagnosed with autism develop epilepsy and about 75 percent suffer from some measurable form of "mental retardation" have contributed to the belief that autism is a biological disorder that affects the brain's operations (Lauritsen and Ewald 2001). Moreover, the high rates of autism in identical twins implicate the role of genetics in influencing development of the disorder. Given such clear evidence that biogenetic factors are implicated in the disorder, much recent research focuses on identifying the specific genes causing the complex array of symptoms whose constellation enables a diagnosis of autism. Sometimes this genetic research also addresses the mediating or catalyzing effects of other biological influences including co-morbid conditions, viruses, and environmental contaminants. These models rarely incorporate socio-cultural influences, perhaps as a consequence of efforts to exorcise the lingering ghost of the refrigerator mother. Across these biogenetic approaches to studying autism one encounters the implicit idea that understanding the genetic *nature* of autism—as a *first cause*—will point to directions for its remediation either through gene or pharmaceutical therapy.

At first, this project seems no more difficult than the project of identifying which gene alleles or genetic errors are found in autistic populations and, perhaps, of identifying potential mediating influences contributing to the presence of the disorder in genetically susceptible individuals. However, as with the case of schizophrenia, sorting out and modeling the complex systemic operations and effects of genetic environments is a vast undertaking. Further, the shifting and multifaceted expressions of autism make it difficult to determine whether or not there exists a single or multiple autism phenotypes. Consequently, it is unclear whether researchers studying the genetics of people with autism are in fact studying a group of people who share the same disorder. Put otherwise, the question arises whether or not people who bear the title "autistic" share the same underlying biological condition given vast differences in the qualitative forms and quantitative degree of their impairments in social interaction, language, and behavioral proclivities.

Complementing the search for the genetic origins of autism is another research approach I describe as "autism brain science." In contrast to the purely genome-driven approach described immediately above, those researchers who conduct "autism brain science" presume that the expression of autistic symptoms traces back to specific neurological abnormalities explainable in terms of genetic errors, gene alleles, or environmental insults. Autism brain science thus faces the challenge of establishing direct equivalences between the phenotypic expression of autism and specific neurological characteristics and then explaining these equivalences in terms of genetic or environmental causal pathways. Thus, autism brain science typically presupposes a linear, unidirectional relationship across neurological abnormalities and the expression of autistic symptoms. The role of the social environment in shaping autistic symptoms has little to no significance in this model. The challenges associated with such linear relationships will also be explored throughout this chapter. I now turn to a more detailed discussion of the scientific quest for discovering the biological "origins" of autism.

Autism: the search for causal agents

An explicit disavowal of the psychoanalytic formulation of autism as rooted in the mother–child relationship motivated the project of defining autism strictly as an organic disorder. Bernard Rimland, a PhD whose son is autistic, helped spearhead the movement in the United States to understand the disorder from a biomedical perspective. Understood from this framework, autism is loosely conceived as a disease or set of diseases caused by underlying genetic errors or variant alleles engendering a variety of neurological and/or physiological conditions believed to cause the development of autism. Across approaches, *observable "autistic" behaviors and cognitive deficits are thus believed to be epiphenomena of the underlying organic disorder(s)*. In order to understand how the biogenetic perspective constructs autism it is first important to understand how research is conducted in the search for the biomedical markers of autism.

Contemporary autism research takes a variety of approaches to discover specific biological markers for the disorder. Perhaps the most publicized approach focuses on identifying a distinct autistic genotype or genotypes across autistic populations. Another related approach explores the relationship between autistic symptoms and other medical conditions in order to understand how biomedical conditions may give rise to the disorder. This second approach does not necessarily construe autism as a distinct disease characterized by exclusive biological markers but it does point to the possibility of the existence of specific gene defects or gene alleles producing biological susceptibilities to agents that can catalyze the disorder. Finally, another popularized approach uses neuroimaging techniques to identify abnormalities in the brain anatomy and brain development of autistic people. Explanations for observed brain abnormalities point to either genetic errors and/or environmental insults suffered early in the prenatal or post-natal environment. Accordingly, I organize my discussion of the search for causal agents by looking at three research trends:

- autistic brains?
- genetic analysis and the search for the autism genotype(s)
- autism and susceptibility: co-morbid disorders and environmental influences.

Autistic brains?

The first research area discussed in this chapter addresses the growing body of literature attempting to identify the distinct characteristics of the "autistic" brain. A disparate and heterogeneous body of literature, the research within its purview shares a commitment to identifying distinct brain profiles of autistic populations using post-mortem analysis or, more frequently, advanced neuroimaging technologies. Using a wide range of technologies, researchers study the brain for evidence of anatomical, chemical, and metabolic abnormalities by asking questions such as:

- Can people with autism be reliably assigned to subgroupings based on the phenotypic expression of specific neurological abnormalities?

- Is it possible to trace autistic cognitive and behavioral deficits to specific neural abnormalities in localized brain centers such as the cerebellum and/or amygdala?
- Is it possible to trace autistic cognitive and behavioral deficits to characteristic imbalances in neural metabolism and/or neural-chemistry, particularly as evidenced by regional cerebral blood flow and/or in neurotransmitter levels (e.g., serotonin and dopamine)?

Although Chapter 5 provides references to these, it is useful to take a brief but focused look at the findings, conclusions, and assumptions of the growing literature I term autism brain science. Before beginning this discussion, I wish to stress that although the research in this literature shares a common belief that autistic behaviors/characteristics can be explained in terms of brain states, researchers diverge greatly in their understanding of the etiological origins of these brain states. Moreover, differences in academic specialization directly influence what researchers look at and the kinds of conclusions they draw. Some researchers, particularly those influenced by cognitive psychology, take a functional approach that suggests that a particular mental content or construct (e.g. depression or theory of mind) can be linked to a particular brain operation or content but caution that all instances of that mental content (depression/theory of mind) cannot necessarily be linked directly to *a* (singular) *specific type* of brain content/operation (see Jackson and Georges 1998). Other researchers, particularly those with backgrounds in medicine or neurology, show less interest in cognitive constructs and instead attempt to link observable behavioral deficits or affective states directly to disrupted brain structures or processes, thereby rendering behavior and mental contents mere epiphenomena of brain states. Because a comprehensive review and critique is beyond the scope of this project, I merely illustrate commonly found findings and their assumptions, beginning with the assumptions that inform most approaches to knowing the brain.

Knowing the brain

Although the brain is a highly integrated organ, the centuries-old project of knowing it often proceeded from the assumption that the brain is organized into specialized substructures with distinct functions. This assumption, that the brain is best represented in terms of distinct structures with specialized functions, may be misleading as it may apply only to specific sensory (e.g., vision) and motor operations (Uttal 2001; Valenstein 1998). However, although the brain may be in fact much more integrated and holistic in its operations than our representations suggest, most introductory accounts begin with a basic anatomical description of what are seen as the brain's distinct, hierarchically organized structures and functions. Accordingly, the brain is often divided into the brain stem and the forebrain (telencephalon)

(Barlow and Durand 1995). The brain stem is composed of the medulla, the pons (midbrain), and the diencephalon. The cerebellum emerges as an out-growth from the medulla. At the top of the brain stem is the diencephalon, located just below the forebrain. The diencephalon is composed of the thalamus and the hypothalamus. At the base of the forebrain (crowning the diencephalon) is the limbic system, composed of the hippocampus, cingulate gyrus, septum, and amygdala. Also at the base is the basal ganglia. The cerebal cortex is the largest part of the forebrain and is composed of the parietal lobes, frontal lobes, corpus callosum, and temporal lobes (Barlow and Durand 1995). Throughout, the brain's operations are affected by the chemicals produced within the glands of the endocrine system: the adrenal gland (produces epinephrine), the thyroid gland (produces thyroxine), and the pituitary gland (produces estrogen and testosterone). The hypothalamus is involved in regulation of the endocrine system. Neurotransmitters such as serotonin and dopamine help constitute the brain's connective pathways, enabling the "transmission" of neural information. Autism brain research has particularly (but not exclusively) addressed the role of the cerebellum (in the brain stem), the hippocampus and amygdala (in the diencephalons), and the mediating impact of neurotransmitters.

Knowledge about the brain's anatomical structure and neural processes has been gained using a variety of techniques. The classical solution for knowing the brain involved pathology studies of deceased patients, an approach utilized in a limited number of autistic brains. However, pathology studies do not reveal *how* the brain works. Therefore, scientists have struggled to devise non-invasive tools for representing aspects of the living brain. In his overview of brain-imaging technologies, Uttal (2001) describes the electroencephalogram (EEG) as an early-twentieth-century innovation in representing electrical activity in the living brain. Although debate exists about what exactly is measured by the EEG, it can reliably detect tumors and lesions, or demonstrate gross brain abnormalities. More narrowly, EEG technologies have been used to try to correlate cognitive processes with the localization of electrical activity in the brain by addressing "evoked brain potentials" (EVBPs), although clear successes have been limited to establishing relations between "cortical activity and particular stimulus or behavior measures" (e.g. eye movements) (Uttal 2001: 56). Nowadays, efforts to represent the brain three-dimensionally include computer-aided tomography (CAT) scans. Tomography enables insight into the internal anatomical structures of the brain by mathematically representing it in a three-dimensional form from X-ray-derived images. Another contemporary technology is positron emission tomography, which entails introducing a radioactive substance into the body and using the energy emitted in its decay as the means for creating a three-dimensional image of the brain (Uttal 2001). PET scans enable insight into the brain's metabolism of particular substances, as well as blood flow into a particular brain region. This technology is particularly useful in providing a representation giving insight into brain processes, although it remains unclear whether the site of the greatest metabolic activity (as measured by the PET scan) is necessarily the site for the operation of a cognitive process. Another representational technique is magnetic resonance imaging, which uses both magnetism and radio frequencies, to make (computer-mediated) three-dimensional representations of scanned tissues based in the magnetic resonance of protons. Although MRI technology is "non-invasive" in that no substance is injected into the patient, the patient is required to lie motionless in a narrow tube *and is subject to very loud noise.* Application of MRIs to functional brain activation is called functional magnetic resonance imaging, which studies the activity of hemoglobin in response to oxygen demand (Uttal 2001). Changes in blood oxygen level are believed to be causally related to variations in neural activity at the respective site. A limitation of fMRI data is that considerable variation in subject response can be found across sessions thereby requiring multiple sessions be conducted to avoid erroneous conclusions (McGonigle et al. 2000). Also, the noise levels and physical restraints of the MRI scanners limit the kinds of stimuli that can be presented to experimental subjects and may affect patients' responses (Scott and Wise 2003).

Representing the autistic brain

Contemporary technologies for studying "autistic" brains involve a wide range of these technologies including pathology studies of brains of deceased autistic people and imaging technologies such as EEGs, PET, CAT, MRI, and fMRIs. Although the vast majority of people with autism do not display any overtly discernible brain abnormalities (Rapin 1998), the range and sophistication of these new technologies may reveal more subtle brain abnormalities in samples of autistic populations, although consistent brain markers of autism have yet to be revealed with the possible exception of increased overall brain size in autism (5 to 10 percent) (Schultz and Klin 2002). However, notwithstanding inconsistencies, post-mortem analysis and neural-imaging studies most frequently cite abnormalities in two areas of the brain. First, research using post-mortem analysis and neural-imaging technologies have detected abnormalities in the cerebellum, although findings are inconsistent across methodologies and across studies. Second, abnormalities of the limbic system, particularly in the area of the amygdala have been detected in select sample populations. In addition to these anatomically specific brain abnormalities, research has also addressed the role of neurotransmitters in the development of autism. I briefly address findings across these research foci.

Cognitive neuropsychologists who support the executive functions theory of autistic deficits (see Chapter 5) are particularly interested in pursuing research addressing the role of anatomical brain abnormalities of the cerebellum, which is involved in motor movement, learning, thought and attention (e.g. see Muratori et al. 2001). Accordingly, brain-imaging studies using MRI and PET scans on the cerebellum of autistic patients have produced a wide range of findings. At an anatomical level, increased total brain tissue volume has been found in the cerebellum of some autistic patients (Buitelaar and Willemsen-Swinkels 2000). One study found an inverse relationship between frontal lobe and cerebellum size in a sample of autistic patients, suggesting wider brain abnormalities may be present (Carper and Courchesne 2000). Although studies document an increase in total brain tissue in some populations, other studies have found a decrease in particular cells within the cerebellum of autistic patients including a decrease in the number of Purkinje cells and granule cells, cells vital to the operations of the cerebellum (Schultz and Klin 2002). Morphological abnormalities have also been found in the cerebellum, although similar abnormalities can be found in many persons with developmental disabilities and mental retardation (Schultz and Klin 2002). Studies using functional imaging technologies have revealed metabolic deficits in the cerebellum (Rumsey and Ernst 2000). In sum, the research studies to date suggest that a wide range of neural abnormalities may exist in the cerebellum and these abnormalities are hypothetically linked to the attention, orientation, adaptability, and sensory integration problems found in people with autism (Kern 2002).

The amygdala, within the limbic system, has also received considerable attention (Baron-Cohen et al. 2000). Cognitive neuropsychologists supporting the theory of mind account of autistic deficits are interested in the amygdala's role because of its purported involvement in emotionality and sociability. In particular, fMRI research suggests the amygdala may be involved in the brain's processes of facial recognition and interpretation (e.g., see Davidson and Slagter 2000; Howard et al. 2000). Accordingly, anatomical abnormalities have been found in the amygdala (e.g., Grady and Keightley 2002; Schultz and Klin 2002) and to a lesser extent in the hippocampus (although this is not yet clear), which is also situated in the limbic system (e.g., Brambilla et al. 2003; Saitoh et al. 2001). Some researchers speculate that these abnormalities may be related to the social deficits found in autistic people; fMRI has also discerned abnormalities in the activation of the amygdala in normal and autistic subjects presented with experimental stimuli (Baron-Cohen et al. 1999; Grady and Keightley 2002; Schultz et al. 2000). The amygdala theory of autism receives support from animal models (monkeys) of autism in which the animals' amygdalas were artificially lesioned (Schultz and Klin 2002). Other research on the role of the amygdala in autism takes a more systemic approach that looks at amygdala dysfunction in the context of broader anatomic connections and neural subsystems (Abu-Akel 2003; Bishop 1993). This more systemic orientation enables a more general discussion of the deficits in mentalizing and/or second-order representation typically associated with autism. In sum, the research points to injuries or problems in the anatomy or activation of the amygdala as playing a role in the "autistic" deficits associated with attending to and decoding others' emotional states.

Also under investigation within the limbic system is the cingulate gyrus. Cognitive researchers have been particularly interested in the role of gyrus in facial recognition and in the capacity to engage in joint attention. Decreased volume and diminished activation of the cingulated gyrus have been found in some populations using PET and structural MRI data (Haznedar et al. 2000). One fMRI study found that a sample of autistic people had unusual patterns (compared to a "normal" sample) of activation in the inferior temporal gyri and fusiform gyrus when engaged in tasks requiring facial recognition (Schultz et al. 2000). Another study suggested deficiencies in the dorsal media-frontal cortex and the anterior cingulate system may together affect the ability to initiate joint attention in infancy (Mundy 2003).

Much of the research on the brain discussed thus far focuses on localized, brain abnormalities primarily evidenced by morphometric anatomical defects in the cerebellum or limbic system. Additional research has targeted morphometric abnormalities in the corpus callosum (Brambilla et al. 2003). Additionally, as mentioned, some studies attempt to correlate observed or inferred anatomical abnormalities with unusual patterns of brain activation (e.g., as evidenced by oxygen consumption). Most of this research attempts to link specific cognitive deficits to special anatomical regions of the brain. Conceptual efforts to synthesize these disparate research findings suggest that "a disturbed neural network probably involving the temporo-parietal cortex, limbic system, cerebellum, prefrontal cortex, and corpus callosum appears to be involved in pathophysiology of autism" (Brambilla et al. 2003: 566).

Supplementing these studies is another line of research exploring how abnormal patterns of brain growth early in a child's development may be linked with and/or cause autism. For example, one such study on sixty autistic boys found that by ages two and three, 90 percent had larger than normal brain volumes, although all were born with normal head circumferences (Courchesne et al. 2001). It is believed that this abnormal brain growth occurs in the first year of life, although the reasons for this abnormal growth are unclear (Courchesne et al. 2003). Some studies point to abnormal brain enlargement in the occipital and parietal lobes (see Buitelaar and Willemsen-Swinkels 2000). However, adolescent subjects with autism do not evidence larger than normal brains (Courchesne et al. 2001). The implications from this finding are unclear although it is possible this rapid brain growth in early life may detrimentally affect the subsequent neural development of other brain centers—e.g., cerebellum and amygdala—discussed above (Cowley 2003). As explained by Courchesne in *Time* magazine, abnormal early growth of gray and white matter in the cerebral cortex may create a kind of signal overload for other areas of the brain, potentially injuring the Purkinje cells of the cerebellum and thereby catalyzing the development of autistic symptomatology (Nash and Bonesteel 2002). Courchesne and his associates are currently investigating specific genes that may play a role in regulating brain growth, particularly vasoactive intestinal peptide (VIP), which also plays a role in the immune system and gastrointestinal tract (Nash and Bonesteel 2002).

Also supplementing these approaches to studying the anatomy, activation, and growth of "autistic brains" are other studies primarily addressing the role of neurotransmitters in autism. I now turn to this research.

Since the 1950s it has been known that neurotransmitters such as serotonin and dopamine play a role in the development of some forms of mental disorder, particularly schizophrenia, obsessive-compulsive disorder, and chronic depression (Stone 1997). Accordingly autism researchers suggest specific neurotransmitters and neuropeptides may be responsible for the key core autistic deficits (communication deficits, social deficits, and restricted interests/obsessive behaviors: e.g. Hollander et al. 1998). For example, researchers hypothesize the restricted interests and obsessive behavior of autistic spectrum people result from serotonin dysregulation. Oxytocin dysregulation is seen as responsible for the social impairments, and dopamine dysregulation is seen as responsible for the speech and communication deficits (Hollander et al. 1998). However, although all of these neurotransmitters may play some role in autism, the research to date has primarily focused on the role of serotonin because an elevation of whole blood serotonin has been found in a significant percentage (30 percent) of sample populations of autistic people (Buitelaar and Willemsen-Swinkels 2000). Moreover, the relative success of the pharmaceutical serotonin reuptake inhibitors in ameliorating obsessive behaviors suggests that serotonin regulation may indeed play some role in the expression of autistic characteristics (McDougle et al. 2002).

Efforts to study the role of neurotransmitters in autism often make use of PET or fMRI technologies allowing researchers some insight into dynamic brain processes. For example, research using PET technology has found abnormalities in neurotransmitter functions—e.g., serotonergic and dopaminergic functions—in an autistic population (Rumsey and Ernst 2000). Another study found that patients with higher metabolic rates in the medial frontal region and anterior cingulate were more likely to respond to the neurotransmitter mediating drug, fluoxetine than were patients with lower metabolic rates (Buchsbaum et al. 2001). Because neurotransmitters are implicated in a wide range of mental illnesses, it is not surprising that they have been found to play a role in autism as well. The challenge is to explain how the variety of symptoms of mental illness traces back to specific chemical imbalances. This challenge of bridging mental symptoms and neurological states has not been met: as Valenstein (1998) explains in his polemic, *Blaming the Brain*, current knowledge about the operation and effects of neurotransmitters remains hypothetical and tentative at best.

Taken as a whole, the autism brain science discussed in this section thus far raises the possibility that sample populations of autistic people do exhibit abnormalities in the form and/or size of specific brain regions and that their patterns of brain activation/metabolism may differ measurably from the patterns exhibited by "normal" populations. However, although possibilities have been raised and tentative hypotheses generated, this research has failed to produce *conclusive findings across studies* (Cody et al. 2002). For example, Cody et al. (2002: 435) observed that in the case of the cerebellum most of the evidence does *not* establish that there are "significant differences in cerebellar size or brainstem structure when total brain size and/or IQ are taken into account." Efforts to reconcile conflicting findings by appealing to the idea of distinct autism phenotypes are sensible but lack conclusive empirical support at this point in time. The tendency for researchers to use small sample size in single-trial studies and the difficulty in establishing adequate controls also undermine the external validity (generalizability) of these studies, rendering conclusions *exploratory* (Cody et al. 2002). What follows offers some additional limitations of the search for the definitive nature of the "autistic brain."

Evaluating findings

Part of the difficulty in establishing conclusive findings from "brain science" stems from the general lack of understanding about the relationship between (1) complex cognitive functions/activities such as consciousness, learning, emotion, and sociability and (2) brain anatomy and functional processes (see Feinberg 2001; Uttal 2001). For example, one MRI study on autistic children found no significant correlation between (1) any dimension of the MRI images of the size of corpus callosum, amygdala, hippocampus, and nucleus caudatus and (2) systemic empirical observation of the children made using the Childhood Autism Rating Scale (CARS) observation scale (Hrdlicka et al. 2002). Thus, although technological progress suggests advances in our ability to *image* brain operations, these technologies raise new challenges for our abilities to make sense of these images. The images revealed by new technologies are not transparent representations of easily discernible processes. Rather, these images must be *interpreted* (Parker-Pope 2003).

A number of interpretive constraints face researchers using neuroimaging technologies. First, it is becoming increasingly clear that neuroscience's lexicon of distinct neural subsystems is a linguistic representation of a brain whose subsystems lack clear demarcation (Valenstein 1998). Consequently, the idea of discrete subsystems reflects the categories of theory/language more than it reflects the categories of the brain. Thus, although new imaging technologies suggest increased electrical or metabolic activity in certain brain regions in response to laboratory-invoked stimuli, this activity is difficult to interpret in terms of its significance and its relevance with respect to the *operation of the brain as a whole* (Uttal 2001).

The problem of interpretation produces the second challenge to our ability to know the brain. The data generated from contemporary representational technologies are not transparent and require a degree of attribution on the part of the people who "read" the results of the images—images which are partially constructed through computer modeling. As one commentator observes, analysis of the brain through neuroimaging technologies is challenged by a number of phenomena:

> Morphometric analysis of the human brain has proved to be challenging. Because the overall sizes and shapes of people's brains differ so much, researchers must employ complex computer algorithms to define normal values for various populations and compare the brains of individuals against these group norms. Moreover, the boundaries between brain structures may be very subtle.
>
> (Hyman 2003: 99)

Additionally, each individual's brain changes over time in response to developmental and environmental stimuli. The variety and plasticity of human brains makes establishing what is "normal" and what is "abnormal" difficult. This plasticity complicates researchers' ability to discern reliable phenotypic groupings because of the intrinsic variation within and across patterns of human cognition. For these reasons, the practice of "reading" the brain remains fraught with interpretive complexities.

The third challenge facing brain science concerns the linking of phenotypic expressions to biologically based causal agents. As Hyman (2003) points out, the utility of brain-imaging technologies depends in part on finding abnormalities that are exclusive and specific to a certain disease or symptom complex. However, the heterogeneity in the degree and content of symptoms, and the seemingly infinite number of causal pathways that can contribute to the production of these symptoms, complicates efforts to link symptoms to first causes in the study of autism, as will be discussed presently.

In essence, autism "brain science" suffers from our general lack of understanding about the relationship between brain structures/functions and human cognition and affect. Brain science cannot explain consciousness nor can it explain how complex mental operations such as language production occur. Moreover, it is very likely that a mechanistic and reductionistic formula will never explain these phenomena because they undoubtedly emerge from the synergistic operations of a holographic brain, a brain whose operations are always/already influenced by its environmental openness.

In sum, two facts fundamentally limit autism brain science: first, human brains are indelibly and uniquely marked/organized in relation to synergistic genetic, environmental, cultural, and individual effect, and second, complex cognitive operations no doubt emerge synergistically from a holographic brain. The materiality of these facts is expressed in the variety of degree and content of autistic symptoms. Consequently, the synergy and openness of the human brain will always bedevil the search for distinct autism phenotypes and genotypes. And yet, despite these limitations the number of studies using neuroimaging technologies to generate empirical support for their research hypotheses is growing. Further, these studies are increasingly appropriated and/or conjoined with studies attempting to address the genetic determinants of "observed" findings on the brain. I turn now to the genetic research on autism, beginning with a discussion of efforts to establish relationships across mental states, brain states and gene states.

Genetic analysis and the search for the autism genotype(s)

There are a number of ways to study the genetic origins of autism. Some approaches presume autism represents a unified genotype whereas other approaches suggest a variety of distinct genetic factors may influence development of the disorder. Some approaches to developing a distinct autistic genotype approach autism by studying the neurochemistry believed to cause its symptomatology and then attempt to identify the genes implicated in that neurochemistry. At times, this research attempts to make linkages across gene states, neurotransmitters (brain states), and patterns of brain activation, as represented by fMRI and PET technologies. Still other approaches skip the role of brain states and attempt to establish direct equivalences between autistic behaviors and chromosomal irregularities. Although beyond the scope of this project to tease out all of the nuances that occur within and across these research approaches, I will briefly describe:

- how genetic influences are inferred from "autistic" brain states
- how genetic influences are inferred from observation of chromosomal irregularities within and across samples of autistic populations.

Establishing equivalences: mental states, brain states and gene states

As explained in the section on autistic brains, some scientists believe that measurable neural-chemical influences cause the behaviors and mental states of autistic people. These scientists believe the discovery of distinct neural-chemical profiles of autistic people will lead to the discovery of the specific genes regulating these chemicals, which through their operations lead to autistic behaviors. This approach currently holds sway over research in mental diseases (e.g., schizophrenia, manic-depressive disorder, depression) and both the pharmaceutical industry and geneticists interested in the genes involved in the regulation of brain chemistry pursue it. Biogenic amines serving as neurotransmitters such as dopamine, serotonin, norepinephrine, and epinephrine have been particularly subject to clinical investigation because their role in mediating information across nerves has been implicated in a variety of important and basic physiological functions. However, while the operation of these neurotransmitters is clearly important to physiological and psychological well-being, a number of issues remain unclear, including the decisive role of genetics in influencing their operation and the relationship between neurotransmitters and mental states (Valenstein 1998). The hypothetical nature of posited relationships will be taken up presently but discussion begins with some examples of the research at issue.

A good example of research attempting to establish direct and linear relationships across gene alleles, brain chemistry, and mental states is found in a study on the role of a particular gene in mediating brain activation of the amygdala (Hariri et al. 2002). The gene (located on the promoter region of the serotonin transporter gene, SLC6A4) under investigation encodes a protein serving a transporter function affecting how neurons assimilate the neurotransmitter serotonin. In this study of twenty-eight people, subjects who had the short form of the gene allele were slightly more likely (3 to 4 percent) to show signs of anxiety or fearfulness on clinical personality tests *and* demonstrated more activity in their right amygdala (as measured by fMRI) when subject to images of frightened or angry people. However, the study's introductory report (Miller 2002) cautioned that the research does not prove that serotonin causes the difference in amygdala activation. A more significant implication is that the suspect gene allele's mere presence only correlated with (not explained) 3–4 percent of the variance in anxiety or fearfulness, leaving 96–97 percent of the variance unexplained. Moreover, chance alone could explain such a low correlation. However, given keen interest in the role of the amygdala in psychiatric disorders (Grady and Keightley 2002), research explaining its patterns of activation in terms of genetic forces will likely receive considerable attention even with tentative conclusions and sample populations too small to generalize to the population as a whole.

Another study illustrating the inferred relationship across mental states/behaviors, brain states, and gene states exists in a study of gene alleles implicated in serotonin transmission. The study "Association of autism severity with monoamine oxidase A functional polymorphism" addressed the relationship between MAOA-uVNTR (monoamine oxidase (MAOA), upstream variable-number tandem repeat region (uVNTR)) alleles and the phenotypic expression of autism in forty-one males diagnosed with the disorder (Cohen 2003). This study forgoes brain-imaging technology focusing instead on the correlation between (1) gene alleles and (2) intelligence and severity of autistic symptoms, as measured by the researchers. The researchers concluded the suspect allele may genetically modify the severity of autism in male populations, as expressed in intelligence. However, another study on the same gene alleles (Yirmiya et al. 2002) found contrasting findings, calling into question the complex interactions between MAOA alleles and other genes implicated in autism and mood disorders.

Moreover, neither study adequately controlled for the role of environmental factors in shaping the observed differences in the behavior and intelligence of the studies' subjects.

As illustrated here, the mediating impact of environmental factors presents a significant difficulty in establishing linear relationships across brain states and gene alleles. Since obstetric complications have been largely ruled out as the primary causal agent for autism (Buitelaar and Willemsen-Swinkels 2000),[2] teratogenic agents are the next most overt form of environmental influence affecting the developing embryo and fetus. Experimental research on animals supported the possibility that such environmental influences may lead to the expression of autistic symptoms. For example, one laboratory study on rats found the teratogens thalidomide and valproic acid directly affected hippocampal serotonin, frontal cortex dopamine, and hyperserotonemia, leading researchers to conclude these teratogens may affect the monoamine system development in the brain and blood, leading to cerebellar abnormalities. Since autistic populations evidence hyperserotonemia in clinical studies, the researchers inferred these teratogens might help explain the pathogenesis of autism (Narita et al. 2002). This type of research affirms the role of brain states in affecting mental and behavioral states but does so in a way that elides the decisive role of gene alleles by centering purely physical environmental influences.

The physical environment is but one important factor that mediates genetic influences. For example, recent research on heart disease finds that lifestyle, not genes, predicts most heart attacks (Sternberg 2003). Likewise, although genetics play a role in the development of Alzheimer's, the most significant predictors for development of the disease are level of education and mental activity across the lifetime (Healy 2003). And yet, the role of *social environments* in mediating/shaping the influence of genetic factors is almost completely elided, even when the researchers report significant variance in socio-economic levels of sample populations.

In sum, taken as a whole, the research exploring the genetics of "autistic" brains suggests the possibilities for establishing very partial correlations between the quantity and operation of neurotransmitters and particular gene alleles. However, a number of challenges remain. First, the relative impact of environmental influences versus genetic influences on brain states remains unclear, as does the possibility for their interdependence. Second, the role of systemic processes implicating multiple gene alleles in the operation of neurotransmitters remains largely unexplored. Third, the posited relationships between gene alleles that affect neurotransmitters and the characteristics of brain structures such as the cerebellum and amygdala are at this point largely if not entirely speculative. Fourth, the decisive role that neurotransmitters play (let alone their gene alleles) in affecting mental and behavioral states remains unclear.

In effect, efforts to establish mechanistic linkages across mental states, brain states, and (ultimately) gene states may be too simplistic. It may be impossible to trace neurological effects to distinct genes when perhaps one-half of all human genes are expressed in the brain (Marcus 2003). Moreover, genes operate synergistically and are always influenced by environmental forces. Environmental forces include the physiological environment of the organism (the role of the body), the physical environment, the cultural/social environment, and the mediating role of *mind*, or the individual's psychological experiences. Berntson and Cacioppo (2000: 9–10) explain that social relations and individual experience mediate physiological and immunological functions thus "comprehensive accounts of psychophysiological relations will likely require multiple analyses across distinct levels of functional organization." To support their position, Berntson and Cacioppo (2000) cite research showing that genotypic high-reactive monkeys become highly reactive themselves when raised by biological or surrogate mothers who are also highly reactive (e.g., high HPA reactivity to stress, aggressive, and maladaptive social behaviors) but become low-reactive when reared by low-reactive caregivers. Social influences trump genetic ones in the case of this example. Specifically, the authors observe that patterns of care modulate genetic actions shaping glucocorticoid binding in the hippocampus and cortex, affecting altered stress reactivity and social behavior in adulthood.

The difficulties inherent in linking brain chemistry with gene alleles is illustrated by a study in which scientists studied the relationship between manic depression and gene alleles of GRK3, a gene which influences the brain's receptivity to chemical messages (Ritter 2003). In this study, the researchers found only 3 percent of their sample population of manic depressives had the suspect allele, although they reported optimistically that they hoped to find more suspect alleles of GRK3. In addition, the researchers were unable to explain why some individuals with the suspect gene allele did not have manic depression. Thus, the ability to discern a relationship between a suspect gene allele and a small portion of a sample is only the first step in the complex and multifaceted project of linking mental state/characteristics, brain states, and gene alleles.

Given the difficulties in establishing correlations across mental states, brain states and gene states, what potential benefits warrant research in this area? The answer to this question rests in the potential pharmaceutical applications of artificially derived brain-altering chemicals, although the manner of their operation is also typically unclear. Specifically, pharmaceutical agents might be helpful in controlling target symptoms such as hyper-activity, aggression and self-injury, stereotypies and rigidity, and anxiety, although environmental and behavioral interventions may prove as productive in alleviating these symptoms (Buitelaar and Willemsen-Swinkels 2000). However, one review of autism published for pharmaceutical audiences pessimistically concluded: "Over recent decades, unfortunately, little progress has been made in developing new and effective pharmacotherapies for autism" (Buitelaar and Willemsen-Swinkels 2000: 78). In sum, it appears that while efforts to correlate mental states with brain states may someday contribute to pharmaceutical innovations that help ameliorate symptoms, these efforts are unlikely to alone explain the origin of or predict the development of these symptoms.

Genomic analysis and identification of the autism genotype

The second approach to studying the genetics of autism skips the role of brain states in its efforts to identify the distinct chromosomal irregularities and/or gene alleles that may engender the disorder. Genetic influences could affect the development of autism in a number of ways:

- Genes could encode harmful mutations such as those responsible for single-gene disorders.
- Genetic dynamics, across and between gene alleles, could trigger the disorder.
- Specific gene alleles could create susceptibilities to environmental influences that ultimately create a cascade of effects that cause the disorder.

(Nash and Bonesteel 2002)

Although genetic research often seems the most promising direction for unraveling the ultimate cause or causes of autism, it is in fact fraught with complications for the following reasons:

1   Autism encompasses a complex genetic predisposition, and does not seem to be inherited as a single gene disorder.
2   There are probably several disease genes involved in autism, resulting in separate genetic disorders in different individuals with similar behavioral phenotypes.
3   The autism behavioral phenotype is complex and might increase the probability that different disorders are being included in the same genetic study.

(Monaco and Bailey 2001: 358)

Given these complicating factors, efforts to identify autism susceptibility genes by selecting candidate genes then testing them genetically in populations with autism face insurmountable challenges, particularly because "most genes expressed in the developing brain become candidates" (Monaco and Bailey 2001: 358).

Therefore, this forces the search for autism susceptibility genes to take a different approach, an approach more open in its search for possible genetic influences. This alternate approach studies large collections of families in which more than one child has autism. Autistic siblings are compared at intervals along each chromosome for similarities or differences using genetic markers. The logic for this comparison holds that chromosomal regions that contain autism susceptibility genes should possess more similarities in affected (autistic) siblings. Using genetic imaging technology, researchers scrutinize the chromosomal regions for inversions or other malformations, as compared to "normal" chromosomes. Research using this approach has identified chromosomal regions 2q, 7q, 16q, as suspect regions for autism susceptibility gene errors or alleles (Monaco and Bailey 2001). Regions on the X chromosome and on chromosomes 2, 3, 15, 19, and 22 have also been implicated as playing a role in the development of the disorder in some autistic individuals ("Another chromosome defect implicated" 1998; Ozand et al. 2003; Shao et al. 2002; Travis 2003). Researchers must now screen regionally defined candidate genes one-by-one to find mutations or variations that could function to alter the encoding of proteins by each gene. Such research has narrowly targeted areas such as 7q32.3–q33 as susceptibility regions (Beyer et al. 2001). Findings pertaining to chromosome 7 excite researchers because that chromosome has also been implicated in other communication/language disorders.

However, problems arise when researchers fail to replicate findings across autistic populations and when family members of autistic people exhibit chromosomal variations yet do not suffer from autism. As Monaco and Bailey (2001) acknowledge in their review of autism and genetics:

> some studies fail to replicate any of these regions, and instead implicate new regions that no other study has seen. This is most likely due to heterogeneity of autism predisposing genes and the complex autistic behavioral phenotypes as well as the relatively small sample sizes of most studies.
>
> (Monaco and Bailey 2001: 358)

Moreover, researchers' efforts to study the encoding of proteins by targeted susceptibility genes are constrained by the mechanistic limitations of their simulations which cannot predict and/or model the range of possible protein encodings that occur in living, developing organisms exposed to an infinite range of environmental influences. Recent research pointing to the role of RNA encoding in the development of autism in one family further expands the range of potential genetic processes that may contribute to the expression of autism symptoms (Graf et al. 2000). Moreover, etiological accounts targeting genes involved in the immune system presuppose that autism emerges from a complex cascade of genetic and environmental events precluding mechanistic, closed representational techniques. The fact that genetic factors do not seem to cause autism in uniform, direct, and predictable ways poses a real problem for the development of drug therapy as illustrated by Monaco and Bailey's observation:

To develop drug therapy, the primary information required is the type of protein encoded by the autism susceptibility gene (ie, is it a good drug target), the expression pattern of the gene during development, and the biological pathway in which it is involved (ie, does it interact with other proteins and are any of those good drug targets).

(Monaco and Bailey 2001: 358)

Identifying the type of proteins encoded by the target gene(s) and the expression patterns of the gene(s) during development, let alone the biological pathways involved (and their susceptibilities to environmental influences) present significant challenges.

Perhaps one of the greatest successes in identifying a distinct gene associated with autism can be found in Dr. Patricia Rodier's (2000) work on mice genetically engineered so that the gene HOXA1 was "knocked-out" of operation. This gene resides on chromosome 7 (7p.15–p14.2) and is highly conserved in evolution, meaning that the sequence of nucleotides constituting its DNA have remained relatively constant over evolution. HOXA1 is active only in very early development and affects the development of the brain stem through production of a protein modulating the activity of other genes. It is believed the invariant operation of HOXA1 is critical because scientists have failed to identify any variant allele of HOXA1 in any mammalian species. However, by focusing on the protein coding regions of HOXA1, Rodier discovered two variant alleles of HOXA1 present in the blood of autistic people, leading to the conclusion that these gene alleles are likely autism susceptibility genes. Focusing on one of the alleles, Rodier found that 40 percent of her sample with autism also had the allele. Disappointingly, her research also revealed that the presence of the allele does not in itself predict autism because in her population about 20 percent of the people with the allele do *not* have autism. Rodier speculates the involvement of multiple gene alleles in the development of the disorder and suggests that some gene alleles may actually help prevent development of the disorder. Further, she concludes that future work must focus on exploring the relationship between targeted autism susceptibility genes and environmental influences that may catalyze or affect the development of the disorder. This additional research is clearly needed as the most recent research summary of the role of HOXA1 suggests that 99.5 percent of the people who have the variant allele do not acquire the disorder and about 60 percent of people with autism do not have the variant allele (Hyman 2003).

Rodier's work and the work of other geneticists reaffirm that genetics plays some kind of role in the development of autism and other related disorders. However, this research also establishes that the model of the gene presuming its efficacy in a mechanistic fashion must be replaced by an open-systems model which recognizes the synergistic effects of genes in relation to environmental influences. The fact that chimpanzees share

98.7 percent of their DNA with humans demonstrates the synergy of genes and suggests it is the complex and unique interactions of genes that enables species differentiation rather than the number or form of the genes themselves. Thus, although research may identify gene alleles or defects correlating with autism in specific populations the presence or absence of these specificities alone is unlikely to predict or explain the development of autism at the level of populations or predict whether or not a specific individual with a suspect gene allele will develop autism.

Frustration over an inability to find consistent chromosomal markers across autistic populations has led many researchers to suggest the search for autism's origins must acknowledge that autism is genetically heterogeneous in origin. Thus, it appears autism may not constitute a distinct disease; rather, it may be more productive to approach autism as a continuum of symptoms reflecting variable biomedical conditions involving a variety of genetic susceptibility factors. The next section explores the question of reliably grouping individuals based on susceptibility.

Autism and susceptibility: co-morbid disorders and environmental influences

As discussed above, the list for suspect gene alleles implicated in autism seems to grow monthly, leaving researchers befuddled about how to make sense of inconsistent research findings. One way of making sense of inconsistent findings is to accept that autism represents distinct genotypes such that autistic individuals can be reliably (sub)grouped according to their genetic profiles. If one accepts this hypothesis, then genomic analysis alone may ultimately reveal distinct autistic populations. And yet, the sheer number of contradictory findings generated to date suggests this strategy may not prove heuristic. However, another way of making sense of the inconsistent genetic findings entails a kind of gestalt switch in which autism is understood as a common final pathway for the expression of a variety of biological cataclysms. Framed within this hypothesis, searching for autistic genotypes may be misdirected because it focuses too exclusively on products—suspect gene alleles—rather than *processes* involving complex and synergistic relations across biological levels. This latter approach, which often rejects the idea of a distinct and generalizable autism genotype, was influenced by research on the co-morbid conditions found within specific populations of people diagnosed with autism.

Autistic populations contain a wide range of relatively easily detectable co-morbid conditions, although the majority of people with autism lack these co-morbid conditions. For example, Fragile X syndrome often is accompanied by the expression of autistic symptoms as are single-gene disorders such as tuberous sclerosis and neurofibromatosis (Lauritsen and Ewald 2001). Co-morbid disorders of the central nervous system account for approximately 10–15 percent of documented autism cases (Szatmari

2003). Although most people diagnosed with autism lack these disorders, the range of possibly autism-related medical disorders (PARMD: Gillberg and Coleman 1996) is much broader and includes disorders of the brain such as hydrocephalus and other known chromosomal disorders such as Angelman's syndrome and sometimes Down's syndrome (Rapin 1998).

Although the existence of clear co-morbid conditions in a minority of autism cases actually reinforces the possibility of identifying at least a few distinct autism genotypes, the majority of conditions cited as potential co-morbid conditions suggest that the development of autistic symptoms may be caused by a complex set of interactions across environmental and genetic factors. For example, autism has been found in untreated phenylketonuria (PKU), a disorder entailing a complex relationship between genetic susceptibility and an environmental influence (Rapin 1998). Additionally, congenital infections with the rubella virus and temporal lobe injury due to herpes simplex encephalitis or tumors have also been associated with autistic behavior (Rapin 1998). Finally, a whole range of traumatic, metabolic, and infectious encephalopathies have been associated with autistic symptoms (Rapin 1998).

Accordingly, the range of possible medical disorders associated with autism leads many researchers to believe the genetic transmission of the disorder operates by engendering biological susceptibilities. That is, this explanation suggests genetics do not cause autism but that they create the conditions of possibility for a person's susceptibility to other agents, which would trigger a synergistic cataclysm expressed in the autistic deficits of communication, sociality, and restricted interests. Although explanations stressing both genetic and environmental forces are gaining currency, they tend to raise more questions than they resolve. What agents play a role in the development of the disorder? Why do some children with biological susceptibilities develop mental retardation while others display autistic symptoms? Moreover, the list of possible biological, environmental, and psychological factors possibly contributing to both autism and mental retardation in genetically susceptible individuals appears endless and, consequently, creates considerable public debate and social anxiety. This more systemic approach also dashes hopes for understanding autism in terms of a distinct genotype or genotypes (although some researchers still persevere with the idea of autistic genotype subgroups) and it suggests preventing and curing autism by biological means may pose more significant difficulties than preventing and curing disorders such as heart disease and cancer that also entail both genetic and environmental contributions because, in the case of the latter, the symptoms can be traced to more definitive biological operations.

However, although this more systemic approach to understanding autism precludes easy answers, it leaves open the possibility that biologically oriented therapeutic strategies may significantly improve the physical and psychological health of people diagnosed with autism. That is, if autistic symptoms are seen as rooted in a complex of factors—of which genetic susceptibility plays a mediating but not exclusive role—then the possibility exists that biological interventions aimed at ameliorating specific dysfunctions may significantly decrease autistic symptoms. This more optimistic orientation runs counter to many of the approaches described in this chapter because the latter typically see autistic symptoms as rooted in relatively *irreparable* genetic or brain defects. The pessimistic approach viewing autism as an irreparable condition is particularly prevalent in clinical approaches to its diagnosis and treatment. As observed by McCandless (2003), the prevailing medical protocols for treating autism are based on the belief that autistic symptoms are "simply behavioral conditions caused by incurable genetic defects" (McCandless 2003: 5). In contrast to this pessimistic formulation, the systemic approach described below offers parents and patients hope for the possibility of ameliorating symptoms or, perhaps, of intervening in the cataclysm of events causing the development of symptoms. Unfortunately, it also creates the possibility for exploitation as some unscrupulous businesses and individuals prey on the hopes of the parents of autistic children, parents desperate to "unlock" the "soul" of their "imprisoned" child. As one physician observed in personal conversation, "autism has become an industry."

Scientists, clinicians, and parents who have pursued this alternative approach to studying autism (using a formulation articulating autism as a heterogeneous condition brought upon by a cataclysm of genetic and/or constitutional susceptibilities and environmental influences) have targeted a variety of environmental factors possibly contributing to the development of autistic symptoms. These environmental factors include but are not limited to viral agents, vaccinations, dietary allergies, and industrial pollutants. Each of these factors will be briefly discussed.

Autism and the immune system

Careful analysis of the immune panels of autistic children suggests that many of these children suffer from altered immune parameters (van Gent et al. 1997; Warren 1998), atypical infections and shifted cell counts (e.g., Binstock 2001). Some researchers believe that susceptible children develop autism due to a faulty immune system that increases their vulnerability to environmental pathogens, particularly viral or bacterial agents (Comi et al. 1999; Warren 1998). One hypothesis suggests a decreased T-cell-mediated immunity could enable an environmental pathogen to directly affect the developing brain (Warren 1998). Another hypothesis suggests an environmental pathogen might trigger an autoimmune mechanism adversely affecting brain functioning (Warren 1998), particularly by affecting a central nervous system protein known as the myelin basic protein (McCandless 2003). A final hypothesis suggests that while in utero, an aberrant immune response by the mother could harm the fetus and/or expose the fetus to a pathogen (Warren 1998). Identifying likely pathogenic agents is an important research focus in this area. For example, the presence of atypical infections and shifted cell counts in autistic populations led Binstock (2001) to hypothesize that the development of autism among several autistic subgroups may be explained by "intra-monocyte pathogens such as measles virus, cytomegalovirus, human herpes virus 6, and Yersinia enterocolitica." Other research pointing more generally to the role of maternal infection in affecting fetal brain development and mental illness give indirect support to the possibility that viral agents may contribute to the development of autism (Patterson 2002).

Although a variety of mechanisms can trigger immunological disorders, the recent interest in the genetic causes of diseases has contributed to efforts to explain which gene alleles (mostly located on chromosome 6) might be implicated in the development of faulty or susceptible immune systems (see Warren 1998). However, when using genetic explanations in this fashion, the model employed is fundamentally systemic in that the genetic susceptibility alone is not seen as the sole source of autistic symptoms. Researchers must also identify the kinds of biological/environmental "insults" contributing to the development of the disorder. The list of potential insults that may affect the immune system (and concomitantly the metabolic and nervous system) of susceptible individuals is potentially endless but the autism research has focused on viral agents (as illustrated above), vaccinations, exposure to toxic metals, and dietary allergies.

Autism and vaccinations

The role of vaccinations in catalyzing autism in genetically susceptible individuals has received particular attention because vaccinations may introduce a variety of "insults" including suspect viral agents or combinations of agents and toxic metals. Accordingly, critics of vaccinations make a number of arguments about how the vaccines might contribute to autism in susceptible individuals. These arguments include claims that:

- The use of thimerosal mercury in childhood vaccinations (since the 1930s) causes autism in individuals whose bodies lack the ability to process heavy metals effectively (e.g. Fehr-Snyder 2001; Geier and Geier 2003a, 2003b).
- The quantity and frequency of exposure to viral agents through vaccinations overwhelms the fragile immune systems of susceptible individuals.
- The particular viral combinations found in the combined Diphtheria, Tetanus and Pertussis (DTP) vaccination and/or Measles, Mumps and Rubella (MMR) vaccination are particularly damaging to children with fragile immune systems (e.g. Wakefield et al. 1998).

Navigating the terrain of studies supporting or disputing these claims presents a difficult task that tends to lead the reader to wonder whether in fact anything at all has been proven. Claims such as that made by the British Public Health Laboratory in 2003 that the MMR vaccination does not overwhelm the immune system of children (McNeil 2003) invariably engender more research questioning such studies' methodology, population, conclusions, or external validity. Moreover, efforts to establish conclusively definitive links between vaccinations and autism present complications because the underlying models presume biological susceptibilities that leave open the possibility for other environmental agents to contribute to the cascade of "insults" ultimately leading to the expression of autistic symptoms.

Autism and heavy metals

Concerns about the potential role of heavy metals in catalyzing autism in genetically susceptible individuals led to the removal of thimerosal mercury from most vaccinations by the year 2000. This move seems essential given the similarity between autistic symptoms and the symptoms of children subject to mercury poisoning (see Bernard et al. 2001). However, although most vaccinations no longer contain thimerosal mercury, methyl mercury is commonly found in many forms of fish, including tuna fish particularly (Shute 2003). Moreover, other suspect metals such as zinc, copper, and lead also pervade the environment and may potentially contribute to the development of autism in susceptible individuals by adversely affecting their immune and/or central nervous systems. The *Autism Research Review International* reported on one study which tested thirty-seven children (twenty-four with autism, five with Asperger's, and eight controls with no disabilities) for toxic heavy metals and found all of the autistic children possessed elevated levels of antimony, 50 percent had elevated lead levels, and 54 percent had elevated aluminum levels ("High heavy metal levels seen in autistic children" 2002). The levels of heavy metals found in the children with Asperger's syndrome were lower than those with classical autism but higher than control subjects with no disorder. Some researchers speculate vitamins, such as B6 and B1, can lessen expression of autistic symptoms by enabling removal of heavy metals from susceptible individuals ("Thiamine benefits autistic children" 2002).

Autism and the metabolic system

Another agent that researchers view as playing a role in the development of autism in some populations is dietary allergies (e.g. see Shaw 1998). The discovery of abnormal urinary peptide patterns in some autistic children led researchers to conclude dietary allergies to casein (a milk protein) and gluten (a wheat protein) might affect development of autistic symptoms. This framework views autism as a metabolic disorder akin to PKU, in which genetic susceptibilities combine with environmental influences to catalyze the disorder. Sometimes, researchers speculate the particular combination of viruses found in the MMR vaccination might also play a role in engendering the metabolic disturbances ultimately resulting in the expression of autism. Efforts to establish gluten, casein-free diets in targeted autistic populations suggest dietary interventions may help reduce expressions of autistic symptoms (Knivsberg et al. 2002); however, these studies often rely on very small sample sizes and are difficult to control for, leaving the success of this intervention strategy unclear.

Autism and other environmental insults

Other environmental agents may also play a role in affecting the development of the disorder in susceptible individuals (see Ozand et al. 2003). Research linking exposure to thalidomide in utero with autism established the precedent for the role of environmental agents contributing to the disorder (Rodier 2000). The possibility of environmental pollutants playing a role in rising rates of autism and PDD seems very likely given vast arrays of environmental pollutants that are routinely released into the environment. In 1998, US companies reported to the federal government that they had released more than one billion pounds of developmental and neurological toxins into the nation's water and air that year alone (Knight 2000). This formal figure is most likely under-reported and does not include release of commonly used neuro-toxic pesticides. The number of industrial products and pesticides associated with developmental problems in children and animals seems to rise daily, as illustrated by the following evidence:

- The chemical PFOA used in Teflon and Goretex, which is found in Americans' blood levels, has been proven to cause developmental problems in rats, and may cause problems in people as well (Borenstein 2003).
- Dursban, the formerly most commonly used household pesticide, has been linked to developmental delays in children. Even low doses of Dursban in pregnancy and early infancy can decrease the manufacture of DNA and negatively reduce the number of particular brain cells, possibly influencing learning and behavior later in life (Eskenazi et al. 1999). It is believed that approximately 10 percent of the population appears to be particularly sensitive to chronic effects from Dursban poisoning (Toxic Chemicals and Health: www.nrdc.org/health/pesticides/bdursban.asp 10/16/2003). Although now banned, Dursban residue still exists widely.
- Organophosphate insecticides, of which Dursban is one, continue to be used widely in US households and one study found that more Rett's syndrome was observed among the children of men who worked in organophosphate industry (Ozand et al. 2003).

- Organic solvents used in the semiconductor industry are known to cause birth defects, although the direct implications for autism are yet unclear (Herbert 2003).
- Toluene, a solvent used in printing facilities, is released in large quantities into the environment, often near urban areas. It is known to cause birth defects including physical abnormalities and cognitive, speech, and motor deficits. In 1998, more than 98 million pounds were released (Knight 2000).
- Air pollution is increasingly linked to birth defects and developmental disorders (Ozand et al. 2003; Vanscoy 2004).

These chemicals represent a small sample of a wide variety of common environmental pollutants that no doubt contribute to neurological and/or immunological problems in susceptible individuals. The possibility that environmental pollutants might contribute to the rise of autism diagnoses has been raised, but tends to be marginalized in research and press accounts capitalizing on genetic influences and the possibility of links to vaccinations. It seems ironic that we scrutinize genetic susceptibility genes more carefully than the myriad environmental pollutants that are ultimately the agents catalyzing neurological injuries in "susceptible individuals." Because environmental pollutants are subject to more direct forms of intervention than gene alleles, the relative lack of research attention to the former is perplexing.

Contemporary practices of toxic waste disposal present researchers a number of opportunities for studying the correlation between the introduction of toxic waste and changes in rates of developmental delays. For example, in the early 1990s, areas in rural China were selected as final resting places for computer and electronic waste because the toxicity of their components prevented disposal in US waste sites ("China villages," 2002). Nowadays, poor Chinese villagers comb through high-tech waste searching for recyclable items thereby exposing themselves to high levels of dangerous chemicals. One villager observed that: "We're worried about our children, sure, but what can I do? This is our livelihood" ("China villages" 2002: A12). Research on whether initial introduction of toxic waste leads to higher incidents of autism could be conducted in situations such as those described here. Within the United States, IBM workers exposed to ethylene glycol ethers (EGE) while making computer chips are now suing the company due to birth defects in their children (Herbert 2003). While unclear whether these birth defects include autism, research on this possibility should be conducted. Finally, it is known that the use of depleted uranium by US and British forces during the 1991 Iraqi war caused terrible birth defects in south Iraq over the subsequent ten years (Kershaw 2001; Schneider 2001). Research on depleted uranium's effects should be expanded to include increased rates of developmental disabilities in children in the region, particularly because low concentrations of uranium are now found in the blood of most western people as well. These examples are designed to highlight the potential role of dangerous chemicals—chemicals that are increasingly ubiquitous in our environment—in causing marked developmental delays and neurological abnormalities in individuals who are "susceptible" due to a wide range of biological and/or genetic vulnerabilities (see WHO http://www.who.int/entity/water_sanitation_health/hygiene/settings/en/ChildrenNM4.pdf).

I believe that the role of industrial pollutants in affecting developmental disorders remains largely unpublicized because it lacks "sex appeal" nor is research on this subject likely to generate large research grants. Although it is unlikely that such pollutants cause developmental delays and/or autistic symptoms in direct and linear ways, it does seem very probable these pollutants may partially explain the etiology of autism in at least some populations.

Concluding thoughts on the search for causal agents

This chapter offered a critical appraisal of the search for the causal agents involved in the development of autism. The research studies reviewed in this chapter suggest the presence of autistic symptoms in specific populations may correlate with a variety of neural abnormalities, genetic alleles, and immunological/metabolic abnormalities. However, the contemporary state of the research cannot provide any definitive, conclusive, and generalizable answers to the question of how autism emerges. As stated from the outset, this chapter's thesis is that no such answers will be forthcoming so long as scientists continue to employ mechanistic and reductionistic models representing autism as a distinct disorder(s) explained and predicted exclusively in terms of very specific causal agents, whether neurological, genetic, or physiological.

From the perspective adopted in this chapter, it is a mistake to presume that autistic cognitive and behavioral symptoms are mere epiphenomena of underlying biogenetic states. Yet, this argument does not preclude the role of biogenetic phenomena in affecting autism. Rather, the argument made here suggests the expression of autistic symptomatology emerges in response to a complex set of interactions within and across genetic, neural, cognitive and social/physical environments. In order to demonstrate the logic of the argument developed in this chapter, I turn briefly to a discussion of the difference between nested and non-nested hierarchies, as this discussion applies to an understanding of the relationship between autistic symptoms and the brain.

The simplest but most pervasive metaphor for the brain's organization and functions implies that the brain is a "non-nested hierarchy" in which higher-order neural subsystems (e.g., the cerebellum) control lower-level neural subsystems (Feinberg 2001: 128). However, a more productive metaphor for the brain entails viewing its subsystems in terms of a "nested hierarchy" in which controls and constraints are embodied within the entire system rather than in specialized subsystems (128). When viewing the brain as a nested hierarchy, every mental operation (e.g., a perception) involves some degree of neural convergence by the whole brain. This nested-hierarchy approach to neural operations does not preclude the possibility for some neural-specialization but it does suggest most mental operations—particularly those involved in perception, language processing and production, and sociality—involve very complex neural operations that cannot be reliably represented (across time/populations) in terms of isolated and specialized neural operations. Moreover, a non-nested approach to the brain recognizes that a wide range of biological and social environments within which the organism is situated influence neural development at a fundamental level. The idea of neural "plasticity" encompasses this idea that the brain's development is fundamentally inscribed by environmental experiences.

What implications for autism research stem from this nested-hierarchy approach to neural operations? If the brain is understood in this fashion, it follows that a wide range of neural variations (both anatomical and metabolic) and/or patterns of neural growth may affect the overall operation of neural subsystems. It also follows that pinpointing a determinate and singular "source" of brain variation or dysfunction presents significant difficulties because the holographic and systemic properties of the brain's operations may preclude simple reductionism.[3] Thus, while it may be the case that the amygdala and the cerebellum are implicated in the expression of autistic symptoms, it would be a mistake to presume the source or "first cause" of autism can be located in a specific defect in these areas of the brain. Likewise, it would be a mistake to presume that "autistic" behaviors or "cognitive styles" can be reduced to—that is, explained exclusively in relation to—specific neural abnormalities. Accordingly, the mere correlation between a suspect neural center and the diagnoses of autism does not mean the observed brain variation exclusively "causes" the symptoms grouped under the label of autism. Finally, it would be a mistake to ignore the complex interactions occurring across neurological and social environments. Although it is known the brain is an open system whose form and operations are fundamentally affected by social phenomena, the role of experience in shaping neurological development in autism seems largely absent from the current literature on autism brain science, wherein mind is mere epiphenomena of brain.

This analysis using the metaphor of a nested hierarchy could apply to a discussion of the genetic origins of autism. As Keller (2000: 136) observes, the metaphor of genes "as clear and distinct causal agents, constituting the basis of all aspects of organismic life" has become deeply embedded in popular and scientific thought although its reductionistic and mechanistic premises stand exposed as inaccuracies. The ubiquity of this way of thinking has contributed to the search for key genetic "defects" believed to "cause" autism in direct and measurable ways akin to the direct operations of the non-nested hierarchies described by Feinberg (2001). And yet, although genetic factors likely play a role in affecting the development of autism, it is a mistake to presume gene alleles directly cause autistic symptoms in mechanistic and measurable ways. Systemic processes whose operations are fundamentally synergistic and open in character always influence genetic processes.

Environmental pollutants that alter DNA production, potentially injuring neurological systems, demonstrate the openness of biological systems to environmental effects most profoundly. Thus, framed from a systemic perspective, the idea that gene alleles (i.e., susceptibility genes) exclusively *cause* autism ceases to make sense. Rather than attempting to explain the etiology of autism *exclusively* in terms of susceptibility genes, researchers would be advised to address the complex interactions across genes and specific environmental agents. For example, recent research pointing to abnormal processes of brain development in some cases of autism would be advised to explore how complex interactions across DNA, RNA, and various environmental phenomena might together catalyze dysfunctions in the regulation of the growth of the brain's white and gray matter.

Furthermore, the role of environmental influences in shaping the expression of "autism"—even in "genetically" susceptible individuals—should broaden to encompass psychological and social phenomena. Thus, the expression of autistic behaviors—which researchers struggle to encompass in autistic phenotypes—should *not* be reductionistically explained in terms of autistic genotypes. Put otherwise:

> The development and expression of *mind* through cognition and behavior should not be reduced exclusively to biological explanations.

The person with autism is a being who has *mind* or consciousness and was thrown into a social and physical environment calling upon him or her to comport self in particular ways. This person may struggle to understand his/her environment—may have difficulty organizing his/her perceptions and responding to others' expectations—and yet this person stands as more than the sum of his or her genetic/neurological/physiological "defects." The term "autism" in fact misleads in this regard because through its etymology it presupposes that someone with autism exists locked in a solipsistic universe when, in reality, they are *not*. The social world imbues their being—their consciousness and bodily comportment—even while its order and significance may at times elude. In this context, autistic symptomatology should be understood as an expression of this lack of fit between the autistic individual's embodiment and their world.

Thus, infants born with biological deficits/injuries/variations affecting their ability to coordinate and regulate their attention and social interactions are prone to behaviors and personality characteristics deemed "strange" and "abnormal." Yet, even while struggling to make sense of a social world that others seem to intuit effortlessly, infants with such deficits are not immune to the influences of their environment nor are they passive beings fully determined by their genes or neurological deficits. Indeed, the research strongly supports the role of caregivers in predicting outcomes for children with autism. For instance, caregivers' efforts to communicate with their autistic children help predict the subsequent development of their children's social abilities, which are inexplicably linked with cognitive skills as well (Siller and Sigman 2002). Accordingly, a non-nested approach to studying autism would emphasize the role of social environments in relation to biological ones, eschewing explanations reducing mind to brain.

Hobson and Bishop (2003) provide an example of this kind of non-nested approach to explaining development of autism. Accordingly, they hypothesize the causes of autism lay less "in the child" and more in the "dysfunction of the system constituted by child-in-relation-to-other" (335). Based on the observation that congenitally blind children exhibit many "autistic-like" symptoms, Hobson and Bishop (2003) remain open to the possibility that a wide range of biological phenomena may contribute to autism's development. But rather than reducing behavioral and cognitive deficits to biological phenomena, their model suggests the expression of autism stems from a failure to make the social contacts necessary for "normal" development to occur. If one cedes the possibility that social contact may itself affect brain development, then the possibility arises that there are no definitive causes for autism or, conversely, there are an infinite number of potential causes for autism.

In conclusion, this chapter encourages a gestalt switch entailing foregrounding, rather than backgrounding, dynamic interactions across biological, physical, and social environments.[4] Framed from this perspective, the individual with autism must be nested (non-hierarchically) within the broader ecological and social subsystems within which he or she is born. Thus, this chapter urges researchers to avoid the reductionism critiqued in this chapter such that:

- Mental states and behaviors should not be reduced to brain states.
- Mental states and behaviors should not be reduced to gene states.
- Brain states should not be reduced to gene states.
- People with autism should not be reduced to a bundle of defective biological and genetic states.

Readers might take issue with this chapter's critical stance and the alternative metaphor offered. Readers might question the value this approach holds for the practical prevention and/or treatment of autism. I now offer several thoughts in response to these questions.

First, this chapter does not argue biogenetic research lacks value. To the contrary, biogenetic research may someday lead to treatment regimes that help prevent or ameliorate the effects of biogenetic susceptibilities. The problems this chapter posed for the success of such developments stemmed from the mechanistic and reductionistic models often employed in the service of such goals.

The search for the specific gene defects or gene alleles implicated in autism will not alone prevent autism from developing, particularly because the presence of suspect alleles does not in itself predict the development of the disorder. Family members of autistic individuals may have the suspect alleles but remain spared from the disorder. Thus, efforts to identify the role of genetics in autism must adopt systemic models emphasizing complex interactions across biological environments. Such models may ultimately reveal that the development of autism in utero or early in the infant's development is at some level fundamentally random. At best, such models may identify particular genetic synergies and/or environmental catalysts contributing to the development of the disorder in genetically susceptible individuals. Such knowledge may lead to treatments attempting to ameliorate or counter the effects of such synergies (e.g., impinge against abnormal brain growth) and/or could finally encourage corporate accountability for the production of environmental pollutants adversely affecting developing beings. But this knowledge will not enable researchers to explain autism as a disease caused definitively and exclusively by specific genetic errors.

Similar comments can be made about the search for the specific neurological deficits that cause autism. In one sense, the search for the "neurological causes" of autism holds a more pessimistic prognosis than the search for the genetic causes of autism. Research seeking to localize the source of autism in specific brain defects suggests that autistic symptoms are mere epiphenomena of irreversible neural abnormalities. Such research ignores the role of biographical and cultural environments in shaping the brain and it ignores the now established fact that older brains continue to grow (Boyd 2000). Further, the brain's "plasticity"—its openness to environmental influences and its regenerative capacities—should be stressed and studied in autism research because this plasticity opens many venues for intervention.

The ghost of the refrigerator mother has, I believe, stymied research into one of the greatest sources of hope today for ameliorating the problematic symptoms and communication barriers associated with a diagnosis of autism.[5] Yet, what little research exists suggests strongly that therapy-based early intervention dramatically improves outcomes for autistic children ("More proof" 2003). These interventions undoubtedly affect the brain by helping the "autistic" child coordinate his/her attention to the shared social world that provides the standards for socially recognized expressions of personhood. Thus, while the biogenetic approaches to studying the causes of autism may capture the imagination of the public and corporate interests, it is the hands-on therapeutic interventions of parents, teachers and therapists that may offer the greatest hope (at least for the foreseeable future) for helping treat and prevent the most troubling expression of autistic symptoms.

In conclusion, it is important to remember that autism is a *developmental* disorder that is fundamentally affected by both physiological and social systems. Autism is not a thing unto itself and it is not a disease with specific biological markers. Autism is a term used to group people exhibiting a wide range of cognitive and behavioral deficits affecting their ability to communicate with others and participate in the shared social world. The research reviewed in this chapter suggests that a whole range of biogenetic phenomena are correlated with a diagnosis of autism. But that does not mean that autistic symptoms are mere epiphenomena of these biogenetic phenomena as this premise invokes the mistaken baggage of classical reductionism— that is "belief that the properties of a system at one level are wholly explainable in terms of the properties of the components present at a 'lower' level" (Lewontin 2000: 27). If classical reductionism were accurate, there would be little hope for helping people with autism in the absence of identifying the primordial causal agents—a quest for a genetic holy grail. However, there is hope because the relationships across the levels of mind, brain, and genes stand loosely coupled rather than mechanistically determined. Early diagnosis of autism through behavioral and cognitive based measures opens up the opportunity space for therapeutic interventions that may shape the very development of the brain.

Notes

1 Although less than 2 percent of the DNA in the human genome codes for proteins, scientists suspect that the remaining 98 percent of DNA is functional; for example, some genes may be involved in regulating other genes' expression by functioning as sites for the protein factors involved in regulating transcription. Other genes may produce RNA fragments that interfere with other genes' expression or may have other unknown biological functions (Insel and Collins 2003).

2 That is, "obstetric hazards are typically seen as consequences of rather than independent aetiological factors" (Buitelaar and Willemsen-Swinkels 2000: 69).

3 Although, by definitional criteria, autism is defined in terms of preservative interests/behaviors and communication disabilities, these same symptoms can be found in people who are not "autistic" but suffer from mental retardation or brain trauma, caused either by infection or environmental insult. For example, the British psychiatrist John Haslam's nineteenth-century account of the inoculation effects on a three-year-old child strikingly resembles late-twentieth-century accounts of childhood disintegrative disorder: the progression of symptoms appear on the surface to be the same. Because so little is really known about how the brain actually operates, it is unclear whether or not distinct capabilities and affective states are actually localized in distinct brain centers, whose operations may be disrupted by genetic mutations or errors or environmental insults. If mind and behavioral states are not in fact necessarily spatially localized in the brain, it may be the case that a variety of different causal agents may engender similar disruptions in mental and behavioral states.

4 Although Hill and Frith in an essay published in 2003: 282 claim that "Research has become focused gradually on genes, brain and mind and their interplay with environmental factors," I would take issue with their claim. Specifically, as I have demonstrated in this chapter, although research addresses relationships across these levels, rarely are they studied systemically; rather, mind is reduced to brain and/or genes.

5 I am aware of the arguments forwarded by "autistic" individuals against "normalization" of the differences. Chapter 7 will address this argument and some of its implications. For the purposes of Chapter 6, the point about "normalization" is intended to convey the idea that people with autism are not indelibly inscribed by biological differences that necessarily preclude involvement in a shared social world.

7 The dialectics of autism
Theorizing autism, performing autism, remediating autism, and resisting autism

> What I write about autism, and the way that I see it, holds true even for the lowest-functioning autistics. In any autistic, there is no such thing as a normal person trapped beneath some sort of shell called autism.
>
> http://home.att.net/~ascaris1/lfa.html

People diagnosed with autism are sites for the operations of complexes of institutional practices and bodies of knowledge. People diagnosed with autism are also human beings whose socially marked forms of *otherness* do not preclude their ability to love and desire, to make some sense of their world, and to seek to act upon it in ways that promote their sense of well-being. So far this book has explored the complexes of institutional practices and bodies of knowledge seeking to know and act upon the purported "essence" of autism. This chapter explores how some of these bodies of knowledge and practices operate upon those people who are labeled "autistic" in the United States. In this respect, the chapter addresses how the disciplinary knowledge produced by psychology and medicine are translated into concrete therapeutic practices. Although the effects of these practices are difficult to determine conclusively, I speculate on how they might shape the expression of autistic symptoms. This chapter also explores how individuals with "high-functioning" autism, particularly Asperger's syndrome, inhabit the identities that have been ascribed to them and how they appropriate and/or resist autistic ascriptions in their efforts to promote their sense of personal well-being.

In essence, this chapter dialectically explores the tension between and across professional practices and bodies of knowledge on the one hand, and individual experience on the other hand. Theoretically, the body of literature that critically investigates the ontology of disease and disability informs this exploration. At a practical level this discussion illustrates how medicalized diagnostic categories can be both constraining and enabling for those diagnosed autistic. As I will explain, disease and disability are not objective or neutral phenomena. At some level, they are produced, at least in part, by the strategies and representational frameworks used to know them. Consequently, individuals who are designated as diseased or disabled are afforded socially produced identities—that is, subject positions—that have implications for the ways that others see them and interact with them. For people identified as autistic, these implications tend to be quite significant because of the social stigmatizations and valuations attached to their symptoms, and because of the quantity and intensity of therapeutic interventions.

Beginning with the idea that autism—as disease or disorder—is a socially constructed idea, this chapter moves to explore how young children diagnosed with autism become sites for medical and psychological interventions. After exploring the social production of autistic children, discussion moves to the forms of self-expression and resistance produced by people who self-identify as autistic. As I shall explain, self-identified autistic individuals simultaneously appropriate and resist historical, cultural and biogenetic constructions of their identity.

Theorizing disease/disablement: autism as socially constructed

The medical model for understanding and managing disease has become the dominant framework for defining autism. This framework focuses almost exclusively on the apparently diseased/pathological autistic body/brain. Accordingly, Chapter 6 discusses in some detail the range of biological pathologies that are implicated in playing a role in the disorder's etiology. The consequence of knowing autism this way is that the characteristics of "mind"—the experiences and behavioral dispositions of "autistic" people—are often represented as mere symptoms of the underlying biogenetic disorder. And yet, the tendency to reduce "mind" to biogenetic processes is not restricted to medical accounts.

Perhaps in an effort to affirm its scientific legitimacy, the discipline of cognitive psychology has increasingly sought to tie its conceptual terms to the concepts and processes specific to the medical model. For example, introductory accounts of autism typically describe the syndrome as a "biologically-based neurodevelopmental disorder" with potentially multiple biologically induced causal pathways (Mash and Wolfe 2002: 274). Defined as such, autism comes under the purview of medical frameworks for understanding the nature and causes of human health and illness, and ability and disability. The complex role of individual and social forces in producing and mediating biological propensities tends to be marginalized. The resulting tendency for biological reductionism is particularly evident in psychological accounts attempting to establish direct equivalences across disparate levels of analysis. For example, the theoretically derived concept of "theory of mind" is increasingly explained in terms of abnormalities or patterns of activation of the amygdala section of the human brain. Accordingly, as described in Chapters 5 and 6, cognitive constructs such as "theory of mind" are biologically essentialized and universalized as they are spatially located in neuro-anatomically defined brain centers. In this fashion, autistic people's minds as well as their brains are pathologized as diseased and/or impaired.

And yet, Chapter 2 presented a challenge to universalizing and ultimately mechanistic models of disease/impairment by introducing the idea that disease is itself a socially constructed phenomenon. This discussion opens the way to an exploration of how it might be possible to view autism as a socially constructed phenomenon, without rejecting the idea that biological processes play a role in the development of the "disorder."

As discussed in Chapter 2, there are a variety of ways of approaching the social construction of a disease or bodily impairment. One can explore the social conditions producing disease, as illustrated by the role of diet in producing diabetes or as illustrated by the role of environmental pollutants in producing developmental delays (e.g., lead poisoning). Or, it is possible to study how ideas about disease define and constrain medical observations, interpretations, and interventions. This latter approach can oscillate between (1) an extreme constructivism whereupon disease is purely socially constructed or is an unknowable facticity rendered intelligible only through its various socially constructed representations and (2) a moderated materialism that views disease in terms of the interaction between biology and cultural practices and interpretive frameworks. However, although a moderated materialism holds theoretical appeal, dialectical accounts stressing the interaction of biology and culture struggle to avoid reifying "biology" and "culture" as distinct phenomena while simultaneously acknowledging, at some level, the brute facticity of corporeality. For example, a migraine headache has a certain undeniable bodily presence that cannot be explainable and/or reducible to cultural constructions of pain's meaning and significance. Thus, the problem with adopting a moderated materialistic approach is that the classical dualisms of object–subject, body–mind, and nature–culture resist transcendence.

The academic field of disability studies has recently addressed these conundrums in its efforts to unravel the social construction of disabled bodies. Although the field of disability studies might, on the surface, appear to have a more narrow scope than the sociology of medicine, it holds direct relevance for understanding how bodies are pathologized and/or normalized because disability functions as an umbrella term that embraces all people who are seen as "disabled," whether from disease, psychiatric condition, or physical limitation. Moreover, the field of disability studies expresses particular interest in how people are socially designated as mentally or physically disabled. Accordingly, in the early 1990s, theorists such as Oliver (1990) proposed a social model for understanding disability by suggesting we draw a distinction between "impairment" and "disability," in order to stress the socially constructed nature of disability. This framework understands impairment in terms of biological or physical "defect" or "lack," whereas it understands disability as the social interpretation of lack/defect and the social organization rendering lack/defect visible as deficiency. This framework stresses the social conditions rendering lack/defect visible but it tends to leave the body unproblematized and untheorized (Tremain 2001) and thereby constructs the "impaired body" as brute, biological facticity, relegating it inadvertently to medical discourse and authority (Hughes and Paterson 1997). Criticism of Oliver's work points to the difficulties in reconciling the corporeality and facticity of the body on the one hand and the social processes of its interpretation and performance on the other. Again, an ability to reconcile social ideas and cultural processes *with* corporeal embodiment and individual experiences of bodily sensations stands at issue.

Recognizing the dualism that accompanying the theoretical distinction between impairment and disability, more recent theorizing within the field of disability studies strives to provide more synthetic accounts embracing biological corporeality, subjective experience, and socially produced interpretive frameworks (Hughes and Paterson 1997; Tremain 2001). Accordingly, efforts to reconcile Cartesian dualisms between body and mind, biology and culture, require retheorizing the body in such a manner as to recognize both the cultural practices inscribing bodies—shaping the possibility of their experiencing—and the facticity of bodies whose sensations and motilities impinge upon conscious experience and thereby demand interpretation and articulation. The cultural practices of diet, architecture, and comportment, for example, provide social conditions of possibility for embodiment by inscribing or producing particular kinds of bodies, which in turn help produce the forms of corporeality enabling particular kinds of experiences. But the productivity of culture or sociality is not limited to the material practices producing particular conditions of embodiment: at the level of the experiencing body, the intrusion of somatic (i.e., bodily) experiences upon individual consciousness is rendered intelligible *only* within cultural vocabularies for naming and interpreting somatic symptoms. Somatic processes are identified and interpreted within cultural matrices of understanding—within language and social practices. Put otherwise, bodily experiences are always/already mediated.[1] Pain and hunger, for example, are somatic forces that demand recognition but are only rendered intelligible (e.g., "I'm hungry because . . .") and attended to in relation to cultural norms and value orientations. Moreover, the experienced body—that nexus of corporeality and culture—is temporally and spatially emergent so that it is always/already *becoming*: for example, cultural practices for fixing somatic distress contribute to the becoming of bodies (socially) designated as ill or disabled. With this in mind, Fox (1999) suggests that dialectical, co-constitutive approaches focus on the *becoming* body–mind as constituted by and in relation to cultural processes.

Therefore, theoretical efforts toward a moderated materialism must acknowledge the co-constitutive processes that produce bodies—including their diseases and/or disabilities—and these processes must include:

- the material, but also cultural, forms of production, sociality, and individual comportment that produce the conditions of possibility for particular forms of embodiment, including particular forms of disease and disablement
- the bodily exigencies posed by somatic forces—pain, hunger, anxiety—that demand conscious recognition and interpretation
- the cultural interpretive frameworks that filter and/or render intelligible bodily symptoms and conditions and that designate normality and pathology within the symbolic universe
- the cultural techniques and remedies used to therapy/remedy/govern bodies identified as different and/or pathological (as diseased and/or impaired) and their effects on/for bodily becomings.

In addition, analysis must address subjective experience—phenomenological embodiment—as it expresses, performs, and resists the cultural frameworks for knowing and "managing" disease and disability. This level of analysis must always/already be contextualized within the forms of cultural analysis identified above. Accordingly, one must address:

- individual interpretations, articulations, and performances of bodily symptoms that are labeled/experienced as "pathological" and/or "disabilities"
- individual expressions of resistance to preferred cultural codes for interpreting and performing bodily symptoms, pathologies, and disabilities.

Individuals' forms of experiential embodiment—their lived bodies—are always situated within historically specific institutional apparatuses constituted by preferred practices and forms of knowledge. Although always/already inscribed by institutional apparatuses, individuals' experiences and expressions may also draw upon alternative practices/frameworks to produce alternate performances of meaning and social practices. Marginalized social discourses/practices and local knowledges offer lived bodies opportunities for resisting dominant frameworks and may thereby be perceived as particularly enabling or malleable. For example, the sets of knowledge and practices that constitute "alternative medicine" are often seen as enabling for people resisting the objectifying practices of technological medicine. Bodily symptoms take on new meanings when "holistic" metaphors of alternative medicine replace the biomedical framework. This example illustrates how a moderated materialism stresses the co-constitutive processes producing biological bodies, cultural frameworks, and individual experience.

One co-constitutive approach to the relationship between the body and culture is explored in the work of Ian Hacking (1998, 1999), who demonstrates the interaction of biology and culture through a variety of examples, as explored in Chapter 2.[2] Although Hacking does not explicitly address issues pertaining to phenomenological embodiment, his framework leaves open a space for this level of analysis. In what follows, I briefly review Hacking's framework in relation to the analytic imperatives identified above.

Hacking introduces the idea of "interactive kinds" to describe phenomena that are indelibly produced in relation to historically specific conditions and interpretive frameworks for identification and classification. As Hacking explains, the dividing practices and frameworks used in classificatory practices emerge within complex matrices of institutions, practices, and bodies of knowledge. To demonstrate his point, Hacking chronicles the development of "niche" disorders; that is, disorders which emerged and were specific to particular socio-historical and economic niche conditions. Using this view, we see how autism illustrates a niche disorder that emerged out of particular material and linguistic practices:[3]

- The historical and cultural developments of child psychiatry, psychology, and mass public schooling, among other forces, produced the conditions of possibility for identifying and naming childhood autism.
- The material but socially produced "built environment" of twentieth-century industrial society may have contributed to, through environmental effects, the production of somatic symptoms that together constitute autism.
- The historical-cultural interpretive frameworks of psychoanalysis, personality theory, cognitive psychology, and the biogenetic medical model have filtered and/or rendered intelligible autistic symptoms throughout the twentieth century.

Accordingly, autism is a niche disorder indebted to particular social and historical conditions of possibility specific to the early nineteenth century while Asperger's syndrome is largely a disorder of the late twentieth century, at least to the extent that it has been constructed as a "medical" rather than personality disorder. This is not to say that the biomedical conditions that engender autism and Asperger's syndrome did not exist prior to the twentieth century. Rather, the point is that the conditions of possibility for naming the disorders and the frameworks of interpretation affording them meaning are socially and historically contingent. Moreover, the built environment of the twentieth century may contribute to producing those biomedical conditions encapsulated and interpreted within the autism spectrum.

However, autistic symptoms are not merely identified and interpreted within cultural matrices, they are also acted upon. That is, the matrices of institutions and knowledge that together produce classificatory systems do not merely divide and interpret individuals in relation to pre-existing objective (i.e., transhistorical) bodily differences. Rather, the matrices of institutions contribute to the production of bodily differences and/or organize bodies in ways that telescope and hypostatize specific bodily differences in ways that could not have been achieved in other historical epoches. Although Hacking does not provide an exhaustive account of how such co-constitutive processes might occur, he does provide a specific example in the form of "biolooping." Using schizophrenia as an example, and alluding to the example's relevance for autism, Hacking illustrates how parental expectations, therapy programs, pharmaceutical agents, and individual experience loop back to affect the expression of biogenetic factors, which Hacking acknowledges play a role in the disorders. Biolooping also has relevance for understanding autism because:

- The various therapeutic regimes of these frameworks have acted upon the bodies–minds of children designated as autistic (and their families) and have contributed to the production and expression of autistic symptoms.
- Individuals designated as autistic have appropriated, performed, and resisted the various therapeutic regimes for identifying, interpreting, and remediating autistic symptoms.

Using these ideas as a foundation, this chapter aims to explore how individuals and their families have experienced, appropriated, and resisted the currently dominant frameworks for interpreting and remediating autism.

Identifying autism, treating autism, experiencing autism

Beginning with a discussion of the production of autistic bodies, I chronicle various operations that are implicated in diagnosing, treating, and experiencing autism in the context of the United States. I also explore how management of the meaning of autism is used to foster the support and understanding of social others.

Diagnosing autism

As established in Chapter 4, historical settings and societal systems produce specific childhood valuations, roles, and practices. In the context of late-twentieth- and early-twenty-first-century life in "industrialized" nations such as the United States and the United Kingdom, children are subject to considerable surveillance by parents, caregivers, pediatricians, and educators in order to ensure that these children reach each and every "developmental" milestone in the formalized chronological framework. Child guidance literature such as *What to Expect the First Year* (Eisenberg et al. 1989) and government-sponsored pamphlets and programs ensure parental familiarity with expert knowledge about child development. In this context, developmental "delays" are rendered relatively visible at increasingly early ages.

For example, parents in the United States who read *What to Expect in the Toddler Years* (Eisenberg et al. 1996) are instructed that toddlers should be able to say at least one word by the fifteenth month. The book also notes that parents should expect toddlers of this age to "communicate pleasure, warmth, interest in new experiences; to play games with parents; to protest; to begin to accept limits" (Eisenberg et al. 1996: 63). The guide encourages parents whose children fail to meet these expected developmental guidelines to express their concerns with pediatricians. Pediatricians thus become the expert authority for assessing the child's development and may be inclined to evaluate cognitive and behavioral development within the medical framework of normality and pathology. Although many pediatricians are unlikely to be alarmed by "mild" developmental "delays," increased public knowledge about autism and pervasive developmental disorders and the purported benefits of early intervention are leading to increased medical vigilance and thereby help increase the rate of psychiatric referrals.

In the case of autism and PDD, age two is the often cited point at which parents or pediatricians initiate the process of psychiatric evaluation. By this age, speech delays and "deficits" in "normal" social interaction become relatively visible in the context of social patterns of childhood surveillance. However, the nature and reason for delays often resist easy diagnosis. Therefore, pediatricians may be inclined to refer children with marked developmental delays (as determined by developmental guidelines) to professionals specializing in pediatric "disorders" including clinical psychologists, pediatric psychiatrists, and developmental pediatricians. In the United States, these experts are apt to use diagnostic guidelines from the DSM-IV in making a psychiatric diagnosis. However, the ambiguity of symptoms and classificatory schemes often requires considerable clinical "guesswork." Even when a child appears to warrant a diagnosis of autism, prognoses are speculative. For example, distinguishing a two or three year old with classical autism from the two or three year old with Asperger's syndrome may prove difficult. Given these uncertainties, clinicians may elect the label of PDD unless the severity of symptoms seems to warrant a diagnosis of classical autism. Across cases, the child has now achieved a label that formally designates a kind of psychological and medical pathology.

Given the increased popularization of genetic explanations for autism, it might be surprising that few children diagnosed with an autistic spectrum disorder actually undergo genetic testing. However, genetic analysis is costly and has little relevance for treatment options, even in the case of known genetic disorders such as Fragile X syndrome. Consequently, despite much media hype, genetic research on autism has very little impact on the diagnoses, treatment or experiences of children with autism. And so, family history reports of psychiatric disorders often constitute the limits of clinical examination of hereditary factors.

The end result of this diagnostic experience is that the parent is presented with a highly charged label capturing and summarizing all of the ambiguous and disturbing behavioral and cognitive symptoms that had led to clinical evaluation. Yet, despite the specificity of the categories used to define autism and PDD, few parents seem to understand what autism means for their children. That is, the diagnostic categories group symptoms but do not explain their source or the prognoses associated with them. All parents have is the label.

How do parents experience this label? In order to understand how parents might react to such a diagnosis one must address the sociological question of how late-capitalist western nations value children. As sociologists have observed for some time, children are valuated in relation to changing cultural and economic relations so that, for example, the child born in medieval England was regarded differently by parents than a child born in the same country in the late nineteenth century (Aries 1962; DeMause 1974; Zelizer 1985). In particular, a number of observers suggest that children took on unprecedented sentimental value in western nations during the early years of the twentieth century as their role as physical laborer was slowly supplemented by the creation of childhood as a special period of life. Now, in the context of late-twentieth- and early-twenty-first-century life in western nations, children may be valued in relation to their sentimentality, their economic costs, and their future ability to maintain or elevate the family's class standing through the acquisition of those skills which will enable them to participate in the increasingly polarized "knowledge-economy" (see Nadesan 2002). Sentimentalized children whose value is in part defined in terms of future economic potential require lengthy and labor-intensive childhoods whose perceived costs tend to put a downward push on family fertility rates (Longman 2004). Thus, each child tends to be highly valued sentimentally and understood in terms of abstract economic costs and potential.

It is, at least partly, in this context that a diagnosis of PDD or autism is likely to be understood. At an emotional level, the typified and formally designated characteristics of PDD and autism imply that so-labeled children are deficient in their ability to reciprocate socially and therefore they (purportedly) lack the foundation upon which sentimental value derives. Moreover, since children with PDD and autism often exhibit cognitive "deficits" and may qualify for a diagnosis of mental retardation, they lose value in terms of their future economic potential and engender costs in terms of their therapeutic needs. Indeed, many parents with autistic children in western nations experience significant economic costs derived from lost wages and behavioral and medical based therapies for their children. In this context, it is not surprising that many parents of newly diagnosed autistic children feel that they have "lost" their child.

However, after an initial period of "mourning," many parents are mobilized to "save" their child from the long-term perils of their diagnosis. Spiritually inspired beliefs that the soul is distinct from the diseased or impaired body lead some parents to believe an autistic "shell" imprisons the essence of their "real" child. Likewise, popularized notions of an "essential inner self" derived from humanistic psychology, particularly Maslow's (1968) Human Potential Movement, contribute to parents' desire to "unlock" their child's buried ("normal") consciousness. The widely shared idea in North American culture that every child has the right to "self-actualize" to the extent of his/her potential also adds to parents' desire to help their children. Indeed, some parents adopt missionary-like zeal pursuing their desire to find the cure for their child's autistic symptoms and in their desire to educate the public about the prevalence and causes of autism.

The next section explores some of these strategies employed by parents to "save their children" and discusses how these strategies have the potential to alter that which they are acting upon. As I shall explain, the therapeutic strategies applied to "saving" autistic children have the potential to shape the expression of autistic symptoms and provide the context within which autistic people advocate for social rights and representation.

Treating autism: biolooping

If autism exists as a niche disorder, how do the institutional practices and bodies of psychological and medical knowledge described above inscribe people labeled as "autistic" and how might biolooping occur such that these inscriptions contribute in an ongoing process to shape the expression and experiences of autism? It seems possible that many of the interventions sketched below, coupled with the understanding and support of primary caregivers, shape the development of the disorder such that the ultimate distinction between low- and high-functioning autism is at least partly *a social outcome rather than a biological given*. The perpetual development of people (bodies/brains/minds) in concert with their environment precludes the idea that autism—or any "disorder"—is a fixed condition.

In the 1930s, an oddly behaved child might have been shunned and/or secluded in the home until that child had reached school age around seven years old. Upon entering the school, such a child would not have received expert attention unless his or her symptoms were particularly overt. A child with overt social difficulties with "normal" intelligence would then have been diagnosed with a morally suspect "personality disorder," cast either within a psychoanalytic frame or within the emerging categories of personality theory. In the case of the former, psychotherapy might be called for in order to avoid future criminality.

However, in the contemporary context, such a child would most likely receive a formal diagnosis of a medicalized psychiatric disorder by the time she/he has turned three or four. Autistic spectrum disorders—pervasive developmental disorders—provide medical and psychiatric authorities with a catch-all category for children with overtly delayed social skills. The medicalization of "developmental disorders" coupled with the humanistic spirit of the self-actualization movement now demand "early intervention." At best, these interventions may potentially help the "autistic" child navigate his/her social environment. At the very least, these interventions shape the expression of a child's behaviors, thereby helping to shape the environment within which she/he exists. Hence, the surveillance, labeling, and therapeutic practices that currently produce "autistic" children also shape the development of their conditions, at the very least by shaping their environments, which in turn affect the child. Therefore, although therapeutic benefits may be difficult to prove or measure and developmental trajectories remain largely inexplicable, it is worthwhile to review commonly adopted therapeutic protocols. These protocols, and their therapeutic assumptions, help constitute the environment within which "autistic" children are produced as such.

The toddler or preschool child diagnosed with autism has already been produced as a particular kind of being—an "autistic child" with particular "cognitive deficits"—within and by the institutional matrices that labeled him or her. Moreover, the degrees of parental surveillance and attention implicated in this early diagnosis also implicate certain institutional matrices. Therefore, the child labeled/produced as "autistic" requires, within the apparatuses of his/her production, certain forms of care—forms of care whose protocols demand expert intervention. Accordingly, the creation of the welfare state in advanced capitalist nations coupled with the professionalization and institutionalization of the "helping professions" such as psychology, social work, speech therapy, and occupational therapy together aid parents who are intent on helping their "autistic" children. Even parents who resist the clinically designated label of autism are likely to avail themselves of these services in their efforts to help/normalize their children.

Available to assist parental efforts are a variety of institutions, therapeutic professionals, and bodies of expert knowledge. Listed here are some of the commonly found institutionalized resources in the United States:

- Government (often state) sponsored intervention programs providing home-based therapeutic programs stressing speech and social interaction. In the state of Arizona, Arizona Early Intervention Programs provide in-house speech and occupational therapy for children under three who receive a formal diagnosis of autism.
- Developmental preschools taught by special education instructors in coordination with speech pathologists and occupational therapists, who stress sensory-integration therapy. In the United States, such developmental preschools are often housed and administered by local school districts.
- Clinic-based and privately funded pediatric speech therapy and occupational therapy.
- Clinic-based and privately funded pediatric psychiatrists and developmental pediatricians who specialize in developmental disabilities.

The institutional practices and philosophies that engendered these programs are discussed at some length in Chapter 4 and include the foundational ethos of humanistic psychology, the institutionalization of child-saving practices (which began early in the twentieth century), and the ethos of the state project of social engineering, which seeks to reduce social and political risk and economic costs by actively engineering the production of citizens (Rose 2001). Cognitive psychology, behaviorism, and neuroscience provide the theoretical frameworks informing contemporary therapeutic interventions. Taken together, these institutions, bodies of knowledge, experts, and therapeutic programs aim to normalize differences in order to assimilate the child as seamlessly as possible into mainstream institutions including the public educational apparatuses and the institutions of work and the economy.

In the case of autism, the cadre of experts who make up these institutions focus on the (cognitive, behavioral, or neurological) modification of autistic symptoms in order to normalize autistic children's behavior and to improve their communication skills. Drawing upon the specialized knowledges and practices of their disciplines, occupational therapists, speech pathologists, behavioral psychologists, and special education teachers target autistic symptoms for intervention. What follows addresses three primary therapeutic regimes that are implemented in the United States and discusses some possible implications for biolooping. Interested readers are encouraged to read Herbert, Sharp, and Gaudiano's (2002) "Separating fact from fiction in the etiology and treatment of autism" for a scientifically based evaluation of these regimes.

Speech and occupational therapies

First, occupational therapists and speech pathologists target the apparent sensory and communication difficulties that are often seen in young children with autism.[4] Both occupational therapy and speech pathology invoke explanatory models stressing cognitive and/or neurological "dysfunctions" within and between implicated brain centers as well as more mechanical models that target anatomical problems and processes. For example, an occupational therapist might explain an autistic child's inability to execute an activity in terms of executive functions deficits and therefore might develop therapeutic strategies that purportedly stimulate the targeted brain area—the cerebellum—such as swinging. A speech pathologist might begin treatment by seeking to exclude purely anatomical accounts for deficits in speech production before developing therapeutic tactics targeting apparently neurologically based difficulties in the interpretation of language (i.e., for a receptive communication disorder) and the encoding of speech (expressive speech disorder). However, although clinical practice presupposes theoretical models to explain deficits and develop treatment, experienced therapists modify and create therapeutic programs based on personal experiences, successes and failures. And yet, therapists' intuitive, tacit, and experientially based knowledge may be difficult to articulate formally and may therefore remain "outside" the formalized domain of professional knowledge, even while it may constitute a significant basis of experienced clinical practice.

Although measuring the effects of these therapies may prove difficult, isolated studies, anecdotal evidence, and autobiographical accounts suggest that they may help some children. For example, autobiographical accounts written by autistic adults often emphasize the import of sensory difficulties for autistic children (see Carlton 1993) and the importance of finding strategies for managing sensory overload.[5] Experienced therapists may help autistic patients develop strategies for reducing sensory overload and for channeling or expressing anxiety in more socially appropriate forms. Skilled speech therapists may help autistic children with phonological awareness to clarify the relationship between speech sounds and the rhythms and meanings of speech (Windham 2004). Social stories may be used to help children understand the pragmatic aspects of communication, which address subtly encoded relational meanings that often escape autistic children. And therapists may maximize the known "cognitive" strength of some autistic children—for example, reading in "hyperlexic" autistics—to find alternative means for teaching information that other children learn intuitively (McGough 2004).

Parental and caretaker efforts to recognize the sensory difficulties of young children with autism or other disabilities may also significantly alter their developmental "trajectory." For example, some parents and therapists either intuitively or deliberately modulate the tempo of their interaction to enable the child to coordinate his/her attention. Autistic children's difficulties in achieving "joint attention" (see Chapter 5) may arise from temporal asymmetries such that the autistic child has difficulty matching the physical and attentional tempo of their relational others. Parents who are sensitive to these temporal asynchronicities and adapt their interaction accordingly facilitate their children's ability to develop communication skills (Siller and Sigman 2002). This form of therapeutic intervention or style of adaptation can potentially alter an autistic child's prognosis even while it lacks formalized protocols, techniques, and standards of measurement.

However, while the possibility remains open that these various therapeutic approaches may help autistic children, there is little firm evidence proving their effectiveness. That is, the "scientific models" from which these therapies originate often fail to establish their effectiveness using "scientific" standards of validity and reliability. For example, in a comprehensive review of scientific evidence, Herbert et al. (2002) found no replicable studies proving the therapeutic success of auditory integration training and sensory integration therapy. In particular, they conclude that the poor experimental design formats of many studies render reported results unclear in terms of their source and significance. To illustrate their point they observe that the purported sensory integration benefits of "brushing" may stem from well-established behavioral principles such as habituation rather than from any specific neurological changes in sensory processing. The lack of "scientifically" validated support for many widely used sensory-based interventions points to the tentativeness in understanding both the nature and treatment of autistic "deficits." Moreover, the heterogeneity of autistic populations may undermine research efforts to find universally effective intervention strategies.

Intensive behavioral intervention

The second most commonly used intervention is intensive behavioral therapy. Although behavioral therapy has been used in clinical practice for decades to modify undesirable behaviors in autism (e.g., self-injurious behaviors), in the 1970s Dr. O. Ivar Lovaas developed an entire autism "treatment" program around behavioral modification (Lovaas 1977). In 1987, Lovaas reported the results of a study using his behavioral modi-fication techniques to train autistic children in the following, progres-sively developed areas: compliance, imitation, receptive and expressive language, and peer integration (Siegel 1996). The purported effectiveness of Lovaas' applied behavioral analysis therapy (ABA) led to its rapid popularization among parents of autistic children, many of whom devel-oped home-based ABA therapy programs. For example, Maurice's (1993) *Let Me Hear your Voice: A Family's Triumph over Autism* chronicles one family's success in "saving" their autistic daughter through intensive behavioral therapy.

The behavior modification program popularized by Lovaas requires children to engage in very specific responses to one-to-one demands. Positive reinforcement in the form of rewards (candy, toys, etc.) serves as the child's primary motivator. However, because autistic children often resist ABA's highly structured and disciplined demands, the program tends to be quite intensive in terms of the efforts exerted by autistic chil-dren and therapists (Siegel 1996). Adults with autism who experienced ABA as children often reflect negatively on their experiences with the therapeutic program because of its demanding, monotonous, and seem-ingly meaningless routines and its tendency to pathologize many charac-teristically "autistic" behaviors (such as "stimming" and hand-flapping: (see e.g. http://home.att.net/~ascaris1/ABA.html, accessed December 30, 2003).

The effectiveness of ABA in treating autism remains controversial despite the program's popularity. In their review of findings on ABA, Herbert et al. (2002) suggest that the measured success of ABA therapy seems most rele-vant in the cases of high-functioning children with autism. Moreover, they observe that most of the research suffers from methodological shortcomings that may have led to an exaggeration of ABA benefits.

Although Lovaas' program most strictly illustrates the doctrine of Skinnerian psychology, other formalized behavior modification programs exist that blend behavior modification techniques with pedagogical principles derived from cognitive psychology and/or psychoanalysis. Stanley Greenspan and Serena Wieder's (1998) "Floor-Time" combines elements of behavior modification therapy with therapeutic "play therapy" practices derived from psychoanalysis and cognitive psychology. Their synergistic model also attempts to help the autistic child learn adaptive cognitive skills and behaviors through intensive one-on-one therapy. Additionally, Project TEACCH, a university-based project started by Eric Schopler, blends a wide range of therapeutic approaches including (but not limited to) behavioral intervention and speech and sensory-based therapies aimed at improving cognitive, academic, and vocational skills (http://www.teacch.com/teacch.htm). Despite variations in specific curricula, programs such as TEACCH and Floor-Time focus on providing highly supported teaching environments emphasizing those "cognitive" and functional skills—attention, imitation, language, social skills—that enable additional academic and vocational learning to occur (Dawson and Osterling 1997).

At best, intensive therapeutic one-on-one programs such as those advocated by Lovaas (1977) and Greenspan and Weider (1998) may help the autistic child develop the basic attentional and communication skills which undergird all other forms of social learning, particularly those that involve social modeling. While it is beyond the scope of this chapter to evaluate the overall effectiveness of these programs, they are relevant and interesting in that they have the *potential*—as a historically unique set of therapeutic practices—to shape the very development of autistic children. At minimum, they introduce a set of therapeutic practices that at a very material level act upon the bodies and minds of children labeled "autistic." That is, they produce autistic children as particular kinds of beings or subjects who require and deserve intensive "professional" surveillance and intervention. While the most rigid forms of ABA often engender resistance from the autistic child, the more "child-centered" early intervention programs may be experienced as tolerable or even enjoyable. The question as to whether or not these programs actually shape the development of those cognitive skills that they presuppose remains unclear.

Although these primary modes of intervention may seem to help some children, parents often find progress slow and frustrating. This frustration is often exacerbated by the continuation of behavior problems such as tantrums and repetitive behaviors that seem unaffected by therapeutic interventions. In these cases, parents may turn to biomedical treatment plans.

Biomedical interventions

Biomedical treatment for autism is a complex and contradictory terrain constituted by conflicting hypotheses about the source of autistic symptoms. Parents who venture into this terrain may follow the guidance of conventional medicine or may opt for the less charted terrain of alternative medicine. Accordingly, there are two primary routes for biomedical intervention. The first route involves the institutional matrix that constitutes professional medicine while the second route combines the medical model with "alternative" biological interventions.

The first route for biomedical intervention draws firmly upon the medical model for knowing and treating autism. Accordingly, licensed pediatric professionals—pediatricians and psychiatrists—may offer parents pharmaceutical agents to address the "psychiatric symptoms" of what are regarded as key biogenetic defects suffered by autistic children. Using the standardized treatments and formalized protocols that constitute mainstream medical practice, licensed medical professionals may treat autistic children with pharmaceutical agents including stimulants such as Ritalin, antidepressants such as Prozac, and in some cases, anti-anxiety agents such as Buspar to better "manage" symptoms. Parents are warned that these drugs will not "cure" their children and will not necessarily alter the "course" or "trajectory" of their development. However, parents may feel that by controlling disruptive behaviors, these drugs enable their children to function better and enable a better quality of life for the autistic child and their family. Clinical research documenting the effectiveness of these medications in controlling autistic symptoms is difficult to find and results vary considerably across individuals.

Parental frustration with the limitations of the medical model is often expressed in autism support groups and advocacy literature. The medical model's stubborn insistence that autistic "defects" are largely and irrevocably determined at birth disturbs parents who aspire to "cure" their children. Moreover, the failure of mainstream pharmaceutical agents to predictably affect symptoms leads to parental disappointment and alienation. Consequently, many parents begin researching autism on their own in order to find alternative treatments. They may start with that body of literature written by parents who claimed to have "cured" their formerly autistic children. Some of these texts argue for the benefits of less established techniques, particularly those that entail "alternative" biomedical interventions. Internet autism support groups and autism research institutes often are particularly focused on alternative biomedical strategies. Organizations such as the American Autism Association, the San Diego Autism Research Institute, which sponsors DAN (Defeat Autism Now), and the various alternative medicine therapeutic regimes found on the Internet all share a loose understanding of autism as a biomedical condition whose behavioral and cognitive symptoms are mere epiphenomena of underlying neurological/genetic/immunological dysfunction (as described in Chapter 6). However, unlike the dominant biomedical model, these organizations suggest that biomedically based interventions may significantly alter the expression and course of development of autistic symptoms. For the sake of simplicity, I refer to this model as the "alternative" biomedical model of autism.

The sheer growth of autism diagnoses, the growing role of the Internet as a source of medical information for non-medical experts, as well as the public's growing awareness of the limitations of traditional medicine help explain the popularity of this "alternative" biomedical model. The alternative medical model draws legitimacy from its appeals to the institutionalized legitimacy of more mainstream medical knowledge. Yet the alternative medical model for autism also appeals to the New Age interest in healing alternatives focusing on the production and maintenance of psychologically and physiologically integrated healthy bodies. This paradigm represents diet, vitamins, and nutritional supplements as tools capable of remedying the disequilibrium of the autistic physiology. Given the model's propensity for systems thinking, these tools are seen as working synergistically to counter autistic metabolic and immunological disturbances. Thus, the model mandates experimentation with the elusive promise of a cure, whose precise nature resists foreknowledge.

Anxious to help their children, parents may elect to try these biologically based intervention strategies. For example, parents may introduce casein and gluten-free diets. They may require that their child take vitamin and dietary supplements. They may attempt to detoxify their children by pursuing chelation therapies. They may inject their children with secretin, a hormone that affects the gastrointestinal system. Commonly used agents include nystatin, folic acid, vitamin B6, DMG, and vitamin C, among others. Although measuring the effectiveness of these programs proves difficult, they afford parents a sense of control over their children's "illness." Parents who pursue alternative-medicine-based interventions often believe that their child's condition is "correctable" if the precise chemical imbalance or dysfunction is identified. For parents, the difference between traditional medicine and the alternative biomedical model is that the latter offers an infinite array of possibilities for intervention, albeit without formalized protocols or safeguards.

Biolooping

Discussion of these intervention strategies demonstrates that parents seeking to help or "save" their children encounter a wide range of institutional matrices—disciplinary knowledge, expert authorities, and therapeutic practices—that facilitate their efforts. Although it is difficult to gauge whether these protocols and practices actually achieve their desired intent, it is clear that they together create new conditions of possibility for the production and emergence of children labeled with autism. In an optimistic example, Ian Hacking (1999) observes in *The Social Construction of What?* that the possibility does exist that biomedical agents may very well transform that which they operate on and, in the case of autism, relieve the most distressing physiological symptoms that impinge against a child's openness to his/her social environment. However, there are also many dangers that can accompany biomedical and psychological experimentation on populations who have no ability to protect themselves from the well-intentioned but potentially harmful (and even deadly) effects of therapeutic interventions.

Thus, the social ideal to "help actualize" or "save" autistic children is ambivalent in its effects. On the one hand, many of the practices described above may help autistic children better synchronize with their environment by providing compensatory tools, developmentally appropriate infrastructures. But on the other hand, these and other intervention strategies may constitute cruel experiments on highly vulnerable subjects.

In sum, the role of therapeutic interventions—whether they be sensory, social, or biologically oriented—cannot be overstated. All children develop in relation to their biological and social environments. Their brains and minds are open systems that reflect all levels of biological, psychological and social synergistic influences. People are produced as particular kinds of beings or becomings in relation to these influences. The therapeutic practices implemented on autistic children likewise produce them in particular kinds of ways. Some of these practices may help autistic children by reducing physiological and/or existential anxiety while others may contribute to their physical and psychic difficulties. In effect, biolooping is inevitable but the pathways of determination may be very difficult to identify and/or predict.

Living with autism

This section briefly explores autism from the perspective of those who experience it most directly. Because this exploration would justify a book in itself, I will limit my discussion to two important themes that are found across popular and academic autism literatures. The first theme centers on what high-functioning autism *means* for parents and social others, particularly with respect to the role of social stigmatization. The second theme centers on autistic children's experience of bullying in the school context. I selected these themes because the role of social stigmatization for both parents and children with autism is often represented as *the* most painful aspect of the disorder. But rather than merely describe the conditions of these experiences, I will also illustrate strategies of resistance and systems of mobilization resulting from the pain of social marginalization. Accordingly, the discussion of school bullying spills over into the final section of this chapter, which addresses autism advocacy.

Defining autism, living with autism

Living with autism follows a difficult path. All parties involved—whether they be parents, siblings, or autistic children—are at risk for experiencing stigmatization and social exclusion. As documented in previous chapters, this pattern of pathologizing those individuals who share characteristically autistic-like traits spans decades of psychiatric history: from psychopath to Asperger's syndrome, people with autistic-like traits have suffered social stigmatization throughout the mid- to late twentieth century. Autobiographies written by parents and by people with autism, on autistic advocacy web sites, and in academic research thoroughly document the paint of social marginalization and stigmatization. Given that these experiences have been well documented in other sources, I will take a more narrow approach and explore how parents cope with real or potential stigmatization by actively managing relational others' perceptions of the disorder, particularly in cases of high-functioning autism.

Young children with autism present their parents with a considerable challenge. Autistic children do not display any discernible physical markers that differentiate them from "normal" children: that is, the appearance of their bodies is not marked by difference. And yet, autistic children—even mildly autistic children—often behave in ways that are viewed as strange: they often violate the subtle codes of non-verbal conduct that regulate social bodies. For example, autistic children may violate others' personal space or, conversely, may avoid any form of physical proximity with others. Autistic children may tiptoe or "flap" their hands or arms. Some may be prone to severe tantrums over the slightest changes in routine or expectations. Others may be unaccountably rude or display mild physical aggression. The juxtaposition of "normal" appearance with "abnormal" behavior renders autistic children ambiguous and violates the binary categories that typically inform social understandings of ability/disability. Social others may therefore be inclined to render inappropriate moral judgments on such children and their parents (see Singer 1999). Indeed, Gray's (2002) research demonstrates that even parents of high-functioning children feel (and often are) stigmatized by their children's unusual behaviors.

One possible coping strategy for contemporary parents experiencing stigmatization is to deliberately pathologize their child (within the medical framework) in order that both the child and the parent be regarded as blameless for the child's transgressions. For example, I have on many occasions witnessed parents of "high-functioning children with autism" explain their child's apparently aberrant behavior by announcing to onlookers that the child is "autistic." This sort of strategy decenters moral integrity by replacing it with medical pathology. Parents stand absolved of parental failure and transform into the objects of sympathy.

Parents of high-functioning autistic children have another strategy for deflecting social stigmatization, a strategy that is growing in popularity.

That strategy centers on emphasizing the unique cognitive strengths of their "autistic" child. For example, one mother of a daughter with Asperger's syndrome proudly announced her daughter's formally assessed IQ score at 130. Another parent downplayed her son's behavioral oddities by stressing to friends and relatives his exceptional early math and reading skills. Such skills tend to be highly valued in the context of late-twentieth-century life wherein facility with abstract symbols and computers distinguishes knowledge workers from service workers.

The idea that autistic people may exhibit particular intellectual skills is not new and can be found in the works of both Kanner and Asperger. For most of the twentieth century, however, those intellectual strengths exhibited by autistic people were typically regarded as "splinter skills" that were vaguely seen as deriving from the foundational autistic psychopathology. This approach harkens back to the idea of an autistic savant as represented in the film, *Rain Man*. The autistic savant was remarkable because *autism* diagnoses were largely restricted to individuals who exhibited "full spectrum" symptoms and were markedly limited in many of their functional abilities.

But the nature of autism diagnoses began to change with the articulation of "Asperger's syndrome" by Lorna Wing in 1981. Wing's research engendered a transformation of classification practices, in addition to expanding research into the "continuum" of autism disorders. Wing transformed classificatory practices by taking a class of people formerly regarded as suffering from personality disorders—in particular, the "schizoid" personality disorder—and reclassifying their condition as an autistic spectrum, developmental disorder. This move deflected the negative social connotations associated with "psychopathic" personality types by rearticulating these personality disorders in relation to "developmental" syndromes. But it also expanded the scope of application for medicalized psychiatric labels.

Hans Asperger rejected defining "autistic psychopathy" as a developmental syndrome because in his social context a non-psychotic developmental syndrome was understood in psychoanalytic terms as a neurosis-derived disorder. However, in the context of the late-twentieth-century psychiatry, developmental syndromes are framed in biogenetic, rather than psychoanalytic, terms. Consequently, Wing's decision to reframe Asperger's syndrome in terms of a developmental disorder opened the door for new therapeutic approaches to, and understandings for, a whole class of people who had formerly been regarded as morally suspect. It medicalized such people but also freed them from psychiatric stigmatization (although cultural stigmatization continues).

Wing's (1981) research eventually interested cognitive psychologists, who felt that high-functioning autism and Asperger's syndrome were effective testing grounds for modular theories of cognition. Autism presented the perfect terrain for testing the modular approach because many autistic people exhibit such singular unevenness in their performance on cognitive tests of discrete abilities. In this respect, Asperger's syndrome was even better. Interest in cognitive modularity, autism, and Asperger's syndrome popularized the disorder among academics and clinicians and helped contribute to the creation of new diagnostic categories in the DSM and ICD (see Chapter 2).

Although it is difficult in retrospect to chart clear paths across disparate events, the popularization of high-functioning autism or Asperger's syndrome in cognitive psychology contributed to new ways of thinking about autistic abilities and engendered the idea of an autistic *cognitive style*. For example, Michael Fitzgerald (2004), a British cognitive psychologist, has published *Autism and Creativity: Is There a Link between Autism in Men and Exceptional Ability*. Likewise, Simon Baron-Cohen, another British psychologist, has gained fame for his approaches to high-functioning autism as a "male" form of cognition. Both researchers view math and science skills as uniquely autistic strengths and tend to view high-functioning autism as a specific "cognitive style."[6] Despite variations in theoretical formation, these academics share a belief that autism is inextricably linked with particular skills and perhaps forms of genius. In effect, we see Hans Asperger's admiration for his students' special perspicuity recloaked in the cognitive jargon of late-twentieth-century psychology (see Chapter 5).

Academic formulations of autism as a unique cognitive style now appear in the genre of literature written by parents about their autistic children. For example, the book *Elijah's Cup: A Family's Journey into the Community and Culture of High Functioning Autism and Asperger's Syndrome*, written by Valerie Paradiz (2002), the mother of an autistic son, suggests that the genius of Andy Warhol, Ludwig Wittgenstein, and Albert Einstein may have derived from the unique perspective afforded by their (purported) underlying autism. Additionally, autism advocacy web sites are often abuzz with speculations by parents that successful individuals, Bill Gates among them, are closet "aspies" (i.e., they have AS).

Popularized media accounts bolster parents' efforts to validate high-functioning autism. The semiotic equation between computer geek and AS has become so pervasive that in 1999 the *Los Angeles Times* ran an article whose headline ran: "Even if 'geekness' is a disorder, there's no rush to find a cure" (Chapman 1999: C1). *Wired* had suggested that "math and tech genes" might be to blame for the sky-rocketing diagnoses of autism in Silicon Valley (Silberman 2001). Following *Wired* magazine's coinage, *Time* magazine referred to AS as "The geek syndrome" (Nash and Bonesteel 2002). Subsequently, *Newsweek* cited Baron-Cohen in suggesting that high-functioning autism might merely be an extreme form of "male intelligence" (Cowley 2003). These writings provide an indication of the beginning of yet another reframing of the culture's perceptions of the amalgamation of the symptoms we call autism.

Although these affirmative representations of high-functioning autism tend to standardize, homogenize, and stereotype the intellectual strengths and weaknesses of all who bear the label of AS, they do de-pathologize the disorder and offer parents and people with high-functioning autism a strategy for reframing behavioral oddities in ways that may, at least partially, valorize, rather than pathologize, their eccentricities. At least, *these new formulations lessen cultural stigmatization by deflecting attention from the "developmental" limitations of a medicalized disorder without invoking the morally inflected baggage of the personality disorder.* And so it is not surprising that more autism advocacy organizations are arguing that high-functioning autism be regarded as a cognitive style, rather than a developmental disability. This formulation affirms autistic difference and de-pathologizes the condition while still maintaining a therapeutic space, particularly with respect to social skills.

In sum, the twentieth century has seen radical transformations in the definition and understanding of what is now called Asperger's syndrome. The constellation of symptoms that roughly define the syndrome have been redefined from an inherent personality disorder "autistic psychopathy," to an autistic spectrum developmental disorder "Asperger's syndrome," to a unique, masculine cognitive style. This latter interpretation still bears the name Asperger's syndrome but it has taken on new meanings through its media popularization and through cognitive researchers' efforts to valorize and essentialize particular intellectual aptitudes in the extreme "male mind" of those designated as "aspies." However, parental and academic efforts to emphasize the unique intellectual strengths of children with autism cannot alone combat the experiences of difference and social marginalization that often accompany an autistic child's life, particularly with respect to his/her inclusion within the regular school system.

Living with autism: children at school

The "autistic" child who acquires speech and exhibits the ability to learn academic material without difficulty finds him- or herself "mainstreamed" into the typical classroom by kindergarten or first grade. School-based experiences then play an important role in autistic children's identity formation, as do these experiences for us all. Without attempting to exhaust the processes of self-formation, I will briefly describe how "mirroring" affects self-development and its implications for children diagnosed with high-functioning autism.

Across many theoretical paradigms, mirroring is seen as playing an important role in the development of self. Psychoanalytic thinkers such as Lacan even describe a "mirror stage" which delineates the emergence of the infant's sense of itself as a discrete, embodied agent while symbolic-interactionists such as C. H. Cooley (1909) described the emergence of consciousness in relation to a "looking-glass self." The mirroring effect of family expectations and reactions is seen as the primary process whereby this occurs in early development. Upon attaining school age, peer relationships and teacher expectations play important roles in self development.

Although the chronology and stages by which these processes occur vary across individuals, few would debate that social expectations affect self-development, even in the case of autism. Thus, although autistic children may have diminished capacities for representing others' internal states, they do evidence other awareness and responsiveness. Autistic children with "normal" intelligence who can be mainstreamed into typical classrooms often pass theory of mind tests and do evidence intellectual awareness of others' emotional states (Bowler 2001), even if they often fail to grasp the subtleties of everyday social pragmatics. This awareness of how others perceive them is evident in many of the published autobiographies of autistic adults. Thus, given the importance of social others in shaping the behaviors and introspections that constitute self, we may wish to ask what experiences might be characteristically representative of those encountered by high-functioning people with autism?

Unfortunately, the written reports of self-identified people with autism tend to emphasize experiences of social marginalization and denigration. These experiences are cited as bringing to the fore differences that might have been experienced by the autistic child as normal or unremarkable until they were accentuated and exacerbated by social others, particularly in the context of the educational apparatuses. As discussed in Chapter 4, educational institutions historically have been places where children have been subject to forms of expert knowledge that divide them in terms of normality and pathology. Moreover, the cultural emphasis in western nations today on interpersonal skills and "image" may amplify social scrutiny by peers. Peer surveillance, perhaps aided and abetted by adult attitudes, inevitably identifies those children most vulnerable to bullying, whether because of physical or psychological differences, differences marked by race, class, ethnicity, or "disability." In particular, children with developmental disabilities—autism, AS, ADHD, etc.—are often readily identified by peers as "different" and are unfortunately subject to bullying and/or manipulation.

In *Freaks, Geeks and Asperger Syndrome: A User Guide to Adolescence*, Luke Jackson (2002), an adolescent with Asperger's, dedicates an entire chapter to bullying. He begins the chapter by stating:

> All my life I have been bullied. Well at least I mean periodically and at school, not at home-not literally every minute of my life. . . . When I started going to school I struggled to understand what was going on, but one thing I did understand was that most of the kids were pretty mean to me. I never knew why.
>
> (Jackson 2002: 135)

Luke chronicles a sad history of bullying across grade levels and schools that encompasses physical and verbal abuse by peers and teachers. Luke observes that his unwillingness to "beat other people" to establish his superiority rendered him "soft" and therefore susceptible to bullying (Jackson 2002: 143).

An online autism advocacy web site also documents the ubiquity of bullying activities experienced by the self-identified "autistic" people who post at the site. Postings describe school experiences of emotional and physical abuse, mostly administered by peers. Painfully recounted experiences are cited as leading to severe depression and social alienation. They are also cited as exacerbating the need for repetitive interests and behaviors, to ameliorate the distress of these experiences. Postings suggest that autistic children's tendency to be solitary singles them out for peer abuse, as do characteristic autistic "oddities" in communications style including flat intonation and avoidance of eye contact, etc. However, the postings also illustrate an acute awareness that peer abuse is not restricted to autistic children and may be targeted against any child who evidences vulnerability and/or difference. This observation led some postings to suggest it is "normal" children's behavior that is pathological, rather than autistics' behavior.

Molloy and Vasil (2002) suggest that the tendency to construct the characteristic behaviors of Asperger's syndrome as pathological is ultimately an arbitrary construction. They suggest that the syndrome has been adopted as a category of pathological difference in the contemporary context because of "its value as a special education category" that serves the interests and needs of educational institutions and their professionals (Molloy and Vasil 2002: 665). This construction has the effect of localizing the source of the child's difficulties in the child, rather than in the educational system. However, as one can see in the case of bullying, it appears that many of the social difficulties experienced by children with Asperger's syndrome reside as much in the informal social culture of the educational system as they do in the Asperger's child. Although such children often lack intuitive understanding of, or appreciation for, tacit social practices, it is often the deliberate and malicious acts of social others that spotlight and exacerbate their differences.

Accordingly, in the case of Asperger's syndrome, the formal determination of pathology is at once arbitrary and political because it preserves the status quo from critical interrogation: for example, bullying behavior is "normal" but specialized and encompassing interests are pathological.

The categorical ambiguity of so-called high-functioning autistic people, including people labeled with Asperger's syndrome and PDD, presents people labeled as such with a contradictory identity, or subject position. On the one hand, their lack of intuitive understanding of the subtleties of social pragmatics and their often acute sensory perceptions engender a sense of difference and/or social alienation that has an important effect in demarcating their identity. Perhaps even more importantly, the mirroring effects of relational others' reactions to their subtle but discernible "differences" amplify the experience of being inexplicably different, particularly by about fifth grade on. However, on the other hand, high-functioning people with autism, by definition, lack the degree of sensory or cognitive impairment that would lead to their physical exclusion from mainstream social life. Moreover, as they mature, high-functioning people with autism may learn—through careful observation—the taken-for-granted and largely intuitive sets of social practices others grasp in their earliest years. And yet, the person who struggled early on with the *sense* of others' implicit expectations and tacit understandings may feel forever haunted by a difference that was mirrored in those early years. The inchoate experience of difference—acquired from a sense of being out of synch—and solidified by the mirroring effects of relational others may come to be an important identity marker organizing their self-concept. The final section of this chapter explores how autism serves as an important identity marker, particularly for high-functioning people with autism.

Identity politics and autism advocacy

Complex historical forces have rendered personal identity an important social force in late-twentieth-century western nations (see Giddens 1991; Rose 1989). As more disparate forces play a role in identity formation, the personal experience of identity is often fragmented in the sense that individuals may articulate their sense of self in relation to a vast range of social roles and cultural forms. Ethnic identities, work or professional identities, and "lifestyle" oriented identities, among others, contribute to each individual's sense of self. The heterogeneous possibilities for identity formation or expression simultaneously produce the potential for existential angst and expand individual's existential space for active self-creation (Holmer-Nadesan 1996). Consequently, identity politics have become an important social force that helps define political processes and cultural movements.

The civil rights movements, the black pride movement, the late-twentieth-century women's movements, and the gay rights movements illustrate the force of identity politics and the ability of such politics to articulate an organized movement out of heterogeneous groupings of individuals. Often times, what unites disparate individuals into a collective movement is a singular identity marker that is socially stigmatized, marginalized, and/or constructed as "other than" a social privileged identity (see Laclau and Mouffe 1985). Although the singular identity marker does not exhaust the subjectivity of those who bear it, they experience this marker as particularly meaningful because of the degree of its social significance/stigmatization. For example, individuals from very different genetic, cultural, educational, and professional backgrounds may share a collective identity only by virtue of the color of their skin. While this singular marker may seem unimportant in the face of considerable group differences, its social significance is such that it becomes critical in that it profoundly organizes/shapes individuals' experiences, particularly experiences of social and political maginalization. Those socially marked differences that are visibly inscribed upon/in bodies are particularly relevant in shaping personal experience because of their seeming "obviousness."

The disabilities rights movement is one of those social movements that embraces and is embraced by individuals who may share little but some bodily difference that has become marked as an important marker of social difference and/or pathology. People who are hearing impaired, asthmatic, obese, or unable to walk all may share the label of disability despite vast differences in their backgrounds and day-to-day experiences. However, what they do share is the experience of difference due to bodily sensations, physical limitations, and/or social constraints.[7] Social value orientations, built environments, and cultural norms all contribute to this experience of difference and render it an important form of demarcating personal identity. Thus, material bodily differences become socially significant identity markers (Albrecht et al. 2001; Corker and Shakespeare 2002; Davis 2002).

And yet, the social and/or personal ascription of "disability" often leads to social resistance. Individuals who are stigmatized by their bodily differences may resist cultural values and governmental or professional practices that "pathologize" their ascribed identities and/or lead to social or physical marginalization. The tactics are multiple and include demands for accommodation to public spaces (e.g. wheel-chair access), governance over service systems and individual care, and appeals to social justice and cultural validation (see Barnartt et al. 2001). Demands for social justice and validation often draw upon the discourse and value orientations of other social movements (e.g. the civil rights movement) and cultural as well as "expert knowledge" derived from the disciplines of law, medicine, biology, and psychology, among others.[8]

Autism advocacy is not a fully formed social movement but it illustrates how a singular identity marker can unite disparate individuals whose socially marked "disabilities" have engendered collective resistance. As explained in Chapter 6, people labeled with autism are most likely a biologically and genetically heterogeneous bunch. What they share are difficulties in communication and social relations and yet these difficulties are not characteristically homogeneous in form or expression. Some people with autism may lack the ability to speak yet others may be very articulate. Some people with autism may evidence strong visual-spatial problem-solving skills while others do not, and so on. And yet, despite considerable heterogeneity, people who are involved in advocacy often embrace "autism" as one of their most important identity markers, even when the subtleness of their symptoms precluded a formal diagnosis until adulthood. It may seem perplexing that some people might choose to label themselves autistic; however, there are important reasons why such a diagnosis might be desired. What follows addresses why people might embrace the label of autism and how it might serve as a force for collective action, despite the paradoxes that might seem to imply.

The unifying experience of being "different" transcends the disparate narratives of individuals who self-identify as autistic. Even the most articulate individuals who claim autism describe this sense of difference as permeating their lives, particularly in relationship to their interactions with social peers and with respect to the intensity of their particular interests. Thus, the noun "autism" summarizes, organizes, and articulates difference in a way that oddly depersonalizes the source of these differences by rendering the syndrome/disorder/personality style as responsible for the individual's dislocation within the social field. Autism becomes the unifying, organizing center that explains and predicts the individual's differences: I am different because I am autistic and autism explains my difference.

This willingness to embrace autism as a label particularly materializes on the autism advocacy Internet sites and in autobiographical texts written by self-described autistic individuals. Popular autobiographical texts include *Pretending to be Normal: Living with Asperger's Syndrome* by Liane Holliday Willey (1999, with a foreword by Tony Attwood), *Emergence: Labeled Autistic* by Temple Grandin and M. M. Scariano (1996), and *Somebody Somewhere: Breaking Free from the World of Autism* by Donna Williams (1995). Although some of these autobiographical accounts of AS represent the individuals' experience with the disorder in terms of personal tragedy, more and more accounts are attempting to de-pathologize the syndrome by contextualizing it in relation to neurological difference rather than medical pathology. For example, an Amazon.com review, posted by "a reader from Los Angeles" of the book *Pretending to be Normal*, reads:

> The title of this book really sums up the most tragic aspect of Asperger's: the self-denying, closeted mentality. Nowadays, autistics are gaining more self-respect. Willey and Attwood's views are a marked improvement over previous depiction of autism as pathology, but ultimately, they reinforce a sense that, while deserving of sympathy, autism is a tragic deficit. *Many autistics now feel that we are a positive neuro-variation, possibly an evolutionary step forward from the mob mentalities that now crush this planet.*
> (my italics, http://www.amazon.com/exec/obidos/tg/detail/-1853027499/qid=1082226560/sr=8-1/ref=sr_8_xs_ap_i1_xgl14/102-9675413-4828127?v=glance&s=books&n=507846)

This idea illustrated in the posting that autism is a potentially positive "neuro-variation" is increasingly promulgated in Internet postings and is slowly finding its way into published media periodicals.

Indeed, autism as "neuro-variation" has become one important theme of the autism advocacy movement. For example, the site titled "Autism Advocacy" authored by Frank Klein (http://home.att.net/~ascaris1/)

describes its mission in relation to a celebration of the "wonders of the autism spectrum" and deliberately distinguishes its focus from sites dedicating to "curing" autism:

> Envisioned as a companion to this site, the *Autistic Advocacy group at Yahoogroups* is a place for parents, professionals, autistics, and anyone else interested in autism spectrum issues to get together and discuss how to parent autistic spectrum kids (AS, autism, PDD, et cetera), and to overcome the various barriers to development that come with autism, while celebrating the wonders of the autism spectrum. This is not a place for the Cure Autism Now! folks . . . there are enough places like that on the net already.

In a series of very thoughtful and articulate postings, the author of this site, Frank Klein, argues for the need to help autistic children without attempting to eradicate the differences that render them special—that is, those that derive from their condition as autistic. Another Internet site, autistics.org. (http://www.autistics.org/library/pschwarz.html) provides an articulate and affirmative statement by Phil Schwarz urging parents to accept their autistic children as "autistic," while also recognizing that these children may face particular challenges due to their underlying neurologically based differences. Autism Network International (http://ani.autistics.org) provides additional examples of this kind of advocacy statement in their philosophical statement of principles:

- The best advocates for autistic people are autistic people themselves.
- Autistic lives are meaningful and worthwhile lives.
- Supports for autistic people should be aimed at helping them to compensate, navigate, and function in the world, *not at changing them into non-autistic people or isolating them from the world.*
- Autistic people of all ages and all levels of ability and skill are entitled to adequate and appropriate support services.
- *Autistic people have characteristically autistic styles of relating to others, which should be respected and appreciated* rather than modified to make them "fit in."
- In addition to promoting self-advocacy for high-functioning autistic adults, ANI also works to improve the lives of autistic people who, whether because they are too young, or because they do not have adequate communication skills, are not able to advocate for themselves.

(my italics: http://ani.autistics.org/intro.html)

As illustrated by these examples, autism advocates are using the Internet to promulgate a more affirmative and activist representation of autism.

A final example of an affirmative approach to autistic difference is found in a radio interview conducted on National Public Radio by Terry Gross

(May 5, 2004) with Michael John Carley, a talented and accomplished individual with Asperger's syndrome. In the program, Carley explained that he was diagnosed with AS in his thirties, one week after the diagnosis of his four-year-old son with the same disorder. Terry Gross asked Carley if the diagnosis came as a surprise, to which Carley responded that although he was initially surprised—it seemed "too ridiculous"—"the more I started to look into it the more it made absolute sense" in "a real epiphanial sort of way" because "I had known that I'd always suspected that you know I really didn't have that sense of shared experience with other people that I had wanted and yearned for in my life." And so by the time the formal diagnosis was made it was "really etched in stone that this is obviously what had been going on my entire life." Carley observed that the diagnosis caused him to reconsider his whole life history: "you have to re-examine" and "re-evaluate" "so many instances in your history." Carley's responses to Gross's questions tended to affirm the positive characteristics associated with AS, such as honesty, and downplayed the disabilities associated with the syndrome. When asked whether Carley observed similarities between himself and his AS son, Carley responded, "a plethora" and added: "it is a joy to raise him." Carley concluded that had he been diagnosed as a child, as is the case with his son, he would have had the opportunity to *know* himself better.

Carley's comments are interesting not only because they affirm autism and attest to its de-stigmatization, at least for people with AS, but also because Carley seems to suggest that autism is his core essence. And yet self-knowledge of that core essence came relatively late in Carley's life. Yet so profound an influence did this knowledge hold that, once received, it led him to reinterpret his whole life in relation to its organizing principle.

As illustrated by Carley's process of self-revelation, many people with high-functioning autism share an implicit belief that autism constitutes a kind of essence that fundamentally defines that person's being. Often times, autism advocates will draw upon neurological research findings to describe this autistic essence. However, autism advocates reject the deficiency model that is often tied to the biogenetic formulations of autism (within which the "autistic brain" and/or "mind" is explained reductively in relation to the composite set of autistic genetic/neural-anatomical "defects" so that autism is essentially defined negatively against a backdrop of normality). Instead, the autism advocacy model suggests that the more troubling symptoms of autism amount to defense strategies mounted by the autistic mind and are not, in most cases, directly tied to neurological or genetic "defects."

Thus, although the advocacy model may reductively trace the autistic mind to biogenetic differences, it is represented as qualitatively *different*, rather than deficient, from typical minds. Framed from this perspective, therapy cannot, and should not attempt to, "cure" autism because the condition constitutes a materially inscribed part of the individual's constitution. Rather, the goal of therapy transforms to helping the "autistic mind" adjust productively to its unique capabilities and disabilities. Therapy should target only those symptoms that directly impair the individual, although the determination of such remains somewhat vague.

Phil Schwarz illustrates this perspective in an essay ("Cure, recovery, prevention of autism?") distinguishing autistic essence from its troubling but non-necessary symptoms in order to dissuade parents from trying to "cure" their autistic children:

> They [parents] make the fundamental mistake of confusing autism itself—which is a set of differences in the way the brain and mind are organized, expressed in different proportions and intensities in each autistic person—with the impediments that arise secondarily to those differences, also in varying proportions and intensities.
>
> (http://www.autistics.org/library/pschwarz.html)

More explicitly, Jim Sinclair writes in a poignant essay ("don't mourn for us") that

> Autism isn't something a person *has*, or a "shell" that a person is trapped inside. There's no normal child hidden behind the autism. Autism is a way of being. It is *pervasive*; it colors every experience, every sensation, perception, thought, emotion, and encounter, every aspect of existence. It is not possible to separate the autism from the person—and if it were possible, the person you'd have left would not be the same person you started with.
>
> This is important, so take a moment to consider it: Autism is a way of being. It is not possible to separate the person from the autism.
>
> (http://web.syr.edu/~jisincla/dontmourn.htm)

This move to distinguish the sometimes troubling and potentially handicapping "symptoms" of autism from an undergirding condition or state of being is an important strategy for de-pathologizing autism while simultaneously acknowledging that people diagnosed with the condition often require forms of assistance not necessary for those who are "neurologically typical." For autism advocates, intervention should aim at helping the autistic child manage and/or surmount his/her particular "surface" sensory or social challenges without attempting to fundamentally alter his or her *essential being*. Again, the determination of which symptoms constitute difference and which constitute impairment remains vague.

The idea that people with autism share some essential being—some unique set of biological (genetic/neurological) differences—rendering them ontologically different in *mind* from the rest of the population of the "neurologically typical"—is simultaneously divisive and affirmative in its representation of autistic difference. First, this deep structure model of autism presupposes an ontological divergence between non-autistic people and autistic people and each group is afforded a certain ontological homogeneity. Accordingly, people designated as autistic are biologically essentialized as ontologically different beings, at least at a neurological level. This essentialization is evident in the ubiquitous tendency for autism advocates to compare themselves with "neurological typicals" or NTs. Advocates are often vague about the source of their essential differences of "mind" but tend to tie them indirectly to neurological and/or genetic variations that are believed to be shared uniquely by autistic populations. Qualitative differences across autistic populations are typically explained by variations of degree rather than by fundamental underlying neurological differences.

Strangely, present-day efforts to represent high-functioning autism as a qualitatively distinct and innate cognitive style parallel early-twentieth-century formulations of personality disorders by Kurt Schneider and Hans Asperger. As explained in Chapter 3, Schneider and Asperger saw psychopathic personalities and "autistic psychopathy" as innate, heritable, and qualitatively distinct personality disorders that could afford special aptitudes as well as social stigmatization. However, while the contemporary cognitive vocabulary avoids the moral baggage of the personality disorder (that infused even Schneider's and Asperger's works), it also represents all people grouped under its labels as sharing a biologically determined and universally applicable set of personality characteristics and cognitive strengths and weaknesses. The greatest advantage of the cognitive vocabulary is that its assumption of modularity affords a therapeutic space for "cognitive deficits" in addition to demanding valorization for "cognitive strengths."

And so, autism advocates embrace autism as a label articulating their unifying, underlying biological and neurological *divergence* from the general population while simultaneously advocating for understanding of and special care for the more troubling autistic deficits or symptoms. Indirect and implicit appeals to the humanistic ethos of tolerance and respect for human variation provide part of the justification for affirming and/or valorizing the differences that make people "autistic." But more frequently the primary justification for affirming autistic difference resides in celebrating those skills, aptitudes, or accomplishments that are viewed as deriving directly from autism.

As explained previously, an important form of argument for valorizing autistic difference appeals to the skills and accomplishments that are viewed as arising directly from "autistic neurology." Advocacy efforts reconstruct formerly pathological autistic "symptoms" in terms of the eccentricities of a unique and meritorious cognitive style. Individuals with high-functioning autism, particularly those labeled with AS, have achieved a kind of cultural affirmation for their purported strength in precisely those skills most valued by post-industrialized economies. Of course, for many people bearing the label of autism, this diffuse culture valorization may have little impact on their daily experiences, trials and challenges. Moreover, family members' ability to mobilize this form of defense in response to others' condemnations of autistic difference is no doubt highly dependent upon their symbolic resources and context, particularly upon their familiarity with these largely media-promulgated arguments. The contradictions arising from media-mediated cultural valorizations of autism and the everyday experiences of marginalization will likely persevere, representing the complex and antagonistic symbolic fields that constitute the source of meaning in social life.

Concluding thoughts: autism as disease/disablement, difference, and genius

This chapter has explored many of the ideas and practices implicated in the social interpretation and production of autistic persons at the turn of the twenty-first century. In this sense, this chapter has explored autism as an "interactive kind": that is, it has explored how people with autism are produced as such in relation to historically specific conditions and interpretive frameworks. It has also explored how some individuals who are inscribed with autistic identities appropriate and resist various interpretations of their experienced difficulties. This dialectically motivated exploration of (1) the institutional matrices of knowledge, practices, and identities on the one hand and (2) the production of—and resistance by—individuals on the other hand illustrates possibilities for exploring the social construction of disease and disability.

People diagnosed with autism and AS do experience difference and are experienced as different. These differences are both produced and rendered visible by complex institutional matrices including built environments, social institutions and professional role identities, and cultural practices and values. Yet, individuals who are singled out and whose behaviors are rendered meaningful by the diagnosis of autism are not passive agents. Although the "symptoms of their disorder" have rendered them visible as different and even "disabled" their differences do not preclude their active participation in self-creation and in the social world. In particular, those people designated with high-functioning autism and/or AS are now actively campaigning for respect and understanding of their uniqueness. Given that the sources for individual and collective agency are typically, if not always, embedded within existing institutional matrices, it is not surprising that efforts to affirm autistic difference are appropriating and reinterpreting biomedical and psychological interpretations of autism as a medical disorder and/or psychopathology. For example, the idea of a genetically coded, neurologically inscribed "autistic difference" forwarded by many autism advocates draws upon and reimagines autistic biogenetic pathology within an affirmative framework. Because this strategy draws upon scientifically legitimized vocabularies and constructs, it demands recognition and commands some level of respect. By invoking preferred "scientific" codes it legitimizes a right to recognition and dialogue.

And yet, contrary to affirmative efforts to reimagine autism as difference rather than disorder, people living with the disorder know it is a difference that ultimately tends to be devalued in relation to a privileged "neurotypical" normality. In particular, people diagnosed with autism and their families do encounter significant social stigmatization. Adolescents with Asperger's syndrome and high-functioning autism are prone to depression and anxiety due to social alienation. Family members of people with autism do experience considerable social stress and emotional exhaustion. Thus, the differences that are organized and labeled by the idea of autism are differences that *matter* in people's lives. Consequently, efforts to reimagine autism, particularly high-functioning autism, as difference often unravel around the cruelty of "normality" and the subsequent experiences of marginality. Efforts to affirm autistic difference in relation to specialized skills and aptitudes that are valorized within the cultural environment may assist in advocacy efforts by generating respect and tolerance or they may lead to resentment from "neurologically typicals" whose subliminated anxieties about economic success in a "winner take all society" get displaced on the apparently intellectually gifted but socially vulnerable AS peer.

The future for people with autism and all its high-functioning variations has yet to be made, yet to be written. However, the advocacy efforts made by self-avowed autistics and their families and friends illustrate a new politics of life that will help shape the social and political tensions of the twenty-first century. Nikolas Rose describes this politics as "the politics of life itself":

> Individuals who identify themselves and their community through their biology challenge the vectors that lead from biological imperfection or abnormality to stigmatization and exclusion. They use their individual and collective lives, the evidence of their own existence and their vital humanity, as antagonistic forces to any attempt to re-assemble strategies of negative eugenics within a new exclusionary biopolitics. . . . As somatic individuals engage with vital politics, a new ethics of life itself its taking shape.
>
> (Rose 2001: 19)

The twenty-first century may present new forms of identity politics embedded in new research in the arenas of genetics and neuroscience. Autism advocacy illustrates how "the politics of life itself" may play out in the social field as those who are rendered different by their biology actively resist their marginalization by illustrating, affirming, and demanding legitimization for their biologically inscribed differences. The biological reductionism that this politics implies and the rejection of social models for the production of individual experience may have effects unintended but these effects as yet remain undisclosed.

Notes

1 The issue of mediation is actually quite contested. Some theorists argue that at least some bodily experiences precede cultural interpretations and enter the realm of sociality through their symbolization. This argument is forwarded by Hughes and Paterson (1997), who suggest that the narratization of bodily symptoms in communication constitutes the transformation of bodily symptoms into cultural phenomenon. Other theorists wish to give the body its due but lean toward accounts that stress the cultural and linguistic mediation of embodied experiences. For example, Weiss (1999) bridges phenomenology and Lacanian psychoanalysis by making the argument that culturally derived bodily images mediate self-concept and bodily experiences. The various writers in the disability studies movement oscillate between mediated and unmediated accounts of bodily experiences. Developing a satisfactory account, free from theoretical dualisms, that fully captures the materiality of the human body and its inscription by cultural forces is very likely impossible. I therefore recognize the limitations inherent in my claim that bodily experiences are always/already mediated.

2 Although Hacking's work is exemplary in its efforts to theorize the co-constitution of nature and culture, brain and mind, body and identity, his works have not gone uncriticized. The project of dialectical theorizing that rejects mechanistic formulas and ontological givens is an ongoing project that, perhaps, is always/already doomed to incompleteness because of the tendency for language to offer the illusion of stable categories of meaning. And so, the model of autism here offered will suffer from the ambiguities and *aporias* specific to this challenge. However, the point of such tentative theorizing is to offer a starting point for exploring, later in this chapter, the complex dividing practices, looping effects, and strategies of resistance characteristic of "autism."

3 The idea that autism is a niche disorder does not preclude affording it a certain brute facticity. Yet that brute facticity is rendered visible and intelligible within social-symbolic institutional matrices.

4 Problems with motor planning, including speech production, are also often targeted for intervention. These difficulties are explained in terms of the "executive functions" account of autistic difficulties (see Chapter 5). However, since the idea of executive functions is fundamentally ambiguous in terms of concrete neurological bases (e.g., relationship to cerebellum is only loosely supported), therapists may have difficulty devising specific therapeutic practices for "stimulating" or developing executive functions skills. In contrast, simply behaviorally based interventions can be implemented to help a child reduce his/her sensory defensiveness.

5 Although the processes by which sensory and social perception occur are unclear, most commentators agree that the ability to filter and interpret sensory data requires complex processes of neural syntheses that are both innate and learned. For unknown reasons, people vary in their perceptual skills and autistic people, in particular, often report a decreased ability to filter unwanted perceptual information and to organize perceptual gestalts, which often lead to considerable experiences of anxiety. Repetitive behaviors and avoidance tactics may be implemented as "defense mechanisms" for the child seeking to reduce his/her sensory-induced anxiety and/or difficulties with executive functions (planning). For such children, sensory-integration and speech therapies that address the child's visual, auditory, or kinetic sensitivities may help the child tolerate, filter and/or organize

their perceptual data, thereby enabling more "normal" or "typical" learning and development to occur. For example, a child whose sensory integration therapy has perhaps enhanced her auditory processing is much more likely to become verbally competent than a child who is unable to make "sense" of an onslaught of auditory stimuli.

6 In contrast to those academics who view certain abilities as emerging from the "autistic mind," Allan Snyder and John Mitchell (1999) at the Centre for the Mind at the Australian National University in Canberra universalize the cognitive attributes associated with autism but argue that although all people possess the ability to engage in hyper-concrete thinking, typical thinking patterns impede against it. For example, they argue that all people actually possess the inherent ability for savant mathematical thinking: "the mechanisms for savant mathematics reside equally in us all but cannot normally be accessed" (Snyder and Mitchell 1999: 591). For Snyder and Mitchell, autistic deficits in synthetic thinking essentially free up this latent capacity for savant thinking.

7 This is *not* to say that other social identity markers such as gender, ethnicity, class, etc. do not mediate and/or inflect the experience of disabled difference (see specific discussion in Barnes and Mercer (2001: 519–520)). Rather, the claim is that as a way of marking social identity, disability (i.e., not abled) becomes a primary material and symbolic marker (see the discussion by Davis 2002).

8 For example, the acknowledgements for the impressive *Handbook of Disability Studies* (2001) states that the ideas for the handbook "germinated in the American civil rights movement of the 1960s and took root in the international human rights impetus of the past 25 years" (Albrecht et al. 2001: ix).

8 Directions in the ontology of personhood

The new genetics, genomics, and opportunities for somatic subjects

> To fix autism would first presuppose that I was broken, then that I needed to be made NT. I don't need to be made NT. I do need to learn how to deal with the world, and to a large extent the world also needs to learn to deal with a much broader range of people than it does.
>
> Amanda

This book has explored the various niche conditions implicated in the production of autism and Asperger's syndrome as diagnostic disorders and the bodies of knowledge implicated in their twentieth-century articulations and valuations. Within these pages no attempt has been made to locate the "truth" of autism because this book contends that no fixed and universal biological or psychological truth of autism may be located. Autism is produced through the nosological clustering of symptoms—symptoms no doubt stemming from diverse etiologies—and through the clinical practices of remediation. It is "produced" through historically unique institutional and representational practices described in this book. Historical matrices not only produced the conditions of possibility for the emergence of autism as a diagnostic category, but also influence contemporary representational practices as historically rooted meanings are smuggled into and shape present understandings. Accordingly, Bleuler's Freudian-influenced idea of "autism" to this day shapes and contributes to the popular notion that the autistic child occupies some solipsistic inner psychological space that can be sundered by bravely administered therapeutic practices. Although these practices may not in fact reveal the space they presuppose, they do operate on and shape the relationship between autistics and their environment. In effect, autism is produced through the effects of its articulations and therapeutic remediations on individuals labeled with this disorder. This argument does not deny biological differences: it does not deny that genetics, ontogenetic socialization factors, and environmental chemicals shape the emergence and expression of our experiential embodiment. Rather, I argue that the processes of identifying, interpreting, and remediating embodied differences are cultural and historically specific and socially and materially mediated. The condition called autism does not stand outside of the symbolic awaiting discovery. Rather, the symbolic inscribes and produces autism. Investigating these processes of inscription/production reveals much about the current desires, anxieties, and opportunities for personhood in the early twenty-first century.

Accordingly, this concluding chapter briefly points to some of the dangers and opportunities presented by current understandings and valuations of autism. In particular, the chapter sketches the contradictions, ambiguities, and opportunities presented by extant genetic and neuropsychological constructions of autism.

As established in Chapter 6, the biogenetic metaphor for understanding autism dominates late-twentieth-century research and social discourse about the disorder. However, although biogenetic autism research may offer new understandings of the complex relationships across behavior, mind, and brain, it also poses challenges. In particular, extant genetic research on autism coupled with efforts to localize neural "abnormalities" in the brains and/or genes of autistic people together pose the threat of a new eugenics. In the context of modern "risk" societies that strive to reduce the economic and social costs of modernization (Beck et al. 1994), autism and other developmental disabilities constitute a form of risk demanding management. The forms of management characteristic of risk society tend to privilege the authority and knowledge of scientific thinking. This holds particularly true within the logic of the new genetics.

Although the new genetics comprises a contradictory matrix of knowledge, professionals, and practices, its unifying nexus involves efforts to explain and predict human variation using genetic explanations. Formally characterized by "neutral scientific representations of bodily processes" whose benefits are tied implicitly to the promise of medically based applications (Kerr and Cunningham-Burley 2000: 295), the new genetics hides normative assumptions and valuations. For instance, the Human Genome Project offers a normative, typified genome ideal against which genetic deviations can be marked. Moreover, the topics, methods, and applications of the human genome project are both reductionistic and deterministic and tend to focus on linking socially marked forms of difference with genetic defects (Kerr and Cunningham-Burley 2000). The new genetics decontextualizes (i.e., strips of social bearing), reifies, naturalizes, and spatializes socially produced and dynamic constructs such as intelligence, aggression, depression, and anxiety (to name but a few) in the brain and/or gene allele.

At times, the new genetics invokes the vocabulary of the old genetics, albeit in new guises. As Kerr and Cunningham-Burley (2000) point out, the old nineteenth-century eugenics' interest in reducing intelligence to genetic factors finds expression in the new genetics search for the gene alleles implicated in distinct "cognitive abilities." Moreover, the purportedly objective and neutral geneticists who have explicitly rejected research into IQ and personality, still accept genetic research into disorders such as schizophrenia and manic depressive illnesses on the grounds that these are pathological conditions, not normal traits (Harper and Clarke 1997). *However, the line between the normal and the pathological is far from clear as new broader continuums of disease are established* (such as the "schizophrenic spectrum" (Rutter and Plomin 1997)) *and the term "cognitive abilities" replaces the older and more politically fraught concept of "intelligence."*

(my italics, Kerr and Cunningham-Burley 2000: 296)

Accordingly, the new genetics medicalizes mental illness to such an extent that syndromes formerly understood as heterogeneous in etiology (e.g., schizophrenia) are now represented as distinct disease entities caused by defective gene alleles. Research funding, practices and publications privilege the causal role of genetic "agents," although they may pay lip service to the mediating role of environmental factors. Efforts to explain why individuals with suspect alleles lack the "positive" symptoms of mental illness (e.g., delusions) necessitate expanding the boundaries of the syndrome to encompass ever more subtle expressions of positive and negative symptoms. Consequently, more and more personality eccentricities are pathologized. Finally, the new genetics inadvertently reintroduce the discourse of heritable degeneracy: by localizing the form and sources of human differences in gene alleles, the new genetics constitutes the individual as the source point and responsible agent for all forms of behavior regarded normatively as undesirable.

The expansion of the "autism spectrum" to include people with the mildest social deficits illustrates the pathologization of differences at issue. And the search for the genetic "origins" of the purportedly unique autistic cognitive strengths and deficits inherits the eugenicists' project of dividing human populations according to characteristics believed both innate and deterministic. Even more affirmative representations of "inherent" autistic differences are shadowed by the specter of genetically inscribed difference.

As discussed in Chapter 5, the media-promulgated valorizations of autistic strengths often implicitly construct autistic intelligence as machine-like and alien. This interpretation is framed in part by cognitive psychology's undergirding computer-based metaphor of mind. Implicitly represented as an ideal testing ground for the modularity of mind thesis, cognitive psychology has constructed the autistic mind—and increasingly brain—in relation to its artificial model of intelligence(s). Within this framework, Asperger's syndrome implicitly represents a threatening apparition—a technological cyborg—as the instanciation of artificial-like intelligence embodied in human corporeality. Those autistic individuals who fail to exhibit specific cognitive strengths are simply constructed in relation to cognitive and social "deficits."

Efforts to trace these cognitive deficits and skills to genetic origins provide the public with few medically viable treatment options and, in times of scarcity, may deflect attention and resources from the less glamorous and commercially unviable forms of practical support for autistic people and their families. Research documents that parents and family members of people with autism require more support than they currently receive, particularly respite and social support (Abelson 1999; Gross 2004). As the rate of autism diagnosis continues to rise, pressures on existing services will likely undermine support capacities for both new and existing families. Identification of autism "susceptibility" genes will fail to address the needs of these individuals.

While writing this book I had the opportunity to meet a family whose children are both diagnosed with autism. One of the children bears a diagnosis of Angelman's syndrome in addition to his autistic diagnosis. Living in the state of Texas, this family's middle-class income renders them ineligible for any form of state support for respite care and provides only limited medical assistance for their two children. Lacking viable daycare for their children, the mother stays home and provides their care. Fearing social censure for the unpredictable behavior of her children, she rarely leaves the house. She and her family live a life of extreme social marginalization. Medical researchers find her family fascinating but numerous genetic analyses revealed no indication of the source of the children's conditions and provided no treatment options.

What benefits would accrue were geneticists able to locate the source gene alleles for this family's autism? The genetic basis of mental health (and most forms of disease) is not conferred in a Mendelian pattern of genetic inheritance. Consequently, susceptibility genes are "neither necessary nor sufficient" to cause disease, are "common within the normal population" and most importantly, "expression of the disease involves the interaction of multiple genetic and environmental factors" (Wilkie 2001: 622). Wilkie demonstrates the lack of practical utility of genetic analysis and testing with the case of the relationship between the *APOE e4* genotype and late onset Alzheimer's disease. Although this genotype is correlated with the disease, a test developed to identify its presence yielded a 71 percent false positive rate (71 percent of individuals with one or two of the alleles never develop the disease) and a 44 percent false negative rate (44 percent of individuals with the disease do not have the *APOE e4* gene allele) (625). Equally important in the lack of utility of genetic testing is the "therapeutic gap" between identifying suspect genes and the provision of treatment and/or prevention (626).

The new genetics' implications for prenatal testing rightly trouble ethicists, disability rights advocates, and religious leaders. Imagine discovering that your child has a 30 percent risk of developing Rett's disorder or Angelman's syndrome, two genetically linked autistic disorders whose susceptibility alleles may have been discovered.[1] That fact alone could condition the decision to maintain a pregnancy, even given a 70 percent probability that the child would not develop the disorder at issue. The stigma of bearing a child with a developmental disorder coupled with the lack of support available to many families in this situation might outweigh the greater probability of having a child who is "normal."

C. S. Friedman explores this issue and the ethical choices and consequences it raises in her *New York Times* Notable Book of the Year, *This Alien Shore* (1998). Friedman imagines two societies' solutions to the problem of genetically transmitted forms of mental illness. In one society, prenatal screening and genetic engineering have eliminated "defective" gene alleles from the genetic pool resulting in an "adjusted" but exceedingly mediocre population. In the other society, elaborate cultural practices and therapeutic regimes serve in the place of genetic engineering to enable the peaceful coexistence of all individuals. The degree of *social* engineering evident in the latter culture enables the occasional brilliance and discovery purportedly stemming from madness and autism. Although Friedman (1998) trades on the romanticist equation of madness and genius, her text aptly illustrates the dangers in genetic engineering and the opportunities possibly afforded to a society stressing support and acceptance for various forms of social difference.

Biogenetic approaches to studying disease—of all varieties—also inadvertently localize the responsibility for disease in the individual. That is, biogenetics represent individuals as possessing genes rendering them "susceptible" to particular physiological processes or environmental effects. This formulation obscures the role of the built environment in shaping and/or catalyzing genetic responses. The built environment includes air pollution, pesticides, and industrial contaminants, all of which are known to negatively affect child development. It is my belief that any *real* increases in (classical) autism rates are a result of environmental toxins adversely affecting developing fetuses and young children. And yet, the search for the genetic "origins" or first causes of autism obscures environmental defects by centering the gene as the locus of defects (Proctor 2004). Therefore, the search for the "genetic" causes of disease conducted in the absence of research on environmental contributions rests on a political foundation because it marginalizes external contributing factors that catalyze disease, contributing factors that reflect the vested interests of vast economic institutional matrices (see Lewontin 1993; Proctor 2004). Further, when one realistically considers the future possibilities of genetic engineering, it appears far simpler to transform the built environment than it does to prevent and shape disease through genetic interventions (Lewontin 1993). As one critic pointed out:

> From the point of view of lives saved per dollar, monies would probably be better spent preventing exposures to mutagens, rather than producing ever more precise analyses of their [genetic diseases] origins and

effects. Sequencing the human genome may be a technological marvel, but it will not give us the key to life.

(Proctor 2004: 27)

The social environment plays an important role in the production and shaping of disease and yet this contribution also tends to be marginalized. The legacy of the refrigerator mother obviously stymied research on the role of family environment in shaping the expression of autistic symptoms. And yet, decades of research on child development indicate that social environments directly affect children, from shaping their stress hormones, to their language development.

When researchers do study the families of people with autism, they tend to focus on identifying purportedly heritable "autistic characteristics" in parents and siblings. Accordingly, researchers exploring the "Broader Autism Phenotype" (e.g. Pickles et al. 2000) presume that personality and communication styles are directly heritable rather than acquired through modeling and socialization. This kind of reductionism ignores the role of cultural and social environments in mediating biogenetic ones and offers family members of people with autism little to no utility.

The body of research most receptive to the role of environment in shaping autism is published by and for kindergarten through twelfth grade (K-12) educators. Educational databases such as Educational Resources Information Center (ERIC) offer a wide variety of research identifying and explaining strategies for helping enable successful outcomes for educators and autistic children. Unfortunately, special education services remain underfunded in many if not most districts across the United States and stand ill-prepared for addressing the diverse needs of large numbers of autistic children. Private interests tend not to support educational programs for children with special needs and thus the economics of school support are contingent upon tax-payer support in an era of tax revolt ("More taxes, anyone?" 2003; New 2003).

As discussed in Chapter 6, the motivations behind the current tendency toward biogenetic reductionism in representing disease are complex but economics represent a compelling force. Private money funds much published medical and psychiatric research making research with potential commercial applications more attractive. Pharmaceutical interests, for example, have few motivations for studying or funding research on social conditioning but many salient motivations for studying the biochemical correlates of mental illness. Although pharmaceutical innovations are always welcome and may play an important role in managing the symptoms of disease, these innovations are less successful in preventing or "curing" physical and mental diseases. This has been particularly true in the case of autism. Pharmaceuticals can help manage "secondary" autistic symptoms but do not redress the core communication and social difficulties associated with autism (Gerlai and Gerlai 2003). Moreover, if autism is understood as the common final pathway for diverse etiologies—cataclysms of disparate biological events—it seems unlikely that pharmaceuticals will ever be successful in eliminating, preventing, or curing all cases of autism, or even most of them. Accordingly, although genetic research can contribute to helping people with autism through pharmaceutical applications, it is unwise to place all faith and resources in genetic solutions.

Autism is after all a social problem. As a term, autism embraces the diverse ways that a heterogeneous group of people do not "fit" within their social environments. Although biogenetic accounts may offer some stories about the source of that lack of fit, their stories are incomplete and offer few resolutions.

What solutions are available for helping to resolve that lack of fit? Early intervention offers one solution. Intensive early intervention for very young children diagnosed with autism seems to predict better outcomes. However, this resolution requires intensive surveillance of all small children and the equalization of health care access. What little research exists suggests that ethnicity, race, and class impact age of diagnosis and access to services (see Cuccaro et al. 1996; Dyches et al. 2001; Mandell et al. 2002). Moreover, this solution does not address the needs of older children and adults with autism (see Choutka 1999). The public's fascination with autistic children fails to sustain an interest in the plight of autistic adults and their families.

Furthermore, there are various paradoxes implicated in the therapeutic ideas and practices employed by those professionals seeking to help autistic children and their families. This book documented how therapeutic regimes presume some implicit or explicit model of the nature of the disease or deficit and this model dictates the form and practice of therapeutic interventions. Some interventions such as the now discredited "holding therapy" may actually engender more harm than good, while other interventions (e.g. ABA) may help some individuals while others regard them as intolerable. Further, the entire discourse of therapeutic regimes presupposes administrative competence and yet any parent who has witnessed therapeutic practice recognizes vast unevenness in the application of therapeutic principles (see Choutka 1999). Thus, therapeutic regimes constituted by theories, professionals, and practices exercise power in asserting their privileged ability to represent and operate upon a "patient's" illness or dis-ability. Therefore, it is of critical importance that such regimes be subject to surveillance, critical assessment, and evaluation by all parties who have a stake in effects and outcomes. In particular, the apparent improvement and well-being of the person at issue must be of central importance.

Disability rights and patient advocate groups have become vocal and articulate in their demands that the subjects of medicalized categories and therapeutic regimes be afforded a new voice in the politics of representing and treating disease or disability. The discourse of the new genetics has responded to these new advocacy movements affirmatively by representing subjects as "active citizens" who weigh options and decide courses of action

(Petersen and Bunton 2002: 182). Although this discourse individualizes disease and dis-ability and regulates actions and choices through this individualization, it also creates new opportunities for social resistance and critical debate (see Rose 1999).

Novas and Rose (2000: 501) suggest that "somatic" individuals who relate to themselves on the basis of some underlying genetic identity do so in a context of inalienable legal rights granting them entitlements as well as obligations. The somatic subject is also embedded within the humanistic psychological discourse of self-actualization that demands certain ethical accountabilities from those providing their services or caring for their well-being. Therefore, the biogenetic medical discourses that construct individuals as "somatic" selves also intersect with other legal and humanistic discourses that stress "autonomy, self-actualization, prudence, responsibility and choice" (502). Disability and patients' rights advocates make use of these legal and humanistic discourses in their efforts to optimize care and social respect and accommodation. For example, disability rights advocates have been successful in the United States in ensuring legal recognition and acceptance for their advocacy rights for equal citizenship (Bagenstos 2004).

In this sense, biogenetic discourses contain and imply the limits of their applications. In recognizing patient rights and choice, genetic discourses present limits to their own operations. These opportunities and limits are increasingly applied to individuals who in previous decades would have been denied the basic rights of citizenship in western nations. However, increasingly the most impaired individuals are afforded some degree of legal and social recognition and choice. Two hundred years of suffrage and civil rights movements have created a cultural–political environment in western nations in which nearly all individuals are afforded legal legitimacy in expressing their rights, although in practice these rights may be curtained by *de facto* principles and practices.

The degree of advocacy occurring on behalf of, and by, autistic individuals illustrates these new recognitions and opportunities. Family members of autistic children and autistic adults increasingly use the Internet to argue for their rights as citizens (Singer 1999) and to argue against eugenicist-driven or eugenicist-seeming research policies seeking to identify and select out autism "susceptibility" genes. Their rhetorical strategies are diverse and multifaceted reflecting the heterogeneous groups who articulate together under the banner of autistic advocacy. Some advocates adopt the same strategy as utilized by C. S. Friedman (1998) in her book *This Alien Shore* by arguing for the potential greatness that is inherent in some forms of mental illness and/or disability. Still other advocates appropriate and reframe the concepts and vocabulary of cognitive psychology in order to argue that cognitive variations are differences rather than pathologies. This strategy has been particularly visible in efforts to represent high-functioning forms of autism as a unique cognitive style. So influential has been this strategy that psychological authorities such as Simon Baron-Cohen now express it.

Other advocates adopt legalistic and humanistic principles derived from still other discourses and other institutional matrices of meanings, practices, and professionals. But all advocates agree that the biogenetic constitution of somatic persons—autistic persons, schizophrenic persons, schizoid persons—does not undermine inalienable legal and humanistic rights deriving from those discourses' constructs of personhood.

Michel Foucault (1988) suggests that all relations of power necessarily imply possibilities for resistance. The discourses of the new genetics and cognitive neuroscience are the extant hegemonic discourses identifying and defining the nature and treatment of autism. But these discourses contain within them ambiguities and contradictions that limit their operations and necessitate recognition of alternative formulations and decision-frameworks. Resistance to these dominant discourses, institutional frameworks, and professional practices has appropriated their vocabularies but recontextualized their meanings in ways affirming the personhood and rights of those deemed autistic. Somatic individuals who self-identify in relation to their biologically defined differences are not passive objects but active subjects. Although they and their families experience social marginalization, new opportunities present themselves for asserting and demanding voice and recognition in the emerging bio-identity politics of the twenty-first century. Part of the politics of the early twenty-first century will involve conflicts over the authority to define the relevance, "truth," and social significance of biogenetic accounts of human differences and to distribute equitably and ethically any practical innovations in biogenetic applications. The politics of truth and value that stem from determinations of truth, equity, and ethics have just begun. In sum, although there are many dangers in the new genetics and psychological discourses, there are also opportunities for a new politics of identity for the twenty-first century.

Note

1 According to Ozand et al. (2003), the mutation of methyl-CpG-binding protein (MECP2) causes Rett's syndrome; however, one study found patients who had the mutation but did not have systemic expression of the disease.

References

Abelson, A. G. (1999) "Respite care needs of parents of children with developmental disabilities," *Focus on Autism and Other Developmental Issues* 14, 2: 96–100.

Abu-Akel, A. (2003) "A neurobiological mapping of theory of mind," *Brain Research Reviews* 43, 1: 29–40.

Albrecht, G. L., Seelman, K. D., and Bury, M. (eds) (2001) *Handbook of Disability Studies*, Thousand Oaks, CA: Sage.

Aldrich, C. A. and Aldrich, M. (1938) *Babies are Human Beings*, New York: Macmillan.

Alexander, F. G. and Selesnick, S. T. (1966) *The History of Psychiatry: An Evaluation of Psychiatric Thought and Practice from Prehistoric Times to the Present*, New York: Harper & Row.

Allen, J. (2003) "Are men obsolete?," *U.S. News and World Report*, June 23: 33.

Amanda (2004) Autism Advocacy http://health.groups.yahoo.com/group/AutAdvo/message/4924 (January 8, 2004).

American Psychiatric Association (APA) (1952) *Diagnostic and Statistical Manual of Mental Disorders*, Washington, DC: APA.

American Psychiatric Association (1968) *Diagnostic and Statistical Manual of Mental Disorders* (2nd edn), Washington, DC: APA.

American Psychiatric Association (1980) *Diagnostic and Statistical Manual of Mental Disorders* (3rd edn), Washington, DC: APA.

American Psychiatric Association (1987) *Diagnostic and Statistical Manual of Mental Disorders* (3rd edn, rev.), Washington, DC: APA.

American Psychiatric Association (1994) *Diagnostic and Statistical Manual of Mental Disorders* (4th edn), Washington, DC: APA.

"Another chromosome defect implicated" (1998) *Autism Research Review International* 12, 3: 4.

Appel, K. E. and Strecker, E. A. (1936) *Practical Examination of Personality and Behavior Disorders: Adults and Children*, New York: Macmillan.

Aries, P. (1962/1992) *Centuries of Childhood: A Social History of Family Life*, trans. R. Baldick, New York: Vintage.

Armstrong, D. (2002) *A New History of Identity: A Sociology of Medical Knowledge*, Basingstoke: Palgrave.

Asperger, H. (1952) Heilpädagogik; Einführung in die Psychopathologie des Kindes für Ärzte, Lehrer, Psychologen und Fürsorgerinnen, Wien: Springer.

Asperger, H. (1979) "Problems of infantile autism," *Communication* 13: 45–52.

Asperger, H. (1991) " 'Autistic psychopathy' in childhood," trans. U. Frith, in U. Frith (ed.) *Autism and Asperger Syndrome*, Cambridge: Cambridge University Press.

"Autistic savant artists: a costly talent" (1998) *Autism Research Review International* 12, 3: 6.

Aylward, G. P. (1997) *Infant and Early Childhood Neuropsychology*, New York: Plenum.

Bagenstos, S. R. (2004) "Justice Ginsburg and the judicial role in expanding 'We The People': the disability rights case," *Columbia Law Review* 104, 1: 49–60.

Baker, B. M. (2001) *In Perpetual Motion: Theories of Power, Educational History, and the Child*, New York: Peter Lang.

Baker, H. C. (2001) "A comparison study of autism spectrum disorder referrals 1997 and 1989," *Journal of Autism and Developmental Disorders* 32, 2: 121–125.

Barlow, D. H. and Durand, V. M. (1999) *Abnormal Psychology: An Integrative Approach* (2nd edn), Pacific Grove, CA: Brooks/Cole.

Barnartt, S., Schriner, K., and Scotch, R. (2001) "Advocacy and political action," in G. L. Albrecht, K. D. Seelman, and M. Bury (eds) *Handbook of Disability Studies*, Thousand Oaks, CA: Sage.

Barnes, C. and Mercer, G. (2001) "Assimilation or inclusion," in G. L. Albrecht, K. D. Seelman, and M. Bury (eds) *Handbook of Disability Studies*, Thousand Oaks, CA: Sage.

Baron-Cohen, S. (1988) "Social and pragmatic deficits in autism: cognitive or affective?," *Journal of Autism and Developmental Disorders* 18: 379–402.

Baron-Cohen, S. (1989) "Perceptual role taking and protodeclarative pointing in autism," *British Journal of Developmental Psychology* 7: 113–127.

Baron-Cohen, S. (1993) "From attention-goal psychology to belief-desire psychology: the development of a theory of mind, and its dysfunction," in S. Baron-Cohen, H. Tager-Flusberg, and D. Cohen (eds) *Understanding Other Minds: Perspectives from Autism*, Oxford: Oxford University Press.

Baron-Cohen, S. (1995) *Mindblindness: An Essay on Autism and Theory of Mind*, Cambridge, MA: Bradford/MIT Press.

Baron-Cohen, S. (1998) "Does the study of autism justify minimalist innate modularity?," *Learning and Individual Differences* 10, 3: 179–191.

Baron-Cohen, S. (2000) "Is Asperger syndrome/high-functioning autism necessarily a disability?," *Development and Psychopathology* 12: 489–500.

Baron-Cohen, S. (2002) "The extreme male brain theory of autism," *Trends in Cognitive Sciences* 6, 6: 248–254.

Baron-Cohen, S., Ring, H. A., Wheelwright, S., Bullmore, E. T., Brammer, M. J., Simmons, A., and Williams, S. C. R. (1999) "Social intelligence in the normal and autistic brain: an fMRI study," *European Journal of Neuroscience* 11, 6: 1891–1898.

Baron-Cohen, S. et al. (2000) "The amygdala theory of autism," *Neuroscience & Biobehavioral Reviews* 24, 3: 355–364.

Baron-Cohen, S., Wheelwright, S., Skinner, R., Martin, J., and Clubley, E. (2001) "The autism-spectrum quotient (AZ): evidence from Asperger syndrome/high function autism, males and females, scientists and mathematicians," *Journal of Autism and Developmental Disorders* 31, 1: 5–17.

Barrett, R. J. (1998) "Conceptual foundations of schizophrenia: I, degeneration," *Australian and New Zealand Journal of Psychiatry* 32, 5: 617–626.

Beck, J. (1986/1967) *How to Raise a Brighter Child*, London: Souvenir.

Beck, U., Giddens, A., and Lash, S. (eds) (1994) *Reflexive Modernization: Politics, Tradition and Aesthetics in the Modern Social Order*, Stanford, CA: Stanford University Press.

Beer, D. M. (1995) "Psychosis: from mental disorder to disease concept," *History of Psychiatry* vi: 177–200.

Beers, C. W. (1908) *A Mind that Found Itself: An Autobiography*, London: Longmans.

Begley, S. (1996) "Your child's brain," *Newsweek* 127, 8: 55–61.

Begley S. (1997) "How to build a baby's brain," *Newsweek* 129: 28–32.

Bender, L. (1947) "Childhood schizophrenia," *American Journal of Orthopsychiatry* 17: 40–56.

Bender, L. (1991) "The historical background of the concept of childhood schizophrenia," in J. G. Howells (ed.) *The Concept of Schizophrenia: Historical Perspectives*, Washington, DC: American Psychiatric Press.

Bernard, S., Enayati, A., Redwood, M. S. N. et al (2001) "Autism: a novel form of mercury poisoning," available online, http://www.autism.com/ari/mercury/html (July 18, 2001).

Berntson, G. G. and Cacioppo, J. T. (2000) "Psychobiology and social psychology: past, present, and future," *Personality and Social Psychology Review* 4, 1: 3–15.

Berrios, G. E. (1993) "European views on personality disorders: a conceptual history," *Comprehensive Psychiatry* 34, 1: 14–30.

Berrios, G. E. (1995) "Delirium and cognate states," in G. E. Berrios and R. Porter (eds) *A History of Clinical Psychiatry: The Origin and History of Psychiatric Disorders*, London: Athlone.

Berrios, G. E. (1996) *The History of Mental Symptoms: Descriptive Psychopathology since the Nineteenth Century*, Cambridge: Cambridge University Press.

Berrios, G. E. and Mumford, D. (1995) "Somatoform disorders," in G. E. Berrios and R. Porter (eds) *A History of Clinical Psychiatry: The Origin and History of Psychiatric Disorders*, London: Athlone.

Bettelheim, B. (1967) *The Empty Fortress: Infantile Autism and the Birth of the Self*, New York: The Free Press.

Beyer, K. S., Klauck, S. M., Wiemann, S., and Poustka, A. (2001) "Construction of a physical map of an autism susceptibility region in 7q32.3–q33," *Gene* 272, 1–2: 85–91.

Binstock, T. (2001) "Intra-monocyte pathogens delineate autism subgroups," *Medical Hypotheses* 56, 4: 523–531.

Bishop, D. V. M. (1989) "Autism, Asperger's syndrome and semantic-pragmatic disorder: where are the boundaries?" *British Journal of Disorders of Communication* 24: 107–121.

Bishop, D. V. M. (1993) "Annotation: Autism, executive functions and theory of mind: a neuropsychological perspective," *Journal of Child Psychology and Psychiatry* 34, 279–293.

Bleuler, E. (1908) "Die prognose der Dementia Praecox (Schizophreniegruppe)," *Allgemeine Zeitschrift fur Psychiatrie und Psychisch-Gerichtliche Medizin* 65: 436–464.

Bleuler, E. (1911) "Dementia praecox oder Gruppe der Schizophrenien," in G. Aschaffenburg (ed.) *Handbuch der Psychiatrie. Spezieller Teil. 4 Abteilung, 1. Halfte*, Leipzig and Vienna: Franz Deuticke.

Borenstein, S. (2003) "Common chemical in doubt," *The Arizona Republic*, April 15: A2.

Bowlby, J. (1952) *Maternal Care and Mental Health*, Geneva: World Health Organization.

Bowlby, J. (1953) *Childcare and the Growth of Love*, Baltimore, MD: Penguin.

Bowler, D. (2001) "Autism: specific cognitive deficit or emergent end point of multiple interacting systems?," in J. Burack, T. Charman, N. Yirmiya, and P. R. Zelazo (eds) *The Development of Autism: Perspectives from Theory and Research*, Mahwah, NJ: Lawrence Erlbaum.

Boyd, R. S. (2000) "Older brains grow, scientists discover," *The Arizona Republic*, May 16: A2.

Boyle, M. (1990) *Schizophrenia: A Scientific Delusion?*, London: Routledge.

Brambilla, P., Hardan, A., di Nemi, S. U. et al. (2003) "Brain anatomy and development of autism: a review of structural MRI studies," *Brain Research Bulletin* 61: 557–569.

Britzman, D. (1998) "Why return to Anna Freud? some reflections of a teacher educator," *Teaching Education* 10, 1: 3–16.

Bromfield, R. (2000) "It's the tortoise race: long-term psychodynamic psychotherapy with a high-functioning autistic adolescent," *Psychoanalytic Inquiry* 20, 5: 732–745.

Brook, S. L. and Bowler, D. M. (1992) "Autism by another name? Semantic and pragmatic impairments in children," *Journal of Autism and Developmental Disorders* 22, 1: 61–81.

Brown, M. (2002) "Introduction: Baudelaire between Rousseau and Freud," in M. Brown (ed.) *Picturing Children: Constructions of Childhood between Rousseau and Freud*, Aldershot: Ashgate.

Buchsbaum, M. S., Hollander, E., Haznader, M. M. et al. (2001) "Effect of fluoxetine on regional cerebral metabolism in autistic spectrum disorders: a pilot study," *International Journal of Neuropsychopharmacology* 4, 2: 119–125.

Buitelaar, J. K. and Willemsen-Swinkels, S. H. (2000) "Autism: current theories regarding its pathogenesis and implications for rational pharmacotherapy," *Paediatric Drugs* 2, 1: 67–81.

Burack, J. A., Charman, T., Yirmiya, N., and Zelazo, P. (eds) (2001) *The Development of Autism: Perspectives from Theory and Research*, Mahwah, NJ: Lawrence Erlbaum.

Burgoine, E. and Wing, L. (1983) "Identical triplets with Asperger's Syndrome," *British Journal of Psychiatry* 143: 261–265.

Cabot, R. C., Adams, F. D. (1938) *Physical Diagnosis*, Baltimore: W. Wood and Company.

"California: $34 million allocated for autism spectrum disorders research" (2000) *Autism Research Review* 14, 2: 1.

Caplan, F. (1971) *The First Twelve Months of Life*, New York: Putnam.

Carlton, S. (1993) *The Other Side of Autism: A Positive Approach*, Worcester, UK: Self Publishing Association.

Carper, R. A. and Courchesne, E. (2000) "Inverse correlation between frontal lobe and cerebellum sizes in children with autism," *Brain* 123, 4: 836–844.

Chapman, G. (1999) "Even if 'geekness' is a disorder, there's no rush to find a cure," *Los Angeles Times*, September 27: C1.

"China villages poisoned by U.S. high-tech trash" (2002) *The Arizona Republic*, March 1: A12.

Chomsky, N. (1968) *Language and Mind*, New York: Harcourt, Brace and World.

Choutka, C. M. (1999) "Experiencing the reality of service delivery: one parent's perspective," *The Journal of the Association for Persons with Severe Handicaps* 24, 3: 213–217.

Church, A. (1936) "An unsolvable problem of elementary number theory," *American Journal of Mathematics* 58: 354–363.

Cody, H., Pelphrey, K., and Piven, J. (2002) "Structural and functional magnetic resonance imaging of autism," *International Journal of Developmental Neuroscience* 20: 421–438.

Cohen, D. J. and Volkmar F. R. (eds) (1997) *Handbook of Autism and Pervasive Developmental Disorders*, New York: John Wiley and Sons.

Cohen, I. L. (2003) "Association of autism severity with a monoamine oxidase A functional polymorphism," *Clinical Genetics* 64: 190–197.

Comi, A. M., Zimmerman, A. W., Frye, V. H. et al. (1999) "Familiar clustering of autoimmune disorders and evaluation of medical risk factors in autism," *Journal of Child Neurology* 14, 6: 338–394.

Conlin, M. (2003) "The new gender gap," *Business Week* May 26: 74–84.

Cooke, R. (2002) "Possible link of violence, gene found," *The Arizona Republic* August 4: A18.

Cooley, C. H. (1909) *Social Organization: A Study of the Larger Mind*, New York: C. Scribner's Sons.

Coolidge, F. L. and Segal, D. L. (1998) "Evolution of personality disorder diagnosis in the *Diagnostic and Statistical Manual of the Mental Disorders*," *Clinical Psychology Review* 18, 5: 585–599.

Corker, M. and Shakespeare, T. (eds) (2002) *Disability/Postmodernity: Embodying Disability Theory*, London: Continuum.

Courchesne, E., Karns, C. M., Davies, H. R. et al. (2001) "Unusual brain growth patterns in early life in patients with autistic disorder: an MRI study," *Neurology* 57, 2: 245–254

Courchesne, E., Carper, R., and Akshoomoff, N. (2003) "Evidence of brain overgrowth in the first year of life in autism," *JAMA-Journal of the American Medical Association* 290, 3: 337–344.

Cowley, G. (2003) "Predicting autism," *Newsweek* July 28: 38–42.

Crain, W. (1992) *Theories of Development: Concepts and Applications* (3rd edn), Englewood Cliffs, NJ: Prentice Hall.

Croen, L. A., Grether, J. K., Hoogstrate, J., and Selvin, S. (2002) "The changing prevalence of autism in California," *Journal of Autism and Developmental Disorders* 32, 3: 207–215.

Cuccaro, M. L., Wright, H. H., and Rownd, C. V. (1996) "Brief report: professional perceptions of children with developmental difficulties: the influence of race and socioeconomic data," *Journal of Autism and Developmental Disorders* 26: 461–469.

Cunningham, H. (1995) *Children and Childhood in Western Society since 1500*, London: Longman.

Darwin, C. (1877) "A biographical sketch of an infant," *Mind* 2: 285–294.

Davidson, R. J. and Slagter, H. A. (2000) "Probing emotion in the developing brain: functional neuroimaging in the assessment of the neural substrates of emotion in normal and disordered children and adolescents," *Mental Retardation and Developmental Disabilities Research Review* 6, 3: 166–170.

Davis, L. J. (2002) *Bending over Backwards: Disability, Dismodernism and Other Difficult Positions*, New York: New York University Press.

Dawson, G. and Osterling, J. (1997) "Early intervention in autism: effectiveness and common elements of current approaches," in M. Guralnick (ed.) *The Effectiveness of Early Intervention*, Baltimore, MD: Brookes.

Dekker, J. (2001) *The Will to Change the Child: Re-education Homes for Children at Risk in Nineteenth Century Western Europe*, Frankfurt: Peter Lang.

DeMause, L. (1974) "The evolution of childhood," in L. DeMause (ed.) *The History of Childhood*, New York: Psychohistory Press.

Doane, J. and Hodges, D. (1992) *From Klein to Kristeva: Psychoanalytic Feminism and the Search for the "Good Enough" Mother*, Ann Arbor, MI: University of Michigan Press.

Donnellan, A. M. (1985) "Introduction," in A. M. Donnellan (ed.) *Classic Readings in Autism*, New York: Teachers College, Columbia University.

Donzelot, J. (1977) *The Policing of Families*, trans. R. Hurley, Baltimore, MD: Johns Hopkins University Press.

Dyches, T. T., Wilder, L. K., and Obiakor, F. E. (2001) "Autism: multicultural perspectives," *Advances in Special Education* 14: 151–177.

Ehrenreich, B. (1989) *Fear of Falling: The Inner Life of the Middle Class*, New York: Pantheon.

Ehrenreich, B. and English, D. (1978) *For Her Own Good: 150 Years of the Expert's Advice to Women*, Garden City, NY: Anchor Press.

Eisenberg, A., Murkoff, H. E., and Hathaway, S. E. (1996) *What to Expect the Toddler Years*, New York: Workman.

Eskenazi, B., Bradman, A., and Castorina, R. (1999) "Exposures of children to organophosphate pesticides and their potential adverse health effects," *Environmental Health Perspectives* 107(Suppl. 3).

"Evidence mounts for epidemic of autism" (2000) *Autism Research Review* 14, 2: 1.

Faris, R. E. L. (1934) "Cultural isolation and the schizophrenic personality," *American Journal of Sociology* 40: 155–164.

Fehr-Snyder, K. (2001) "More study urged in possible link of mercury," *The Arizona Republic* October 2: A5.

Feinberg, T. E. (2001) *Altered Egos: How the Brain Creates the Self*, Oxford: Oxford University Press.

Fisher, H. (2004) *Why We Love: The Nature and Chemistry of Romantic Love*, New York: Henry Holt.

Fitzgerald, M. (2000) "Is the cognitive style of the persons with the Asperger's syndrome also a 'mathematical style'?," *Journal of Autism and Developmental Disorders* 30, 2: 175–176.

Fitzgerald, M. (2002) "Asperger's disorder and mathematicians of genius," *Journal of Autism and Developmental Disorders* 32, 1: 59–60.

Fitzgerald, M. (2004) *Autism and Creativity: Is There a Link between Autism in Men and Exceptional Ability*, London: Brunner-Routledge.

Flew, A. (1979) *A Dictionary of Philosophy* (2nd rev. edn), New York: St. Martin's Press.

Fodor, J. (1983) *The Modularity of Mind: An Essay on Faculty Psychology*, Cambridge, MA: MIT Press.

Fodor, J. (2000) *The Mind Doesn't Work that Way: The Scope and Limits of Computational Psychology*, Cambridge, MA: MIT Press.

Foucault, M. (1965) *Madness and Civilization: A History of Insanity in the Age of Reason*, trans. R. Howard, New York: Pantheon.

Foucault, M. (1979) *Discipline and Punish*, trans. A. Sheridan, New York: Vintage.

Foucault, M. (1988) "The ethic of care for self as a practice of freedom: an interview with Michel Foucault, conducted by R. Fornet-Betancourt, H. Becker, A. Gomez-Muller," trans. J. D. Gautheir, in D. Rasmussen (ed.) *The Final Foucault*, Cambridge, MA: MIT Press.

Foucault, M. (1991) "Governmentality," in G. Burchell, C. Gordon, and P. Miller (eds) *The Foucault Effect*, London: Harvester Wheatsheaf.

Fox, N. (1999) *Beyond Health: Postmodernism and Embodiment*, London: Free Association.

Freud, A. and Sandler, J. (1985) *The Analysis of Defense: The Ego and Mechanisms of Defense Revisited*, New York: International Universities Press.

Freud, S. (1910/1957) *The Standard Edition . . . Five Lectures on Psychoanalysis, Leonardo da Vinci and Other Works Vol. 11*, London: Hogarth Press.

Freund, P. E. S. and McGuire, M. B. (1991) *Health, Illness, and the Social Body: A Critical Sociology*, Englewood Cliffs, NJ: Prentice Hall.

Friedman, C. S. (1998) *This Alien Shore*, New York: Daw.

Frith, U. (1989) *Autism: Explaining the Enigma*, Oxford: Basil Blackwell.

Frith, U. (1991) "Asperger and his syndrome," in U. Frith (ed.) *Autism and Asperger Syndrome*, Cambridge: Cambridge University Press.

Frith, U. and Happe', F. (1999) "Theory of mind and self-consciousness: what is it like to be autistic?," *Mind and Language* 14: 1–22.

Fromm-Reichmann, F. (1948) "Notes on the development of treatment of schizophrenia by psychoanalytic psychotherapy," Psychiatry 11: 263–273.

Galton, F. (1883) *Inquiries into Human Faculty and its Development*, London: Macmillan.

Gardner, M. (2000) "The brutality of Dr. Bettelheim," *Skeptical-Inquirer* 24, 6: 12–14.

Geier, M. R. and Geier, D. A. (2003a) "Neurodevelopmental disorders after thimerosal-containing vaccines: a brief communication," *Journal of Experimental Biology and Medicine* 228, 6: 660–664.

Geier, M. R. and Geier, D. A. (2003b) "Thimerosal in childhood vaccines, neurodevelopmental disorders, and heart disease in the United States," *Journal of American Physicians and Surgeons* 8, 1: 6–11.

Gerlai, J. and Gerlai, R. (2003) "Autism: a large unmet medical need and a complex research problem," *Physiology and Behavior* 79: 461–470.

Gesell, A. (1952) *Infant Development: The Embryology of Early Human Behavior*, Westport, CT: Greenwood Press.

Gesell, A. and Amatruda, C. S. (1941) *Developmental Diagnosis: Normal and Abnormal Child Development*, New York: Hoeber.

Giddens, A. (1991) *Modernity and Self-Identity: Self and Society in the Late Modern Age*, Stanford, CA: Stanford University Press.

Gillberg, C. and Coleman, M. (1996) "Autism and medical disorders: a review of the literature," *Developmental Medicine and Child Neurology* 38: 191–202.

Grady, C. L. and Keightley, M. L. (2002) "Studies of altered social cognition in neuropsychiatric disorders using function neuroimaging," *Canadian Journal of Psychiatry* 47, 4: 327–336.

Graf, W. D., Garcia-Marin, J., Gao, H. G. et al. (2000) "Autism associated with the mitochrondrial DNA G8363A transfer RNA(Lys) mutation," *Journal of Child Neurology* 15, 6: 357–361.

Grandin, T. and Scariano, M. M. (1996) *Emergence: Labeled Autistic*, New York: Warner.

Grant, J. (1998) *Raising Baby by the Book: The Education of American Mothers*, New Haven, CT: Yale University Press.

Gray, D. E. (2002). "Everybody just freezes. Everybody is just embarrassed': felt and enacted stigma among parents of children with high functioning autism," *Sociology of Health and Illness* 24, 6: 743–749.

Greenspan, S. I. and Wieder, S. (1998) *The Child with Special Needs: Encouraging Intellectual and Emotional Growth*, Reading, MA: Perseus.

Gross, J. (2004) "As autism cases rise, parents run frenzied race to get help," *New York Times*, January 30: A1–2.

Gross, T. (2004) "Michael John Carley on Asperger's Syndrome," on *Fresh Air*, National Public Radio, May 5.

Gueguen, J. P. (1996) "History of the concept of schizophrenia," in J. T. Dalby (ed.) *Mental Disease in History*, New York: Peter Lang.

Gundel, H. and Rudolf, G. A. E. (1993) "Schizophrenic autism: historical evolution and perspectives," *Psychopathology* 26: 294–303.

Hacking, I. (1998) *Mad Travelers*, Charlottesville, VA: University Press of Virginia.

Hacking, I. (1999) *The Social Construction of What?*, Cambridge, MA: Harvard University Press.

Hale, N. G. (1995) *The Rise and Crisis of Psychoanalysis in the United States: Freud and the Americans 1917–1985*, New York: Oxford University Press.

Hall, S. G. (1904) Adolescence; its Psychology and its Relations to Physiology, Anthropology, Sociology, Sex, Crime, Religion and Education, New York: D. Appleton and Company.

Hall, S. G. (1907) Youth; its Education, Regimen and Hygiene, New York: Appleton.

Halpern, D. F. (2000) *Sex Differences in Cognitive Abilities* (3rd edn), Mahwah, NJ: Lawrence Erlbaum.

Happe, F. (1999) "Autism: cognitive deficit or cognitive style," *Trends in Cognitive Sciences* 3: 216–222.

Hardcastle, V. G. (1995) "A critique of information processing theories of consciousness," *Minds and Machines* 5: 89–107.

Hariri, A. R., Mattay, V. S., Tessitoire, A. et al. (2002) "Serotonin transporter genetic variation and the response of the human amygdala," *Science* 297: 400–403.

Harper, P., Clarke, A. (1997) *Genetics, Society and Clinical Practice*, Oxford: BIOS.

Haslam, J. (1809) *Observations on Madness and Melancholy*, London: Callow.

Hawkins, A. H. (1999) *Reconstructing Illness: Studies in Pathography* (2nd edn), West Lafayette, IN: Purdue University Press.

Haznedar, M. M., Buchsbaum, M., Wei, T. C. et al. (2000) "Limbic circuitry in patients with autism spectrum disorders studied with positron emission tomography and magnetic resonance imaging," *American Journal Psychiatry* 157: 1994–2001

Healy, B. (2003) "Pumping the neurons," *U.S. News and World Report*, June 30/July 7: 29.

Hedgecoe, A. (2001) "Schizophrenia and the narrative of enlightened geneticization," *Social Studies of Science* 31, 6: 875–911.

Heil, J. (1981) "Does cognitive psychology rest on a mistake?," *Mind* 90, 359: 321–342.

Henley, D. (2001) "Annihilation anxiety and fantasy in the art of children with Asperger's syndrome and others on the autistic spectrum," *American Journal of Art Therapy: Art in Psychotherapy Rehabilitation and Education* 39, 4: 113–121.

Herbert, B. (2003) "Early warnings," *The New York Times*, September 12, available online, http:// www.nytimes.com/2003/09/12opinion/12HERB.html?th.

Herbert, J. D., Sharp, I. R., and Gaudiano, B. A. (2002) "Separating fact from fiction in the etiology and treatment of autism: a scientific review of the evidence," *The Scientific Review of Mental Health Practice* 1, 1: 23–43.

Herman, E. (1995) *The Romance of American Psychology: Political Culture in the Age of Experts*, Berkeley, CA: University of California Press.

High heavy metal levels seen in autistic children (2002). *Autism Research Review* 16, 3: 2. Study by Gordon Bell, not published.

Hill, E. L. and Frith, U. (2003) "Understanding autism: insights from mind and brain," *Philosophical Transactions of the Royal Society of London Series B Biological Sciences* 358, 1430: 281–289.

Hobson, R. P. and Bishop, M. (2003) "The pathogenesis of autism: insights from congenital blindness," *Philosophical Transactions of the Royal Society of London Series-B Biological Sciences* 358, 1430: 335–340.

Hoenig, J. (1995) "Schizophrenia: clinical section," in G. E. Berrios and R. Porter (eds) *A History of Clinical Psychiatry: The Origin and History of Psychiatric Disorders*, London: Athlone.

Hollander, E., Cartwright, C., Wong, C. M. et al (1998) "A dimensional approach to autism spectrum," *CNS Spectrums* 3, 3: 22–39.

Holmer-Nadesan, M. (1996) "Organization, identity and space of action," *Organizations Studies* 16: 49–81.

Horn, M. (1989) *"Before it's Too Late": The Child Guidance Movement in the United States, 1922–1945*, Philadelphia, PA: Temple University Press.

Houston, R. and Frith, U. (2000) *Autism in History: The Case of Hugh Blair of Borgue*, Padstow, Cornwall: Blackwell.

Howard, M. A., Cowell, P., Boucher, J., et al. (2000) "Convergent neuroanatomical and behavioral evidence of an amygdala hypothesis of autism," *Neuroreport* 11, 13: 2931–2935.

Howard, D. V. (1983) *Cognitive Psychology: Memory, Language and Thought*. New York: Macmillan.

Hrdlicka, M., Lulisek, R., Propper, L. et al. (2002) "Child autism and other pervasive disorders: the relation of autistic psychopathology to selected brain structures," *Ceskoslovenska Psychologie* 46, 4: 289–298.

Hubbard, R. and Wald, E. (1999). *Exploding the Gene Myth: How Genetic Information is Produced and Manipulated by Scientists, Physicians, Employers, Insurance Companies, Educators, and Law Enforcers*, Boston: Boston.

Hudson, R. P. (1983) *Disease and its Control: The Shaping of Modern Thought*, Westport, CT: Greenwood Press.

Hughes, B. and Paterson, K. (1997) "The social model of disability and the disappearing body: towards a sociology of impairment," *Disability and Society* 12: 325–340.

Hughes, J. M. (1989) *Reshaping the Psychoanalytic Domain: The Work of Melanie Klein, W.R.D. Fairburn, and D.W. Winnicott*, Berkeley, CA: University of California Press.

Hunt, M. (1993) *The Story of Psychology*, New York: Doubleday.

Husserl, E. (1913/1967) *Ideas: General Introduction to Phenomenology*, trans. W. R. Boyce Gibson, New York: Collier.

Hyman, S. (2003) "Diagnosing disorders," *Scientific American* 289, 3: 96–104.

Insel, T. R. and Collins, F. S. (2003) "Psychiatry in the genomics era," *American Journal of Psychiatry* 160, 4: 616–620.

Jablensky, A. (1999a) "The concept of schizophrenia: pro et contra," *Epidemiologia e Psichiatria Sociale* 8, 4: 242–247.

Jablensky, A. (1999b) "The conflict of the nosologists: views on schizophrenia and manic-depressive illness in the early part of the 20th century," *Schizophrenia Research* 39: 95–100.

Jackson, F. and Georges, R. (1998) "Mind, philosophy of," in E. Craig (ed.) *Routledge Encyclopedia of Philosophy*, London: Routledge, available online, http://www.rep.routledge.com./article/V038 (July 7, 2003).

Jackson, L. (2002) *Freaks, Geeks and Asperger Syndrome: A User Guide to Adolescence*, London: Jessica Kingsley.

Johnson, S. (2004) *Mind Wide Open: Your Brain and the Neuroscience of Everyday Life*, New York: Scribner.

Jones, D. and Elcock, J. (2001) *History and Theories of Psychology: A Critical Perspective*, London: Arnold.

Jones, K. W. (1999) *Taming the Troublesome Child: American Families, Child Guidance, and the Limits of Psychiatric Authority*, Cambridge, MA: Harvard University Press.

Kagan, J. (1989) *Unstable Ideas: Temperament, Cognition, and Self*, Cambridge, MA: Harvard University Press.

Kanner, L. (1935/1972) *Child Psychiatry* (4th edn), Springfield, IL: Charles C. Thomas.

Kanner, L. (1943/1985) "Autistic disturbances of affective contact," in A. M. Donnellan (ed.) *Classic Readings in Autism*, New York: Teachers College, Columbia University.

Kanner, L. and Eisenberg, L. (1956) "Early infantile autism 1943–1955," *American Journal of Orthopsychiatry* 26: 55–65.

Keller, E. F. (1995) *Refiguring Life: Metaphors of Twentieth-Century Biology*, New York: Columbia University Press.

Keller, E. F. (2000) *The Century of the Gene*, Cambridge, MA: Harvard University Press.

Kern, J. K. (2002) "The possible role of the cerebellum in autism/PDD: disruption of a multisensory feedback loop," *Medical Hypotheses* 59, 3: 255–260.

Kerr, A. and Cunningham-Burley, S. (2000) "On ambivalence and risk: reflexive modernity and the new human genetics," *Sociology* 34, 2: 283–304.

Kershaw (2001) "In foreign parts: a chamber of horrors so close to the 'Garden of Eden'," *The Independent* (London) December 1: 19.

Kirschner, S. R. (1996) "Sources of redemption in psychoanalytic developmental psychology," in C. F. Graumann and K. Gergen (eds) *Historical Dimensions of Psychological Discourses*, Cambridge: Cambridge University Press.

Klein, M. (1931/1950) "A contribution to the theory of intellectual inhibition," in E. Jones (ed.) *Contributions to Psycho-analysis 1921–1945 Melanie Klein*, London: Hogarth Press.

Klein, M. (1946/2000) "Notes on some schizoid mechanisms," in P. DuGay, J. Evans, and P. Redman (eds) *Identity: A Reader*, London: Sage.

Klin, A. and Volkmar, F. R. (1997) "Asperger's syndrome," in D. J. Cohen and F. R. Volkmar (eds) *Handbook of Autism and Pervasive Developmental Disorders*, New York: John Wiley & Sons.

Knight, D. (2000) "Pollution may trigger child disabilities," Washington, DC: Inter Press Service, September 7.

Knivsberg, A. M., Reichelt, K. L., Hoien, T., and Nodland, M. (2002) "A randomized, controlled study of dietary intervention in autistic syndromes," *Nutritional Neuroscience 5*, 4: 251–261.

Koffka, K. (1921) *The Growth of the Mind*, New York: Harcourt.

Lacan, J. (1968) *The Language of the Self: The Function of Language in Psychoanalysis*, trans. A. Wilden, Baltimore, MD: Johns Hopkins University Press.

Laclau, E. and Mouffe, C. (1985) *Hegemony and Socialist Strategy*, London: Verso.

Lauritsen, M. B. and Ewald, H. (2001) "The genetics of autism," *Acta Psychiatrica Scandinavica 103*: 411–427.

Leekam, S. and Moore, C. (2001) "The development of attention and joint attention in children with autism," in J. A. Burack, T. Charman, N. Yirmiya, and P. R. Zelazo (eds) *The Development of Autism: Perspectives from Theory and Research*, Mahwah, NJ: Lawrence Erlbaum.

Lewontin, R. (1993) *Doctrine of DNA: Biology as Ideology*, London: Penguin.

Lewontin, R. (2000) *It Ain't Necessarily So: The Dream of the Human Genome and Other Illusions*, New York: New York Review Books.

Likierman, M. (1995) "The debate between Anna Freud and Melanie Klein: a historical survey," *Journal of Psychotherapy 21*, 3: 313–325.

Lippman, A. (1991) "Prenatal genetic testing and screening," *American Journal of Law and Medicine 1*: 15–50.

Locke, J. (1690/1961) *Essay Concerning Human Understanding*, vol. 1, J. W. Yolton (ed.), London: J. M. Dent and Sons.

Locke, J. (1693/1964) *Some Thoughts Concerning Education*, in P. Gay (ed.) *John Locke on Education*, New York: Bureau of Publications, Teachers College, Columbia University.

Longman, P. (2004) "Which nations will go forth and multiply?," *Fortune*, April 19: 60–61.

Lormand, E. (1998) "Consciousness," in E. Craig (ed.) *Routledge Encyclopedia of Philosophy*, London: Routledge, available online, http://www.rep.routledge.com/article/W011 (July 3, 2003).

Lovaas, O. I. (1977) *The Autistic Child : Language Development through Behavior Modification*, New York: Irvington.

Loveland, K. A. (2001) "Toward an ecological theory of autism," in J. A. Burack, T. Charman, N. Yirmiya, and P. R. Zelazo (eds) *The Development of Autism: Perspectives from Theory and Research*, Mahwah, NJ: Lawrence Erlbaum.

McCallum, D. (2001) *Personality and Dangerousness: Genealogies of Antisocial Personality Disorder*, Cambridge: Cambridge University Press.

McCandless, J. (2003) *Children with Starving Brains: A Medical Treatment Guide for Autism Spectrum Disorders* (2nd edn), North Bergen, NJ: Bramble Books.

McCarley, R. W., Shenton, M. E., O'Donnell, B. F., and Nestor, P. G. (2004) "Uniting Kraepelin and Bleuler: the psychology of schizophrenia and the biology of temporal lobe abnormalities," available online at http://splweb.bwh.harvard.edu:8000/pages/papers/szrev.rwm/szrevrwm.html (June 26, 2004).

McDougle, C. J., Naylor, S. T., Cohen, D. J. et al (2002) "A double-blind, placebo-controlled study of fluvoxamine in adults with autistic disorder," *Current Opinion in Neurobiology* 12, 1: 115–118.

McGonigle, D. J., Howseman, A. M., Athwal, B. S. et al (2000) "Variability in fMRI: an examination of intersession differences," *NeuroImage* 11: 708–734.

McGough, R. (2004) "Disorder hints at how brain learns to read," *The Wall Street Journal,* January 8: A1, A20.

McLaughlin, B. (1998) "Connectionism," in E. Craig (ed.) *Routledge Encyclopedia of Philosophy*, London: Routledge, available online, http://www.rep.routledge.com/article/W010 (July 7, 2003).

Macleod, D. I. (1998) *The Age of the Child: Children in America, 1890–1920*, New York: Twayne.

McNeil, D. G. (2003) "No risk found in childhood shot, study says," *The Arizona Republic,* February 20: A19.

Mahler, M. (1952) "On child psychosis and schizophrenia: autistic and symbiotic infantile psychoses," *The Psychoanalytic Study of the Child* 7: 286–305.

Mahler, M. (1965) "On early infantile psychosis," *Journal of the American Academy of Child Psychiatry* 4, 4: 554–568.

Mandell, D. S., Listerud, J., Levy, S., and Pinto, M. (2002) "Race differences in the age of diagnosis among Medicaid eligible children with autism," *Journal of the American Academy of Child and Adolescent Psychiatry* 41, 12: 1447–1453.

Marcus, G. (2003) *The Birth of the Mind: How a Tiny Number of Genes Creates the Complexities of Human Thought*, New York: Basic Books.

Mash, E. J., Wolfe, D. A. (2002) *Abnormal Child Psychology*, Belmont: CA: Wadsworth/Thomson Learning.

Maslow, A. H. (1968) *Toward a Psychology of Being* (2nd edn), Princeton, NJ: D. Van Nostrand.

Maurice, C. (1993) *Let Me Hear your Voice: A Family's Triumph over Autism*, New York: Fawcett Columbine.

Mayes, S. D., Calhoun, S. L., and Crites, D. L. (2001) "Does DSM-IV Asperger's Disorder exist?," *Journal of Abnormal Psychology* 29, 3: 263–272.

Miller, G. (2002) "Genes' effect seen in brain's fear response," *Science* 297: 319.

Miller, J. N. and Ozonoff, S. (1997) "Did Asperger's cases have Asperger's Disorder? A research note," *Journal of Child Psychology and Psychiatry* 38, 2: 247–251.

Molloy, H. and Vasil, L. (2002) "The social construction of Asperger Syndrome: that pathologizing of difference?," *Disability and Society* 6: 659–669.

Monaco, A. P. and Bailey, A. J. (2001) "The search for susceptibility genes," *Lancet* 358, 3: s3.

"More proof of dramatic results of intensive early intervention reported," (2003) *Autism Research Review* 17, 3: 1.

"More taxes, anyone?" (2003) *Economist* 366, 8304: 22–24.

Morss, J. R. (1990) *The Biologising of Childhood: Developmental Psychology and the Darwinian Myth*, Hove: Lawrence Erlbaum.

Mukoff, H. E., Hathaway, S. E., and Eisenberg, A. (1989) *What to Expect the First Year*, New York: Workman.

Mundy, P. (2003) "Annotation: the neural basis of social impairments in autism: the role of the dorsal medial-frontal cortex and anterior cingulated system," *Journal of Child Psychology and Psychiatry and Allied Disciplines* 44, 6: 793–810.

Muratori, F., Cesari, A., and Casella, C. (2001) "Autism and cerebellum: an unusual finding with MRI," *Panminerva Medica* 43, 4: 311–315.

Nadesan, M. (2002) "Engineering the entrepreneurial infant: brain science, infant development toys, and governmentality," *Cultural Studies* 16, 3: 401–432.

Napoli, D. S. (1981) *Architects of Adjustment: A History of the Psychological Profession in the United States*, Port Washington, NY: National University Publications Kennikat Press.

Narita, N., Kato, M., Tazoe, M. et al. (2002) "Increased monoamine concentration in the brain and blood of fetal thalidomide and valproic acid exposed rats: putative animal models for autism," *Pediatric Research* 2, 4: 576–579.

Nash, M. J. and Bonesteel, A. (2002) "The geek syndrome," *Time*, May 6: 46.

Neumarker, K. J. (2003) "Leo Kanner: his years in Berlin, 1906–1924. The roots of Autistic Disorder," *History of Psychiatry* 14, 2: 205–218.

New, M. (2003) "The tax revolt turns 25," *Human Events* 59, 20: 22.

Newell, A. and Simon, H. (1972) *Human Problem Solving*, Englewood Cliffs, NJ: Prentice Hall.

"(Not) all talk" (2003) *U.S. News and World Report*, June 16: 14.

Novas, C. and Rose, N. (2000) "Genetic risk and the birth of the somatic individual," *Economy and Society* 29, 4: 485–513.

Oliver, M. (1990) *The Politics of Disability*, London: Macmillan.

Ovsiew, F. (2000) "An end to Kraepelinian nosology?," *Journal of Neuropsychiatry and Clinical Neurosciences* 12, 3: 297–299.

Ozand, P., Al-Odaib, A., Merza, H., and Al Harbi, S. (2003) "Autism: a review," *Journal of Pediatric Neurology* 1, 2: 55–67.

Ozonoff, S. (1995) "Executive functions in autism," in E. Schopler and G. B. Mesibov (eds) *Learning and Cognition in Autism*, New York: Plenum.

Paradiz, V. (2002) *Elijah's Cup: A Family's Journey into the Community and Culture of High Functioning Autism and Asperger's Syndrome*, New York: Free Press.

"Parent perspective in raising special kids," (2002) *Connect Connecting* 7, 5: 12–13.

Parker-Pope, T. (2003) "Warning your MRI may be out of focus: why scans often miss what's wrong," *The Wall Street Journal*, February 18: D1.

Parsons, T. (1963) *The Social System*, New York: The Free Press.

Patterson, P. H. (2002) "Maternal infection: window on neuroimmune interactions in fetal brain development and mental illness," *Current Opinion in Neurobiology* 12, 1: 115–118.

Petersen, A. and Bunton, R. (2002) *The New Genetics and the Public's Health*, London: Routledge.

Phillips, J. (1999) "The hermeneutic critique of cognitive psychology," *Philosophy, Psychiatry, and Psychology* 6, 4: 259–264.

Piaget, J. (1923/1959) *The Language and Thought of the Child*, trans. M. Gabain, London: Routledge and Kegal Paul.

Piaget, J. (1924/1972) *Judgment and Reasoning in the Child*, trans. M. Warden, Savage, MD: Littlefield, Adams.

Pickles, A., Starr, E., Kazak, S. et al. (2000) "Variable expression of the broader autism phenotype: findings from extended pedigrees," *Journal of Child Psychological Psychiatry* 41: 491–502.

Pinker, S. (1997) *How the Mind Works*, New York: Norton.

Plotkin, H. (1997) *Evolution in Mind*, London: Alan Lane.

Pollock, L. A. (1983) *Forgotten Children: Parent–Child Relations from 1500 to 1900*, Cambridge: Cambridge University Press.

Pollock, L. A. (1992) "Foreword," in M. R. Brown (ed.) *Picturing Children: Constructions of Childhood between Rousseau and Freud*, Aldershot, UK: Ashgate.

Porter, R. (2002) *Madness: A Brief History*, Oxford: Oxford University Press.

Post, E. L. (1936) "Finite combinatory processes—formulation I," *Journal of Symbolic Logic*, 1: 103–105.

Potter, H. W. (1933) "Schizophrenia in children," *American Journal of Psychiatry* 89: 1933.

Preston, S. H. and Haines, M. R. (1991) *Fatal Years: Child Mortality in Late Nineteenth Century America*, Princeton, NJ: Princeton University Press.

Proctor, R. N. (2004) "Genomics and eugenics: how fair is the comparison?" available online, http://www.bumc.bu.edu/www/sph/lw/pvl/book2/4–Genomics%20and% (July 19, 2004).

Rabinow, P. (1999) *French DNA: Trouble in Purgatory*, Chicago: University of Chicago Press.

Rafalovich, A. (2001) "The conceptual history of attention deficit hyperactivity disorder: idiocy, imbecility, encephalitis and the child deviant, 1877–1929," *Deviant Behavior: An Interdisciplinary Journal* 22: 93–115.

Ramsay, F. P. (1931) *The Foundations of Mathematics and other Logical Essays*, R. B. Braithwaite (ed) London: Routledge & Keegan Paul.

Rapin, I. (1998) "Progress in the neurobiology of autism," *CNS Spectrum* 3, 3: 50–79.

Rapin, I. (2002) "Diagnostic dilemmas in developmental disabilities: fuzzy margins at the edges of normality. An essay prompted by Thomas Sowell's new book: *The Einstein Syndrome*," *Journal of Autism and Developmental Disorders* 32: 49–57.

Ratey, J. and Johnson, C. (1997) *Shadow Syndromes: The Mild Forms of Major Mental Disorders that Sabotage Us*, New York: Bantam.

Reef, C. (2002) *Childhood in America: An Eyewitness History*, New York: Facts on File.

Richards, G. (1996) *Putting Psychology in its Place: An Introduction from a Critical Historical Perspective*, London: Routledge.

Richardson, T. (1989) *The Century of the Child: The Mental Hygiene Movement and Social Policy in the United States and Canada*, Albany, NY: State University of New York Press.

Ritter, M. (2003) "Manic-depression gene identified, scientists say," *The Arizona Republic*, July 16: A7.

Rodier, P. (2000) "The early origins of autism," *Scientific American* 282, 2: 56–63.

Rodrigue, E. (1955) "The analysis of a three-year-old mute schizophrenic," in M. Klein, P. Heimann, and R. E. Money-Kyrle (eds) *New Directions in Psycho-Analysis: The Significance of Infant Conflict in the Pattern of Adult Behavior*, London: Tavistock.

Rose, N. (1989) *Governing the Soul: The Shaping of the Private Self*, London: Routledge.

Rose, N. (1994) "Medicine, history and the present," in C. Jones and R. Porter (eds) *Reassessing Foucault: Power, Medicine and the Body*, London: Routledge.

Rose, N. (1999) *Powers of Freedom: Reframing Political Thought*, Cambridge: Cambridge University Press.

Rose, N. (2001) "The politics of life itself," *Theory, Culture and Society* 18, 6: 1–30.

Rousseau, J. J. (1762/1948) *Emile, or Education*, trans. B. Foxley, London: J. M. Dent and Sons.

Rudin, E. (1916) Studien über vererbung und entstehung geistiger Störungen, Berlin: Springer.

Rumsey, J. M. and Ernst, M. (2000) "Functional neuroimaging of autistic disorders," *Mental Retardation and Developmental Disabilities Research Review* 6, 3: 171–179.

Rutter, M., Plomin, R. (1997) "Opportunities for psychiatry from genetic findings." *British Journal of Psychiatry* 171: 209–219.

Saitoh, O., Karns, C. M., and Courchesne, E. (2001) "Development of the hippocampal formation from 2 to 42 years: MRI evidence of smaller area dentate in autism," *Brain* 124, pt 7: 1317–1324.

Samet, J. (1998) "Nativism," in E. Craig (ed.) *Routledge Encyclopedia of Philosophy*, London: Routledge, available online, http://www.rep.routledge.com/article/W028 (July 10, 2003).

Sass, H. and Herpertz, S. (1995) "Personality disorders," in G. E. Berrios and R. Porter (eds) *A History of Clinical Psychiatry*, London: Athlone.

Sayers, J. (1991) *Mothering Psychoanalysis: Helene Deutsch, Karen Horney, Anna Freud and Melanie Klein*, London: Hamish Hamilton.

Scharfetter, C. (1996) "An examination of the history of concepts of schizophrenia," in J. T. Dalby (ed.) *Mental Disease in History*, New York: Peter Lang.

Schneider, H. (2001) "WHO to study health effects of depleted uranium in Iraq," *The Washington Post*, March 15: A20.

Schneider, K. (1923) *Die Psychopathischen Persönlichkeiten (The Psychopathic Personalities)*, Leipzig: Thieme.

Schneider, K. (1953) "Ueber die Grenzen der Psychologisierung" (The limits of psychologization), *Nervenarzt* 24: 89–90.

Schopler, E., Reichler, R. J., Renner, B. R. (1988). CARS (Childhood Autism Rating Scale), Los Angeles: Western Psychological Services.

Schultz, D. P. and Schultz, S. E. (1987) *A History of Modern Psychology*, (4th edn), San Diego, CA: Harcourt Brace Jovanovich.

Schultz, R. T. and Klin, A. (2002) "Genetics of childhood disorders: XLIII. Autism, Part 2: Neural Foundation," *Journal of the American Academy of Child and Adolescent Psychiatry* 41, 10: 1259–1262.

Schultz, R. T., Gauthier, L., Klin, A., et al. (2000) "Abnormal ventral temporal cortical activity during face discrimination among individuals with autism and Asperger's syndrome," *Archives of General Psychiatry* 57, 4: 331–340.

Scott, S. K. and Wise, R. J. S. (2003) "Functional imaging and language: a critical guide to methodology and analysis," *Speech Communication* 41, 1: 7–21.

Shahar, S. (1990) *Childhood in the Middle Ages*, London: Routledge.

Shannon, C. E. and Weaver, W. (1949) *The Mathematical Theory of Communication*, Urbana, IL: University of Illinois Press.

Shao, Y., Wolpert, C., Raiford, K. et al. (2002) "Genomic screen and follow-up analysis for autistic disorder," *American Journal of Medical Genetics* 114: 99–105.

Shaw, W. (1998) *Biological Treatments for Autism and PDD*, Overland Park, KS: Great Plains Laboratory.

Shorter, E. (1997) *A History of Psychiatry: From the Era of the Asylum to the Age of Prozac*, New York: John Wiley and Sons.

Shute, N. (2003) "Heavy metal fish," *U.S. News and World Report*, March 17: 42–43.

Sibley, D. (1995) *Geographies of Exclusion: Society and Difference in the West*, New York: Routledge.

Siegel, B. (1996) *The World of the Autistic Child*, New York: Oxford University Press.

Silberman, S. (2000) "The geek syndrome," *Wired Magazine* 9, 12: 174–183.

Siller, M. and Sigman, M. (2002) "The behaviors of children with autism predict the subsequent development of their children's communication," *Journal of Autism and Developmental Disorders* 32, 2: 77–89.

Simon, H. (1957) *Administrative Behavior* (3rd edn), New York: The Free Press.

Singer, E. (1992) *Child-Care and the Psychology of Development*, trans. A. Porcelijn, London: Routledge.

Singer, J. (1999) "Why can't you be normal for once in your life? From a 'problem with no name' to the emergence of a new category of difference," in M. Corker and S. French (eds) *Disability Discourse*, Buckingham: Open University Press.

Snyder, A. W. and Mitchell, D. J. (1999) "Is integer arithmetic fundamental to mental processing? The mind's secret arithmetic," *Proceedings of the Royal Society of London B* 266: 587–592.

Snyder, A. W. and Thomas, M. (1997) "Autistic artists give clues to perception," *Perception* 26: 93–96.

Sowell, T. (1997) *Late-Talking Children*, New York: Basic Books.

Sowell, T. (2001) *The Einstein Syndrome*, New York: Basic Books.

Spitz, R. (1945) "Hospitalism: an inquiry into the genesis of psychiatric conditions in early childhood," *The Psychoanalytic Study of the Child* 1: 53–74.

Spock, B. (1946) *Common Sense Book of Baby and Child Care*, New York: Duell, Sloan and Pearce.

Sternberg, S. (2003) "Most heart attacks tied to lifestyle, not genes," *The Arizona Republic*, August 20: A5.

Stone, M. H. (1973) "Child psychiatry before the twentieth century," *International Journal of Child Psychotherapy* 2: 264–308.

Stone, M. H. (1997) *Healing the Mind: A History of Psychiatry from Antiquity to the Present*, New York: Norton.

Stotz-Ingenlath, G. (2000) "Epistemological aspects of Eugene Bleuler's conception of schizophrenia in 1911," *Medicine, Health Care and Philosophy* 3: 153–159.

Strasser, S. (1957) "Phenomenological trends in European psychology," *Philosophy and Phenomenological Research* 18, 1: 18–34.

Suplee, C. (2000) "Scientists claim to have pinpointed source of human IQ," *The Arizona Republic*, July 23, A26.

Szatmari, P. (2003) "The causes of autism spectrum disorders," *British Medical Journal* 326, 7382: 173–174.

Szatmari, P., Archer, L., Fisman, S., Streiner, D. L., and Wilson, F. (1995) "Asperger's syndrome and autism: differences in behavior, cognition, and adaptive functioning," *Journal of the American Academy of Child and Adolescent Psychiatry* 34: 1662–1671.

Tager-Flusberg, H., Baron-Cohen, S., and Cohen, D. (1993) "Introduction to the debate," in S. Baron-Cohen, H. Tager-Flusberg, and D. Cohen (eds) *Understanding Other Minds: Perspectives from Autism*, Oxford: Oxford University Press.

Talan, J. (2002) "Scientists link anxiety to specific gene," *The Arizona Republic*, July 19: A8.

ten Have, H. A. M. J. (2001) "Genetics and culture: the geneticization thesis," *Medicine, Health Care and Philosophy* 4: 295–304.

"Thiamine benefits autistic children; may work by removing heavy metals," (2002) *Autism Research Review International* 16, 3: 4.

Thompson, P., Cannon, T. D., and Toga, A. W. (2002) "Mapping genetic influences on human brain structure," *Annuals of Medicine* 34, 7–8: 523–536.

"Toxic Chemicals and Health: Pesticides: In Depth Technical Brief. Natural Resources Defense Council," available online, www.nrdc.org/health/pesticides/bdursban.asp (October 16, 2003).

Travis, J. (2003) "Autism advance," *Science News* 163, 14: 212–213.

Treffers, P. D. A. and Silverman, W. K. (2001) "Anxiety and its disorders in children and adolescents before the twentieth century," in W. K. Silverman and P. D. A. Treffers (eds) *Anxiety Disorders in Children and Adolescents: Research, Assessment and Intervention*, Cambridge: Cambridge University Press.

Tremain, S. (2001) "On the government of disability," *Social Theory and Practice* 27, 4: 617–636.

Trent, J. W. (1994) *Inventing the Feeble Mind: A History of Mental Retardation in the United States*, Berkeley, CA: University of California Press.

Trillat, E. (1995) "Conversion disorder and hysteria," in G. E. Berrios and R. Porter (eds) *A History of Clinical Psychiatry*, London: Athlone.

Tsai, L. (2004) "Diagnostic confusion in Asperger's Disorder," available online, http://www.med.umich.edu/psych/child/dd/sum2002nwsltr.htm (November 7, 2004).

Turing, A. M. (1936) "On computable numbers, with an application to the Entscheidungs problem," *Proceedings of the London Mathematics Society* (series 2) 42: 230–265.

Turner, T. (1995) "Schizophrenia: social section," in G. E. Berrios and R. Porter (eds) *A History of Clinical Psychiatry: The Origin and History of Psychiatric Disorders*, London: Athlone.

Tustin, F. (1969) "Autistic processes," *Journal of Child Psychotherapy* 2, 3: 23–42.

Tustin, F. (1991) "Revised understandings of psychogenic autism," *International Journal of Psycho-Analysis* 72: 585–591.

Tustin, F. (1992) *Autistic States in Children* (rev. edn), London: Routledge.

Tversky, A. and Kahneman, D. (1974) "Judgment under uncertainty: heuristics and biases," *Science* 185: 1124–1131.

Uttal, W. R. (2001) *The New Phrenology: The Limits of Localizing Cognitive Processes in the Brain*, Boston, MA: MIT Press.

Valenstein, E. S. (1998) *Blaming the Brain: The Truth about Drugs and Mental Health*, New York: The Free Press.

Van Gent, T., Heijnen, C. J. and Treffers, P. D. (1997) "Autism and the immune system," *Journal of Child Psychology and Psychiatry* 38: 337–349.

Vanscoy, H. (2004) "Damage from air pollution starts before birth, study says," *The Arizona Republic*, April 1: E1, E3.

Vedantam, S. (2003) "Researchers find stress, depression have genetic link," *The Arizona Republic*, July 18: A10.

Volkmar, F. R. (2000) "Understanding autism: implications for psychoanalysis," *Psychoanalytic Inquiry* 20, 5: 660–624.

Volkmar, F. R., Klin, A., and Cohen, D. J. (1997a) "Diagnosis and classification of autism and related conditions: consensus and issues," in D. J. Cohen and F. R. Volkmar (eds) *Handbook of Autism and Pervasive Developmental Disorders*, New York: John Wiley and Sons.

Volkmar, F. R., Klin, A., Marans, W., and Cohen, D. J. (1997b) "Childhood disintegrative disorder," in D. J. Cohen and F. R. Volkmar (eds) *Handbook of Autism and Pervasive Developmental Disorders*, New York: John Wiley and Sons.

Wakefield, A. J., Murch, S., Anthony, A. et al. (1998) "Ileal-lymphoid-nodular hyperplasia, non-specific colitis, and pervasive developmental disorder in children," *Lancet* 351, 9103: 637–641.

Walk, A. (1964) "The pre-history of child psychiatry," *British Journal of Psychiatry* 110: 754–767.

Wardle, C. (1991) "Twentieth-century influences on the development in Britain of services for child and adolescent psychiatry," *British Journal of Psychiatry* 159: 53–68.

Warren, R. P. (1998) "An immunological theory for the development of some cases of autism," *CNS Spectrums* 3, 3: 71–79.

Waterhouse, L. and Fein, D. (1997) "Perspectives on social impairments," in D. J. Cohen and F. R. Volkmar (eds) *Handbook of Autism and Pervasive Developmental Disorders*, New York: John Wiley and Sons.

Weiss, G. (1999) *Body Images: Embodiment as Intercorporeality*, New York: Routledge.

West, E. (1996) *Growing up in Twentieth-Century America: A History and Reference Guide*, Westport, CT: Greenwood Press.

Wetzell, R. F. (2000) *Inventing the Criminal: A History of German Criminology, 1880–1945*, Chapel Hill, NC: University of North Carolina Press.

Wilkie, A. (2001) "Genetic prediction: what are the limits?," *Studies in History and Philosophy of Science, Part C, Biology and Biomedical Sciences* 32, 4: 619–633.

Willey, L. H. (1999) *Pretending to be Normal: Living with Asperger's Syndrome*, London: Jessica Kingsley.

Williams, D. (1995) *Somebody Somewhere: Breaking Free from the World of Autism*, New York: Three Rivers Press.

Windham, C. (2004) "Brain imaging provides a window on speech, learning problems," *The Wall Street Journal*, January 23: A11.

Wing, L. (1981) "Asperger's Syndrome: a clinical account," *Psychological Medicine* 11: 115–130.

Wing, L. (1991) "The relationship between Asperger's syndrome and Kanner's autism," in U. Frith (ed.) *Autism and Asperger's Syndrome*, Cambridge: Cambridge University Press.

Wing, L. (1993) "The definition and prevalence of autism: a review," *European Child and Adolescent Psychiatry* 2, 2: 61–75.

Wing, L. (1997) "Syndromes of autism and atypical development," in D. J. Cohen and F. R. Volkmar (eds) *Handbook of Autism and Pervasive Developmental Disorders*, New York: John Wiley and Sons.

Winnicott, D. W. (1951/2000) "Transitional objects and transitional phenomena," in P. DuGay, J. Evans, and P. Redman (eds) *Identity: A Reader*, London: Sage.

Winnicott, D. W. (1967/2000) "Mirror-role of mother and family in child development," in P. DuGay, J. Evans, and P. Redman (eds) *Identity: A Reader*, London: Sage.

Wolff, S. (1996) "The first account of the syndrome Asperger described? Translation of a paper entitled 'Die Schizoiden Pychopathien im Kindesalter' by Dr. G. E. Ssucharewa; scientific assistant, which appeared in 1926 in the Monatsschrift fur Psychiatrie und Neurologie 60: 235–261," *European Child and Adolescent Psychiatry* 5: 119–132.

World Health Organization (WHO) (1992) *The ICD-10 Classification of Mental and Behavioral Disorders: Clinical Descriptions and Diagnostic Guidelines*, Geneva: Author.

World Health Organization (2004) "Environmental threats to children," available online, http://www.who.int/entity/water_sanitation_health/hygiene/settings/en/ChildrenNM4.pdf (February 6, 2004).

Wright, D. and Digby, A. (eds) (1996) *From Idiocy to Mental Deficiency: Historical Perspectives on People with Learning Disabilities*, London: Routledge.

Yirmiya, N., Pilowsky, T., Tidhar, S. et al. (2002) "Family-based and population study of a functional promoter-region monoamine oxidase A polymorphism in autism: possible association with IQ," *American Journal of Medical Genetics* 114: 284–287.

Zelazo, P. D., Burack, J. A., Boseovski, J. J., Jacques, S., and Frye, D. (2001) "A cognitive complexity and control framework for the study of autism," in J. A. Burack, T. Charman, N. Yirmiya, and P. R. Zelazo (eds) *The Development of Autism: Perspectives from Theory and Research*, Mahwah, NJ: Lawrence Erlbaum.

Zelizer, V. A. (1985) *Pricing the Priceless Child: The Changing Social Value of Children*, New York: Basic Books.

Index